D0205671

Peter Manoleas, MSW
Editor

The Cross-Cultural Practice of Clinical Case Management in Mental Health

Pre-publication
REVIEWS,
COMMENTARIES,
EVALUATIONS . . .

"**T**he cross-cultural emphasis in this book is a substantive and viable contribution to the literature in case management. The editor has selected writers who utilize their expertise to offer the reader major practice themes on diversity. The cultural content throughout the book is very focused on the mentally ill population. . . . Each chapter offers unique cultural perspectives for the ethnic/racial group being addressed. Many do a creative job of presenting newer insights with culturally driven options to traditional intervention modes.

This is a comprehensive, must-read book for any practitioner–regardless of discipline–working in the mental health arena who is committed to providing culturally appropriate services to diverse groups, especially within the persistently mentally ill population."

Maria E. Zuniga, PhD
Professor of Social Work,
San Diego State University

"**M**anoleas has done a comprehensive job of pulling together a valuable collection of writings that address practice concepts, sociodemographics, and research findings that are necessary for informed case management practice of clinical concerns with diverse populations. The various chapters approach assessment and intervention considerations related to ethnicity, gender, and developmental factors. In balance this text is superb in its review of the meaning and function of culture in the lives of our clients, and the application of insights derived from that literature into effective case management interventions with a clinical focus. The text also provides a worthwhile resource in its review of the core tenets of case management.

This work is a wonderful addition to the growing literature on multicultural practice because of its fine-tuned focus on clinical work within a case management framework."

Betty Garcia
Associate Professor,
Department of Social Work Education,
California State University–Fresno

"*T he Cross-Cultural Practice of Clinical Case Management in Mental Health* is truly a book which is long overdue in social work practice. Mr. Manoleas has very effectively addressed the issues of two emerging trends in the field of human service professionals: clinical case management for serious mental disorders and delivery of mental health services to ethnically and culturally diverse populations, which constitute an increasing proportion of clients in publicly funded mental health facilities. This book is both comprehensive and ambitious in its scope, covering a broad range of developmental, gender, and social factors as well as specific strategies of case management with four major ethnic groups, i.e., African American, Native American, Latinos, and Southeast Asians.

This book provides a useful framework for understanding the fundamental impact of culture and ethnicity on clients' world views,

The Haworth Press, Inc.

The Cross-Cultural Practice of Clinical Case Management in Mental Health

The Cross-Cultural Practice of Clinical Case Management in Mental Health

Peter Manoleas, MSW
Editor

The Haworth Press
New York • London

The Haworth Press, Inc., 10 Alice Street, Binghamton, NY 13904-1580

Library of Congress Cataloging-in-Publication Data

The cross-cultural practice of clinical case management in mental health / Peter Manoleas, editor.
    p.   cm.
   Includes bibliographical references and index.
   ISBN 1-56024-874-2
   1. Minorities–Mental health services–United States. 2. Psychiatry, Transcultural–United States. 3. Psychiatric social work–United States. 4. Social work with minorities–United States. I. Manoleas, Peter.
   [DNLM: 1. Social Work, Psychiatric–methods–United States. 2. Culture. 3. Socioeconomic Factors. 4. Mental Health. 5. Mental Disorders–therapy. WM 30.5 C951 1994]
   RC451.4.M57C76 1994
   362.2'08'693–dc20
   DNLM/DLC
   for Library of Congress
                                               94-47017
                                                 CIP

For Francine and Joseph

ABOUT THE EDITOR

Peter Manoleas, MSW, has been a lecturer and field work consultant at the University of California at Berkeley School of Social Welfare since 1983. Mr. Manoleas has worked in the fields of mental health and substance abuse as a clinician, administrator, and consultant for 24 years and has been teaching since 1977. A member of several professional organizations, including the Council on Social Work Education and the National Coalition of Hispanic Health & Human Services Organizations, he has published in the areas of cross-cultural training, mental health, and the disease model of addictions.

CONTENTS

Preface   **xi**

Acknowledgements   **xv**

Chapter 1. Culture and Case Management   **1**
    Peter Manoleas

Introduction   1
The Emergence of Case Management   3
Characteristics of Case Management   5
The Role of Culture   7
The Culture of Psychiatry   8
Culture and Mental Illness   15
Culture and the Activities of Case Management   17
The Culture Broker   26
Language   27
The Use of Metaphors   29
Cultural Reframing   31
Conclusion   33

Chapter 2. The Culture of Homelessness   **41**
    Phillip Fellin

Homelessness as Culture   43
The Study of Homeless People   46
Cultural Traits   48
Poverty and Homelessness   48
General Lifestyles   50
Disaffiliation   52
Treatment/Service Resistance   53
Subcultures of Homelessness   57
Case Management with Homeless Clients   61
Evaluation of Case Management   63
Conclusion   67

Chapter 3. Demoralization: A Useful Concept for Case Management with Native Americans   **79**
Felicia Schanche Hodge
Patricia Kipnis

Introduction   79
Native Americans and Depression: An Overview   80
Problem Definition and Previous Research   81
Utilization of the CES-D Scale in a Native American
     Population   83
The Study   83
Study Results   85
Discussion   90
Conclusion   95

Chapter 4. Crisis Intervention: An Essential Component of Culturally Competent Clinical Case Management   **99**
Rafael Herrera

Introduction   99
Case Management   100
Latinos Are a High Risk Population   101
Utilization   102
Barriers   104
Most Therapeutic Encounters Are Brief   105
Crisis and Brief Therapy Are Effective   106
What Is Crisis Intervention?   106
Cultural Variations in the Definitions of Crisis   107
Eclectic Crisis Intervention Theory   110
Cultural Knowledge and Help-Seeking Patterns   111
Summary and Conclusions   113

Chapter 5. Clinical Case Management and Cognitive-Behavioral Therapy: Integrated Psychosocial Services for Depressed Latino Primary Care Patients   **119**
Kurt C. Organista
Eleanor Valdes Dwyer

Depression in Primary Care   119
Relevance of the Problem to Latinos   120

Decreasing Traditional Barriers to Mental Health
    Utilization   121
Addressing Psychosocial Stressors in Low Income
    and Minority Clients   121
Responding to Depressed Latinos in Primary Care   122
Integrated CCM and CBT: A Culturally Responsive
    Approach to Depression in Latino Primary Care Patients   126
Conclusions   139

**Chapter 6. Culturally Responsive Psychiatric Case
Management with Southeast Asians**   **145**
        Yeunhee Joyce Kim
        Birgitta Oey Snyder
        Alice Y. Lai-Bitker

A Diverse Population   145
One Program's Experience   146
Lack of Service Availability   148
Service Delivery Strategies for the Refugee Population   150
Case Management Issues   151
Cultural Appreciation and Assessment of Service Needs   151
Components of Culturally Competent Assessment   156
Dependence vs. Empowerment   158
Trust-Building   159
Culture-Syntonic Treatment Intervention   162
Advocacy   164
Conclusion   165

**Chapter 7. Clinical Case Management with Severely
Mentally Ill African Americans**   **169**
        Valerie Roxanne Edwards

Introduction   169
Africentric Perspective   170
An Africentric Matrix of Support   171
The Intersection of Family and Community Support   176
The Dynamics of Biculturalism   178
The Role of Religion   180
The Impact of Racism on Mental Health Care Delivery   181
Conclusion   182

Chapter 8. Gender as Culture: Competent Case Management for Women with Major Psychiatric Disorders 185

Joanne R. Wile
Anna M. Spielvogel

Introduction 185
Major Areas of Evaluation 186
Health Care Needs 187
Family Planning 189
Motherhood 192
Sequelae of Early Sexual Trauma 194
Relationships 196
Substance Abuse 198
HIV Disease 200
Violence 201
"Treatment-Resistant" Women 204
Conclusion 206

Chapter 9. Culturally Competent Health and Human Services for Emotionally Troubled Children and Youth: Only Through Intensive Case Management 211

Abner J. Boles III
Harriet A. Curtis-Boles

Introduction 211
Systems of Care 213
Family Mosaic Project 215
Coordinated Case Management 217
Services 220
Individualized Care 220
"Wrap-Around Care" 223
Measuring Success 223
Cultural Competence 224
Flexible Funding 227
Obstacles to Change 228
Recommendations 230

Index 233

Preface

Having recently faced the challenge of devising a new practice course for graduate social work students who will be working in public mental health settings, my thought processes scanned the skills such students should have to work with the clients typically found in the public system of care. High on my list were: psycho-diagnostics and psychosocial assessment skills, group and family skills, case management skills, and the cultural competence necessary to work with the great ethnic diversity of clients found in public mental health systems throughout this country. Case management has, of course, been an integral part of social work practice with the seriously mentally ill for a long time, even before the term became popularized. Despite the fact that skill-based training of practitioners has included case management functions, the theoretical and knowledge bases have continued to emphasize the contributions of psychology, and, to a lesser degree, sociology. It is my contention that training effective cross-cultural practitioners requires us to make use of the vast contributions of cultural anthropology in the preparation of social workers and other professionals. Also, insofar as all practitioners are professional communicators, some of the work done in the area of linguistics should be looked at for practitioner preparation.

This volume uses the term culture in a broad sense. By doing this, it is possible to look at the treatment needs of certain groups of people who, in the aggregate, are highly represented in public mental health systems; namely, ethnic minorites of color, women, and the homeless. The book aims to provide a useful conceptual framework as well as reviewing current research, presenting case vignettes, and including several brief descriptions of innovative programs. Contributors, by design, represent researchers, program planners, and practitioners in the hope that the resultant product will be a collective description of the state-of-the-art practice of culturally competent clinical case management with public mental health clients. The book is roughly organized into sections reflecting conceptual models, research findings, clinical experiences, and program descriptions.

It is designed to be of use to graduate and advanced undergraduate social work students preparing to work in the mental health field. It is also designed for use by journey therapists and social workers who find themselves working in public mental health systems that are "retooling" their service delivery models to work more effectively with the seriously mentally ill and ethnic minorities.

In the first chapter, I attempt to review and synthesize current thinking about case management and cross-cultural work into a conceptual model that will hopefully be useful to practitioners. The second and third chapters focus on research. In Chapter 2, Fellin does a skillful job of demonstrating how the concept of culture can be used to better understand the needs of the mentally ill homeless. In Chapter 3, Hodge and Kipnis provide empirical evidence for the utility of the concept of demoralization in working with Native American clients. In Chapter 4, Herrera takes on the age-old notion of the once per week session and makes a convincing case for the use of a crisis intervention model with Latinos and other ethnic minorities. In Chapter 5, Organista and Dwyer describe an innovative approach for providing culturally relevant treatment to depressed Latinos that integrates case management and cognitive-behavioral therapy. In Chapter 6, Kim, Snyder, and Lai-Bitker provide special insights into the issues involved in working with Southeast Asian clients. Valerie Edwards provides us with fresh insights about psychiatric case management with African-Americans in Chapter 7, and in Chapter 8, Wile and Spielvogel draw upon the unique experiences of a specialized program in delineating clinical issues facing seriously mentally ill women. In the final chapter, Boles and Curtis-Boles describe a state-of-the-art approach to providing comprehensive case management services to seriously emotionally disturbed children and youth.

Though this book is primarily intended for practitioners and students, several chapters contain important findings for program planners, researchers, and policy analysts. Organista and Dwyer (Chapter 5) and Hodge and Kipnis (Chapter 3) make very clear cases for the principle that any systems serious about providing competent treatment to depressed Latinos and Native Americans should be focusing on primary care clinics and not on mental health outpatient centers where these populations are far less likely to present. In his thorough literature review, Fellin (Chapter 2) substantiates the assertion that the clinical needs of the homeless can only be addressed in settings that first address their survival needs. Similarly, Wile and Spielvogel (Chapter 8) show us how the psychiatric and medical needs of seriously mentally ill women cannot be separated. All of these authors describe elements of culturally responsive treatment models, and, in the aggregate, clearly demonstrate that, "one size does not fit all," when it comes to program design.

Peter Manoleas

Acknowledgements

This project would not have been possible without the inspiration of many people. The ideas contained in this volume come from the real experiences of many committed people. They are researchers, clinicians, teachers, planners, and above all, the consumers of mental health services whose lives are, essentially, summarized here. I would like to thank Jewelle Taylor Gibbs for her encouragement to undertake this project, Bart Grossman for his technological help with computer matters, and Loretta Morales for her secretarial support. My deepest gratitude, however, is reserved for my family. To my parents, who, while several strides further along in the journey of life, never fail to provide support and guidance for me. To my long-time companion Francine Masiello for her constant support, encouragement, and feedback, and to our son Joseph, who every day inspires me with his youthful energy and perspective.

Chapter 1

Culture and Case Management

Peter Manoleas

INTRODUCTION

The period from the mid-1970s to the present has seen the emergence of case management as a viable modality for the rehabilitation and treatment of the seriously mentally ill. A plethora of publications have described the tasks of mental health case managers (Rose, 1992; Harrod, 1986; Rapp and Chamberlain, 1985; Morin and Seidman, 1986; Goldstrom and Manderscheid, 1983); the effectiveness of the approach (Bond et al., 1988; Deitchman, 1980; Goering et al., 1988); and the refinement of the model to clinical case management (Surber, 1994; Lamb, 1980; Kanter, 1988; Harris and Bachrach, 1988). The same period has witnessed the growth of literature devoted to examining the impact of culture and ethnicity on service utilization (Snowden and Cheung, 1990; Cheung and Snowden, 1990; Scheffler and Miller, 1989); the development of cross-cultural approaches to counseling and psychotherapy (Jones and Korchin, 1982; Gibbs and Huang, 1989; Acosta, Yamamoto, and Evans, 1982; Wilkinson, 1986; Pederson and Pederson, 1989; Comas-Diaz and Griffith, 1988); and cross-cultural considerations in psychiatric diagnoses (Loring and Powell, 1988; Adebimpe, 1984; Westermeyer, 1985; Fabrega, 1987). The contributions to these parallel literature streams have been multidisciplinary in nature, with the fields of psychiatry, social work, psychology, sociology, and anthropology being abundantly represented. While covering the same time span, however, the trends in the literature have tended to speak to the topic of cross-cultural work *or* of case management with the seriously mentally ill. These two separate and distinct literature streams rarely, if ever, refer to each other. To some degree, this represents the bifurcated thinking of mental health planners and others who have been charged with identifying "priority populations," in the face of vastly inadequate resources. Funding for both research and treatment has tended to be earmarked for either the seriously mentally ill, or for ethnic minorities of color. There is evidence, however, that there is considerable overlap among these two groups (Snowden and Cheung, 1990). While the former group is defined by the severity of their symptoms and the duration of their illness, the latter is characterized by chronic exposure to serious environmental stressors that often result in acute symptom syndromes somewhat different from those manifested by majority culture members (Draguns, 1980). Both groups tend to suffer from catastrophic stressors such as unemployment, homelessness, poverty, and domestic violence, but the latter group also often suffers from the effects of translocation, racism, and even torture. Indeed, there is also ample evidence that ethnic minorities of color comprise a growing percentage of the users of public mental health services (Cheung and Snowden, 1990). The time has come for a more comprehensive definition of what constitutes "at risk" populations, variously defined as at risk for psychiatric hospitalization, criminal incarceration, the development of serious medical illness complicated by stress, or other manifestations of severe life stressors.

The person-in-environment approach of clinical case management allows us to view the client and his or her needs holistically. Therapeutic interventions can be targeted toward the client, a variety of points in the client's environment, or both. The realization that the client's environment is composed of agencies, professionals, and informal support systems, each with their own distinct subculture, allows us to integrate the two previously mentioned bodies of literature. In addition to their other tasks, each case manager must act as a cultural bridge between the client, his or her own culture, and the various subcultures the client must deal with in the mental health environment. This chapter synthesizes existing thinking on case management and cross-cultural practice and provides a framework that will underpin the culturally competent practice of clinical case management in public mental health settings. It proposes a role for case managers as "culture brokers," that will make some of the work on ethnic culture more useful to them. Some contributions from the fields of linguistics and medical anthropology are included and the resultant fresh approach to case management is illustrated with case vignettes.

THE EMERGENCE OF CASE MANAGEMENT

The group of clients usually targeted for case management services is that designated as the seriously mentally ill. Most mental health systems include in this group persons suffering from psychoses and major affective disorders on Axis I of the DSM-III-R. With the limited resources available, people with Axis II disorders generally do not qualify for services. Diagnostic criteria alone, however, do not give us a very clear picture of the range of people who are recipients of public mental health services. The past decade has seen a drastic increase in the number of homeless people in the United States, and the mentally ill are generally thought to comprise between 28 and 40 percent of this population (Koegel, Burnham, and Farr, 1990). The ranks of the chronically mentally ill have been swollen by the addition of a whole new generation of young adult patients who, while generally socially disenfranchised and suffering from multiple problems, have not spent long periods of time in state mental hospitals (McCreath, 1984; Bender, 1986). Added to this are the ever-increasing number of "dually diagnosed" mentally ill individuals who also have substance abuse problems, and the large numbers of immigrants and refugees (Lee and Lu, 1989) who often suffer from the effects of war, racism, and even torture. From this we can get a picture of the current need for community-based mental health services, whose resources, in constant dollars, have been shrinking annually for more than a decade (Elpers, 1989). Meanwhile, the individuals needing such services are more ethnically diverse than at any time in the past (Sands, 1991, p. 155), and ethnic minorities of color comprise a growing percentage of the users of mental health services (Cheung and Snowden, 1990).

Three factors affect the appropriate service package for a given client. The first, of course, is availability. Community mental health services have never been funded at levels adequate to replace services that "deinstitutionalized" clients needed. A variety of factors, including the cessation of direct federal participation in community mental health care, local "taxpayer revolts," and ongoing indifference, if not hostility, toward the mentally disabled have resulted in treatment systems that have seen declining support for several years. Very few communities in this country have the comprehensive service networks needed to sustain seriously mentally ill individuals outside of the hospital with a reasonable quality of life (Gerhart, 1990, p. 11). The second factor is that services must also be accessible to clients. This means geographically, physically, linguistically, and culturally. Changing demographic trends among the users of public mental health services require concurrent changes in services if these services are to be culturally accessible. Finally, the services that do exist need to be carefully coordinated for the client. Perhaps this latter requirement has contributed most to the rising popularity of case management.

Given the diverse forces behind deinstitutionalization, researchers have looked at the need for case management from a variety of perspectives. Inherent in the nature of deinstitutionalization was the mandate to attempt to keep clients out of the hospital. This was reinforced by increasing cost consciousness and by the fact that inpatient services have invariably been the most expensive. One of the primary justifications for the case management approach, therefore, has been that it reduces "recidivism" (Morin and Seidman, 1986; Harris and Bergman, 1988). Increasing evidence supports that indeed it does (Bond et al., 1988; Goering et al., 1988). Others saw a need to reduce duplications of service and general inefficiencies in the delivery system (Deitchman, 1980). Recent thinking, however, has come back to the realization that treating serious mental illness is a long-term process and that relapses requiring brief hospitalizations can be expected to occur periodically in some patients. This wisdom seems to free us from the ongoing paradox of identifying the sole goal of one service (case management) as the reduced utilization of another service (hospital recidivism). Contemporary conceptualizations of the practice of case management, however, see it as a process that should be driven by the needs of the client (Anthony et al., 1988; Kanter, 1991). Such notions have focused upon the needs of the client within the context of functional limitations imposed by long-term mental illness. We should add to these considerations the dimension of the client's ethnic culture. The ethnic culture of the clients blends with their "socialized" culture as mental patients to form complex and often confusing identity amalgams that profoundly affect their attitudes, beliefs, and behavior.

CHARACTERISTICS OF CASE MANAGEMENT

While a variety of definitions of case management have emerged in the literature, they tend to be descriptions of case management tasks that lack a common conceptual base (Goldstrom and Manderscheid, 1983; Spitz and Abramson, 1987). These descriptions have looked at the activities of case managers in public, for-profit, and non-profit settings. Consistent with the two-tiered system of mental health care represented by the public and private sectors respectively, each of these sectors has developed separate models of case management. Public sector case management, the focus of this volume, attempts to secure needed services for an individual from a patchwork of poorly coordinated and underfunded services either operated by, or on contract to, public entities. Private case management is exemplified by the "managed care" field and often takes the form of regulating access to insurance benefits and pre-authorization of service utilization. The practice of case management, nevertheless, is commonly acknowledged to be part of social work's person-in-environment tradition (Leukefeld, 1990). A controversy, however, has arisen over the relative weighting of personal and environmental interventions. This is understandable given the triple historical mandates of maintaining clients out of the hospital, improving their quality of life, and coordinating inadequate and fragmented community services. The emphasis on referral, advocacy, linkage, and service coordination (Turner and TenHoor, 1978; Leavitt, 1983; Johnson and Rubin, 1983) has come to be known as the service brokerage model. Critics have variously called this model too bureaucratic and pathology/deficit-focused. In addition, it has been seen as contributing to a trend to de-professionalize the practice of case management. A modification of the brokerage model is the developmental-acquisition model (Rapp and Chamberlain, 1985; Modrcin, Rapp, and Poertner, 1988). This model emphasizes the development of the client's potential (utilizing his/her strengths) and the acquisition of community resources. The most recent thinking, and that embraced by many of the contributors to this volume, encompasses all of the above, *and* emphasizes, moreover, the importance of the therapeutic relationship between client and case manager. It adds periodic psychotherapy to the list of tasks performed by case managers, and has come to be known as clinical case management (Lamb, 1980; Kanter, 1988; Surber, 1994).

All in all, clinical case management for the seriously mentally ill is "fundamentally a putting into practice of the concept of continuity of care" (Harris and Bachrach, 1988, p. 1). Perhaps the simplest way to conceive of the clinical component of case management is that it involves the conscious use of self by the case manager. Concepts of transference and countertransference arise and often must be interpreted in the context of serious mental illness (Kanter, 1989). Nevertheless, two other levels of relationships must be examined in the practice of clinical case management. While, of course, transference and countertransference classically refer to the relationship between the therapist and client, two other important relationships–that of the client and the environment, here understood as the network of agencies, professionals, and significant others in the client's life, and that of clinical case manager and this environment.

We thus get a picture of a triangular relationship between client, clinical case manager, and the environment.

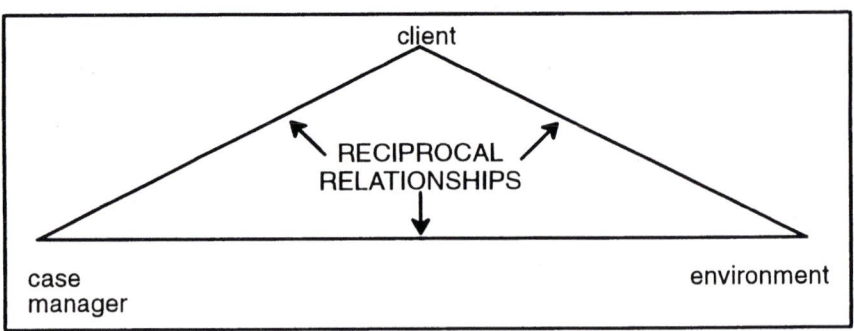

Each side of the triangle consists of a diadic relationship between two of the entities and is a possible target for therapeutic intervention. Consequently, the case manager must make ongoing assessments of both the client's level of functioning and the environment's responsiveness to the client's needs in order to arrive at a systematic and informed judgment about an appropriate point of intervention. This is the main difference between clinical case management and traditional office-based psychotherapy. The central thesis of this volume is that each side of this triangle represents a relationship between either the client and case manager, client and environment, or case manager and environment; that each of these entities has its own complex culture; and that effective clinical case management demands that these three key relationships reflect appropriate cultural bridging between the three entities.

THE ROLE OF CULTURE

Culture can be defined as the vehicle through which one generation passes on to the next its ways of seeing, experiencing, interpreting, and *being*. It serves the purpose of teaching the new generation ways of coping and surviving in the world as the previous generation understood it. Indeed, as D'Andrade (1984, p. 116) explains, it consists of

> learned systems of meaning, communicated by means of natural language and other symbol systems having representational, directive, and affective functions, and capable of creating cultural entities and particular senses of reality. Through these systems of meaning, groups of people adapt to their environment and structure interpersonal activities.

Consequently, culture shapes the basic characteristics of human beings, such as beliefs, emotions, sense of self, and even, as some have claimed, the *diseases* to which one is susceptible. While such a broad definition of culture allows us to interpret behavioral data from a variety of perspectives, and indeed, allows us to practice cultural relativism (Fabrega, 1989a) in public mental health, care must be taken not to overly attribute physical and mental phenomena to cultural influences. Overgeneralization can result in cultural reification, harmful stereotyping, and loss of the individuality that is so important in effective treatment and case management. In fact, intracultural differences may exceed intercultural differences in some cases (Sue, 1981). As Roll, Millen, and Martinez (1980, p. 165) illustrate, "there are some ways in which any particular Chicano is like *all* other Chicanos and there are some ways in which a particular Chicano is like *some* other Chicanos, and there are ways in which a particular Chicano is like *no* other Chicano."

A slightly divergent trend among anthropologists has focused on culture as a set of coherent subsystems or domains of shared knowledge (D'Andrade, 1981), behavioral domains (Roberts, 1964), or semantic domains that feature ways of classifying and talking about phenomena (Romney, Weller, and Batchelder, 1986). This framework allows us to conceive of the professional and bureaucratic environments our clients encounter as having their own cultural characteristics. These environments, for each client, comprise agencies, professionals, formal and informal support networks, and other systems, with each of these groups having its own culture or, more properly, subculture. These subcultures are generally professional and organizational in nature, and members are socialized to advance the mission of the profession or agency in question.

THE CULTURE OF PSYCHIATRY

The term *mental health* itself is an omnipresent reminder to us that perhaps the most pervasive environmental culture with which our clients must interact is the medical/psychiatric culture and its "stepchildren" represented by certain traditional forms of psychotherapy. Disease theory describes the parameters of illness—cause, manifestation, distribution, course, and response to treatment (Fabrega, 1989a). The notions of causality inherent in these parameters have their roots in the scientific method developed over 400 years ago by Galileo and Keppler. Indeed, science is a product of the European cultural tradition and its emphasis on understanding. These European roots require that we consider alternative formulations of problem etiology when serving clients of non-European background. Sigmund Freud, a neurologist by training, was perhaps the first to apply a topographical model in describing the mind. Though the functions of the id, ego, and superego could be abundantly described, one could not dissect them from a brain as one could a frontal lobe or amygdala. Because there is the tendency in medicine to partition human beings into organs, tissues, and chemical processes, the challenge of viewing humans as complex biopsychosocial beings is most acute. Psychiatry has followed this tradition and the practice of partitioning is carried over in the delivery of services in public mental health systems.

Most often, recipients of service from public mental health systems are provided treatment by a team of professionals, each with a specific role in the delivery of services. The effectiveness of the approach depends upon the relationships and communication between team members. There are often large gaps in such communication with the resulting treatment proving ineffective. Case managers are in the unique position of being able to restore the biopsychosocial and holistic viewpoints in the treatment of their clients. Generally, when a person is referred for case management services, he or she has been through the mental health treatment system at least once. At each point in the system, such as the psychiatric emergency service, outpatient clinic, and rehabilitation center, a diagnosis has been made, with the more thorough diagnostic workups usually occurring in inpatient settings. The ongoing diagnostic process is part of the partitioning process that the client goes through. Often this phase of treatment lasts for years and may include multiple exposures to different parts of the treatment system, including hospitalization. By the time a client reaches the case manager, considerable psychodiagnostic work has occurred. The clinical case manager has the unique opportunity to prepare an ongoing treatment plan that is based upon a true biopsychosocial *and* cultural assessment. This may be one of the most important, and least mentioned, functions of clinical case management. Once implemented, the reintegrating effect of case management can mitigate against years of partitioning of the client engendered by the mental health system itself, but may require a change in the thinking of some professional case managers who over-identify with psychiatric culture.

Fabrega (1989b) describes the discipline of psychiatry as consisting of a complex amalgam of the traditions, knowledge, institutions, and practices involved in understanding psychiatric illness that has evolved in Western societies. Central to this practice is the identification and treatment of mental disorder or psychopathology. The field of medical anthropology has adapted the terms *etic* and *emic* from the discipline of linguistic studies. An etic perspective (Snowden and Todman, 1982) describes syndromes, illnesses, and other medical phenomena as scientifically derived, presumably universal, and based upon clearly specified symptoms and processes. The indicators of major disorders are held to be culture free. Diagnosis is arrived at objectively and dispassionately after consulting a listing of standardized classifications of disorders, in this case, the DSM-III. Mirowsky and Ross (1989, p. 16) lay the foundation for exploring the cultural bias in this process by noting:

> The absence of gold standards, the paucity and the uncertain relevance of latent biological classes, and the symptom factors that bear little resemblance to diagnostic [syndromes] lead us to believe that psychiatric diagnoses, whether simulated or clinical, are mythical entities. The diagnoses add nothing to the direct assessment of the feelings, thoughts, acts, and histories (or biochemistries) on which they are based. On the contrary, they degrade information, obscure patterns, and misdirect attention.

The opposing view, called the *emic* perspective, claims that emotional and behavioral phenomena must be evaluated within the context of the affected person's ethnic culture (Breslin, Lonner, and Thorndike, 1973). This line of investigation has brought us research on culture-bound syndromes. Such syndromes have been documented for a variety of ethnic groups. The term *culture-bound syndrome* is used to describe "dramatic behavior, usually of short duration, which is specific to a given culture and without biological cause" (Littlewood and Lipsedge, 1987, p. 94). There are many culture-bound syndromes found in Western society, and a common interpretation is that such syndromes represent a protest of the weak against the strong. Many examples of such syndromes have been documented. Weidman (1979) describes "falling out" among North Americans and Caribbeans of African descent as consisting of sudden collapse and paralysis with the inability to see or speak while hearing and understanding remain intact. Similarly, *ataques de nervios* is a syndrome affecting Puerto Ricans that is taken to constitute an expression of deep anger or sadness and is characterized by shaking, heart palpitations, a sense of heat in the chest rising into the head, and numbness of the hands (Good and DelVecchio-Good, 1980). Bulimia, food binging followed by self-induced vomiting, is found almost exclusively among North American Euro-Americans, mostly women (Westermeyer, 1985; Littlewood and Lipsedge, 1986).

The conflict between Western psychiatric culture and individual ethnic cultures, as an example of etic bias, is not found only in the area of psychodiagnostics. Other concepts central to treatment approaches and symptom assessment such as "physical health," "relaxing," "anxiety," "control over thinking," and "feeling depressed" are integral to Western psychiatry (Fabrega, 1989a). Many of these concepts, when they do translate, have vastly different meanings. Kinzie and associates (1988), for example, report teaching progressive relaxation techniques accompanied by lowered light and voice tones to a group of Southeast Asian Mien clients. Instead of relaxation, the approach elicited anxiety and apprehension. It was subsequently learned that dim light and low voices are associated with a Mien shamanistic ritual to exorcise spirits. Other conflicts with psychiatric culture arise from the less than voluntary status of a large number of public mental health clients.

Many clients of public mental health systems can be said to be involuntary in one sense or another. Either they are court ordered into treatment, pressured by relatives or some other source, or otherwise less than willing consumers of the services. At the very least, the element of choice available to those able to pay for private services is absent. This situation arises from the dual mandates given to public mental health: to provide treatment and to protect society. As resources become scarce, the latter mandate is emphasized and danger to self or others often becomes one of the criteria for service eligibility. All of this means that more and more people are being involuntarily exposed to the culture of psychiatry. Berry (1975) has used the term *imposed etic* to describe such situations where the perspective of one culture is imposed upon another. It is clear, then, that treatment will be most effective when there is the greatest degree of agreement regarding treatment goals between client and system, that is to say, when there is client "buy in." In this sense, the cultural bridging role of the case manager is central. Before examining some specific techniques for doing this, however, we will first turn our attention to several additional sectors of environmental culture faced by the long-term mental health client, and in which the case manager should serve as a bridge.

An alternative, or supplement to the medical model of psychiatric care is the functional or rehabilitation model. This model has evolved from the world of physical disability and entails doing a functional (behavioral) assessment of the client's strengths and deficits. Once this baseline is established, stepwise goals are established for the client in order to be able to progress, presumably in linear fashion, to higher functional levels. This thinking has found programmatic expression in the development of social skills and increasingly independent living situations. Underpinning all of this approach, however, is the implicit goal that clients will eventually engage in some type of employment if they are at all able. The thrust of such rehabilitation is therefore to ingrain work habits and teach work culture to clients who either were never oriented this way or had lost this orientation due to their psychiatric histories. The importance of establishing work culture cannot be overstated. This is the process by which the client gradually abandons the "sick person" self-concept and adopts a "worker" self-concept. It is clear that this happens only with massive support and immersion in the culture of work. Minkoff (1978) found that 30 to 50 percent of patients studied were working within the six-month period following hospital discharge, but these numbers were only 20 to 30 percent at one year following discharge. Fairweather (1969) found that clients in a lodge-type group living setting with a positive work culture had significantly higher rates of full-time employment than did a control group not living in the lodge. Furthermore, those who moved away from the lodge were not able to sustain the higher employment rate. The vocational rehabilitation model is one that is culturally syntonic for members of many ethnic minority cultures, especially males. The "male as breadwinner role" is still valued and sought after by many minorities of color, both males and females, who feel it has been denied them (De La Cancela, 1990). Indeed, among such clients there is still a great deal of belief that connects being employed with masculinity (Staples, 1971). Program participation is much more ego acceptable when the justification for such participation is preparation for employment. The shame of being regarded as crazy, or even the perceived weakness of being ill can be overcome when one sees oneself as preparing to be able to meet one's familial obligations by attending "job classes" rather than group therapy, for example. Clearly many clients who, by virtue of functional disability, will not be able to engage in unsubsidized employment may still be able to gain immense benefit from the dignity and structure that goes with being engaged in some sort of meaningful and productive activity measured to their interests and abilities.

Of course, a very large number of diagnosed mentally ill people will probably never be gainfully employed due to disability, discrimination, lack of useful skills, discouragement, the permanent rate of "structural unemployment" inherent in a capitalist system, or, most likely, as a result of a combination of these factors. There is still enough of a safety net left in the United States to provide subsistence levels of support to such individuals, primarily through Supplemental Security Income (SSI), Social Security Disability Income (SSDI), and Social Security (SS). In some sense, however, the safety net is also a trap. The largest share of individuals who receive such support receive SSI payments. SSI requires the individual to profess his or her disability with certification from a qualified physician; that is, they must formally acknowledge their inability to work. Given the fact that almost all individuals in our society live in a money economy based upon the exchange of labor, goods, and expertise for remuneration, the chronically mentally ill people in question are usually unable or unwilling to participate conventionally in this economic system. This fact suggests the hypothesis that what the clients do exchange or provide (intentionally or unintentionally) for their wages are their disabilities, diagnoses, and deficits. It becomes apparent "that their *disabilities* function as do others *abilities,* that their *incompetence* reaps for them what others *competence* earns" (Estroff, 1981 p. 119). At this point the illness metaphor and the work metaphor get paradoxically intertwined. The clients' perception of their sanity or health status may be influenced and their ability and motivation to work may be undermined simply by being in the treatment system. "The system conveys the messages of poor health, inability to work, and confirmed disability, connecting them with an alternative, secure form of income based on maintaining these conditions" (Estroff, 1981, p. 167). It is the task of the case manager, insofar as possible, to help the client to rationalize these paradoxical dilemmas in a way that preserves maximum dignity for clients. If they are comfortable and adjusted to the notion of being "disabled persons," that adjustment should not be disrupted by pushing them into work programs. On the other hand, if they need financial support but are not comfortable with the welfare culture surrounding SSI, participation in a workshop or sheltered employment can be framed in a way that lets them see they are earning wages and are, in fact, entitled to them. Finally, first time applicants need to be made aware, insofar as they are capable of processing such information, that to receive SSI is to "wear one's disability on one's sleeve," inviting discrimination and stigma. Sharing this perspective is empowering for clients and allows them some choice.

The clinical case manager should examine the characteristics of other subcultures to which the client is exposed and assess areas of potential cultural conflict. Day treatment programs, for example, are usually quite group-oriented. This may be an alien environment for clients who are either not group-oriented, or, more likely, extremely group-oriented within their own families or perhaps within their own ethnic group. For them not to adapt well to a multi-ethnic therapeutic group or milieu does not necessarily mean they are evidencing symptomatic "isolative behavior." Segal, Silverman, and Baumohl (1989) have examined the covariance between a number of client characteristics and a variety of environmental characteristics in a board and care home sample. While they did not specifically look at culture, it is clear that different board and care homes have different cultures. Some have a rehabilitation focus, others a "home-like" atmosphere, and others simply provide lodging. The case manager must exercise whatever influence he or she has to ascertain that this living environment is culturally syntonic for the client. Finally, many public mental health clients have had contact with law enforcement personnel, and may again. The orientation of the police is to protect the public safety, to prioritize their responses, and to seek the most expedient solutions to problems while enforcing the law. The case manager who frames his or her consultation with the police in terms of helping them perform their difficult job is likely to be more successful at protecting his or her client from unnecessary harm than one who professes to be "educating the police about mental illness." This is an example of appropriate cultural bridging.

CULTURE AND MENTAL ILLNESS

While the characteristics of interactions between individual ethnic cultures and serious mental illness will be left for discussion elsewhere in this volume, we must here consider several cultural dimensions and perspectives crucial to effective cross-cultural case management. Sartorius (1992) demonstrated a better prognosis for schizophrenia in developing countries than in the industrialized West. Other studies have found high remission rates and shorter disease courses in developing nations (Murphy and Raman, 1971; Lo and Lo, 1977), and a body of opinion has emerged that *chronicity* in major psychotic disorders is an artifact of cultural belief systems and expectations regarding etiology, duration, and curability (Lefley, 1990). A common explanation for reduced incidences of chronicity in certain non-Western cultures has to do with the perceived causes of behavioral phenomena, or "symptoms," seen as external to the person and thus conveyed through a somatic or supernatural idiom. In this view of causality, the patient is freed from blame; there is less social rejection, less self-devaluation among patients; and expectations are created that aberrations will be brief and temporary (Lin and Kleinman, 1988). It is crucial to assess in both the client and family members their belief regarding the causation of the aberrations suffered by the identified patient. If external or supernatural causes that are culturally syntonic are believed to be involved, some attention to ritualistic cures, ranging from community healers and religious practices to medicinal herbs, may be given. This may have the effect of increasing trust and treatment "buy in" or, at the very least, enhancing placebo effect. From a different perspective it has been suggested, in the dominant North American culture, that chronicity may be a product of the belief system of the clinical establishment, which holds that for most people who suffer from serious mental illness, this disease is inherently chronic (Harding, Zubin, and Strauss, 1987). The "external cause" view tends to maintain existing support systems while the Western view "tracks" a client into the formal treatment system with its psychiatric culture and attendant conflicts. Chronicity is generally felt to be more prevalent in situations where stress is high and social supports have been eroded. Anything that can strengthen these supports will tend to reduce stress on the client. Shamis (1976) notes that many categories of behavior such as evasiveness, impatience, deference, and others are universal, but find culturally specific expressions. Consequently it is preferable to evoke a metaphor to describe the malady drawn from a culture familiar to the client and his/her family. In most cases, this facilitates communication with the case manager and increases agreement on treatment goals. Often such a metaphor serves to explain unacceptable behavior in a way that does not affix blame to any particular family member, but in fact might suggest a "cure." Temporary "loss of the mind" due to supernatural causes is one such metaphor that can be used in conjunction with standard psychopharmacological treatment.

An understanding of personhood consistent with the client's culture is particularly important for people who have been diagnosed as schizophrenics. This is because schizophrenia is a disorder that fragments the self and such an understanding is key to how self-disorganization is experienced and evaluated (Lefley, 1990). In Western culture, loss of self entails a loss of autonomy, control, and meaning that makes it difficult for afflicted persons to distance themselves from the illness. This fusion of identity with illness leads to alienation, despair, and chronicity (Fabrega, 1989c). Related to this is the concept of the degree of personal interdependence considered normal within a given culture. Since greater interdependence is generally associated with non-Western cultures, case managers must have an appropriate understanding of this reality in order to properly apply such terminology as "ego boundaries," "enmeshed family," or "pathological dependence." Fabrega (1989a, p. 424) describes schizophrenic psychopathology as reflecting "an alteration of the ability of the self to orient symbolically in its culturally created and structured world." Such a conceptualization avoids the etic bias inherent in the terminology previously described.

In addition to the partitioning of human beings introduced by Western medical traditions, we also see a tendency to "psychologize" explanations for disfunction. Members of many non-European cultures tend to express imbalance or discomfort in their lives through the somatic sphere. In those cultures, changes in bodily perceptions and reports of bodily symptoms and complaints are accepted as describing a "real" medical entity. Symptoms of depression are often expressed via stomach, neck, and other physical complaints. Fabrega (1989a, p. 422), for example, has observed, "In all types of societies hidden things (e.g., spirits, viruses, genes, sorcery) play a role in accounting for illnesses, and culture stipulates their reality." Western psychiatry, by contrast, places emphasis on cognition, emotion, and related *mentalistic* structures, events, processes, or attitudes as the critical parameters of psychiatric illness (Kirmayer, 1984). The areas of thought and emotion are typical of the "mentalistic sphere" emphasized by the Western psychiatric tradition. Such an emphasis, with its etic bias may partially explain the underdiagnosis of certain syndromes, particularly depression, among groups that employ the somatic idiom, such as African Americans, Asians, and Latinos. Kleinman and Good (1985) attempt to minimize etic bias by suggesting that "neurovegetative symptoms of depression flow from the altered meanings life now has for the altered [depressed] self." In this regard, a cognitive therapy approach is probably the one that is most free of cultural bias as it works with the connections between the client's existing cognitions while basically validating healthy cultural beliefs. In any event, case managers must be attuned to the client's cultural preference for voicing complaints, whether it is via the somatic vehicle, the mentalistic vehicle, or a combination of the two.

CULTURE AND THE ACTIVITIES OF CASE MANAGEMENT

Case management has been described as a process for mobilizing, coordinating, and linking the components of the service delivery system (Billig and Levinson, 1989). A plethora of authors have described the tasks of case managers serving the seriously mentally ill (Intagliata, 1982; Harrod, 1986; Harris and Bergman, 1988; Kanter, 1989; Gerhart, 1990). It is now possible to review some of the major tasks and look at the role culture may play in each of them.

The initial task of the case manager is the formation of positive relationships. Unquestionably, the effectiveness of any case manager depends, in part, upon the relationship (s)he is able to form with the client, family, and other key people in the client's environment. This can be especially challenging with clients whose very disability makes interpersonal relating and intimacy difficult, as is the case with those suffering from psychotic disorders (Harris and Bergman, 1988). Many chronically mentally ill people are lonely, isolated, and have difficulty forming and maintaining relationships (Deitchman, 1980). Almost certainly, this type of client will have had extensive experience with the mental health system by the time his/her case reaches the case manager. The quality of that experience will shape the expectations the client and the family have for future interventions and treatment. This is part of the "institutional transference" that most clients experience. In order to form an effective and positive therapeutic relationship with clients and their families, case managers will have to work through feelings about previous experiences with the mental health system that may have been disappointing or outright negative. This may include working sensitively with the client's reactions to the psychiatric culture itself. Most clients will form quick opinions about the degree of identification the case manager has with the psychiatric culture based upon the clinician's behavior. Case managers must also form effective working relationships with key community providers of service and others in the client's environment. As a general rule, the best relationships are those based upon mutual respect. Case managers will benefit their efforts in forming such relationships by attempting to learn all they can about agency and organizational subcultures as well as their clients' ethnic cultures. This knowledge can lead to better understanding of the difficult jobs others face and of challenges inherent in some of the other subcultures. Conversely, exhaustive efforts need to be made to educate others about the perspective of clinical case management. Communication can be facilitated by reframing areas of disagreement around the fact that all parties involved are there for the best interests of the client.

The overall goal of clinical case management is to support the optimal functioning and quality of life of the client by attempting to remove barriers, both internal and external, to this objective. Thus defined, it is a process that combines elements of classical casework and psychotherapy. Case managers must affirmatively deal with environmental barriers to client success, but also must be involved with symptom management. The latter can entail working with clients' behaviors, cognitions, and feelings. The debate about casework *versus* psychotherapy consequently represents a false and reductionistic dichotomy insofar as clinical case management with the seriously mentally ill is concerned. A thorough assessment of the client's needs, both material and clinical, must be combined with an evaluation of the environment's responsiveness to those needs.

As mentioned, most clients have had considerable experience in the mental health system by the time the case manager sees them. They have received one or several diagnoses, and as Draguns (1977) notes,

> . . . the decision about who is disturbed and who is not has already been made for the assessor [in this situation, the case manager], in part by previous professionals, and in part by family members and others in the community by having directed the individual to services.

The task of the case manager is to assess independently the client's condition and needs in a culturally sensitive manner, taking into account the dimensions mentioned in the previous section, and to evaluate the client's behavior within the standards of her/his own community. Where etic bias is found to exist in evaluations inherited by the case manager, it is his or her obligation to reformulate the assessment, perhaps even the diagnosis if warranted, and to advocate for such revisions within the network of treatment providers. This is extremely important insofar as all case planning and decisions about subsequent interventions will be based upon this assessment.

The assessment should be holistic and comprehensive, not only evaluating the client's pathology and limitations, but emphasizing the client's strengths and potential for growth in self-esteem and in other areas such as independent living and productive activity. Looking at where along the acculturation continuum the person falls comprises an important part of the assessment. Such an assessment should include evaluating their biculturality and/or cultural blend if applicable. In evaluating the degree of importance of the person's ethnic culture, decisions must be made about how much emphasis to place upon the values and perspectives of the culture in question.

Such an assessment provides safeguards against possible *emic* bias, that is to say, attributing the client's experiences to cultural factors when they are in fact due to psychopathology.

The second part of the assessment entails an evaluation of the client's environment. Case managers must identify stressors and areas of conflict that may lead to symptom activation or exacerbation as well as social supports that will tend to act in a positive way for the client. Such stressors may consist of loss, change, isolation, or deprivation. Each stressor, once identified, must be evaluated for the degree to which it may affect the client's functioning, and the degree to which the client sees it as important. Recommendations can then be made for managing these stressors (Leavitt, 1983). They must also evaluate family members, staff of community living facilities, and other individuals with whom the client will come in frequent contact for their level of tolerance of symptomatic behavior. It is also necessary, at times, for case managers to identify any ideological rigidity the client may encounter among various agencies or professionals. When this exists, it usually emanates from that particular environmental subculture. Examples of such ideological rigidity can be found in outpatient clinics that accept clients based upon their capacity for "insight," or substance abuse programs that will not accept clients who also carry psychiatric diagnoses. These rigidities act as barriers to service when clients must meet eligibility requirements based upon their "prognosis" for responding favorably to the particular approach in question. This often results in a "blaming the victim" approach to serving the seriously mentally ill.

The case manager has a variety of possible tools for interacting with the client's environment. First of all, psychoeducation, which has generally been thought of as a technique for use with family members, can be adapted for others in the client's environment including professionals. Specific techniques such as culture brokering and the cross-cultural reframe will be examined later. Advocacy, a key function of case management, will also be addressed in a separate section.

The planning process the case manager goes through for any given client is a natural extension of the assessment. In this phase, problems are prioritized and goals are established. Global goals generally have to do with reducing or managing active symptoms, maintaining a stable community adjustment, supporting the client for risking new behaviors and intimacies, and improving the client's quality of life. Inherent in the goal of symptom management is generally the notion of increasing internal locus of control over behavior and also increasing the client's ability to focus extrinsically, that is to say, socially. The much-abused notion of "appropriate" behavior clearly carries with it the possibility of cultural bias. While behavior must be evaluated in its cultural context, care must be taken not to under-identify symptomatic behavior. The goal of increasing internal locus of control of behavior must be consistent with culturally syntonic notions of behavioral causality. Perhaps nowhere is this more difficult to evaluate than in the proper identification of "religious preoccupation," which is generally taken to be symptomatic. Such behavior must be evaluated not only against prevailing community and cultural norms, but also against the client's own premorbid level of functioning. Sudden onsets of religiosity, without obvious external precipitant (such as a major catastrophe), are generally suspect. "Visions," or talking to God clearly cannot be assumed to be symptomatic without further evidence. Culturally relevant community baseline data must often be gathered as the following case illustrates.

> A clinical case manager in the San Francisco Bay Area recently reported in a case conference on a 29-year-old male Vietnamese immigrant who had attempted to burn off two of his fingers. When questioned, the client responded that he had been performing a Buddhist ritual. The clinician, being uninformed about such practices and recalling Vietnam War era television images of self-immolating Buddhist monks, decided she needed further information. After consulting with family members and a local Buddhist priest, she decided that the behavior was a product of internal psychotic stimulation and not a culturally appropriate religious response.

Goals must always include making sure the client's material needs are met first before any goals of a psychological nature. Deitchman (1980) discusses how beginning with the provision of tangibles such as food, clothing, and shelter can serve to establish trust. Expanding upon this, it is important to begin in a way that is consistent with the cultural expectations of the client, family, and significant others. In other words, the case manager must investigate just what type of "help" is expected by clients.

Assuring continuity of care and coordinating services for clients requires the case manager to be involved in the *linking* function. This term implies a much more active approach than that which is usually involved in making a "referral." Unquestionably, there is an extreme scarcity of services for the mentally ill, and there probably never will be an adequate quantity of programs available. This results in a situation where there are lines, waiting lists, and, in fact, competition for available services. Consequently, like it or not, part of the case manager's role is in "marketing" the client, or getting him or her accepted for necessary community services. The effectiveness of the case manager in the linking function depends, in part, on *how* referrals are made. This often involves a good deal of informal interpersonal negotiation (Riffer and Freedman, 1980). Case managers can enhance their personal credibility and hence their effectiveness by being knowledgeable about various agency priorities and subcultures. Kanter (1991), for example, has commented on the often hierarchical medical structures of hospital settings versus the relatively egalitarian structures of community programs. These structures clearly have implications for decision making about clients. The case manager should feel at home in either subculture, and in a sense use this "biculturality" to facilitate acceptance of the client in the appropriate program(s). Often, dispositional decisions are made about clients not only without their input, but also on the basis of distorted views of how different programs operate. Case managers should play a major role in reducing such misperceptions and in promoting optimal collaboration.

Closely related to the case manager's linking function is his or her advocacy function. Advocacy generally will be needed at both the individual and system levels (Intagliata, 1982). Individual advocacy efforts are geared toward securing goods and services needed by clients, and helping them to be supported in both their ethnic community *and* the various agency subcultures. Such advocacy serves as an attempt to help the mentally ill person to mainstream into these various subcultures without fragmenting his or her ethnic self. At the same time, the case manager may have to intervene with family members and others to confront certain ethnic-based attitudes about mental illness when the client is negatively affected by them. All advocacy on the individual level must strengthen social supports. The personal style of the case manager when advocating for the client is as important an issue as is style in the psychotherapeutic context. Methods used in advocacy are dictated by the situation and range along a continuum from educating, consulting, and "reframing" to confrontation.

System-level advocacy generally occurs around developing more services, and against the loss of existing services. In an era of mental health cutbacks, every case manager should also be a "mental health activist." Such efforts can involve coalition building, single issue community organizing, and lobbying. They can also be geared toward increasing access by people labeled mentally ill to services and institutions not specifically designed to serve them. This involves confronting barriers supported by discrimination and stigma. Especially important in this era of profound cultural diversity is not adopting "one size fits all" attitudes toward services. Mental health and related services should be physically, linguistically, and culturally accessible to clients and their families. Advocating for such services in an active manner is an integral part of being a good clinical case manager.

Clinical case managers, though they are non-medical professionals, have a major role in medications, as a great number of the seriously mentally ill take some form of neuroleptic or another. In an attempt to guard against negative side effects and to maximize client compliance and satisfaction, case managers often play a key role in recommending dosage levels and monitoring effects. Case managers may act as the gatekeepers who determine whether or not an individual needs to be seen by the physician. In all of these ways, case managers exercise some indirect discretion about medications and should be as knowledgeable about them as possible. Recently, investigators have been looking increasingly at the comparative effects of psychotropic medications across ethnic groups (Keltner and Folks, 1992). Lawson (1986) found that Asian Americans tended to develop extrapyramidal side effects at lower dosage levels than either African Americans or Euro-Americans. In several studies reported by Lin (1986), Chinese patients responded to neuroleptics with higher plasma levels than did Caucasians, and received a therapeutic effect at appreciably lower doses. Latino patients taking tricyclic antidepressants have been reported to experience side effects at half the dosages seen in Anglos (Marcos and Cancro, 1982). Lefley (1990) suggests that action-oriented clients such as Anglo-Americans, with a need to control their environment, require larger dosages of sedating drugs than other patients. Rivera (1988) noted that among Latinos in New York City, typically Puerto Ricans or Cubans, polypharmacy and sharing medications within the family was a common practice. African Americans have significantly higher plasma levels of tricyclic antidepressants than whites when weight and age are controlled for (Zeigler and Biggs, 1977). Since tricyclic overdose accounts for more than 25 percent of all hospital admissions (Harsch and Holt, 1988), cultural differences must be carefully considered. Dworkin and Adams (1987) found no correlation between the dropout rate of Latino outpatients and receiving injectable medications. Case managers need to be as familiar with these findings and others that comprise the body of knowledge that looks at inter-ethnic differences in medication usage and effect as they are with the etically derived literature on psychopharmacology. Furthermore, routinely educating other professionals about this body of knowledge should be an integral part of their practice.

Working with families is a very important part of the practice of case management. Goldman, Morrissey, and Bachrach (1982) reported that about 65 percent of hospitalized patients return to live with their families, thus creating a need for provider-family alliances. Dynamic approaches to family therapy with the seriously mentally ill that emphasize the family's role in the etiology of the disorder, as in the "schizophrenogenic" family, are no longer thought to be viable as the biological basis for the disorder is more frequently cited. A psychoeducational approach that addresses client and family concerns, when adapted to the family's ethnicity, can be useful for the family living with a mentally ill person and can encourage family members to take an active role in the treatment plan. In these sessions, the case manager works to find ways to help the client and family conceptualize the experiences of the identified patient and metaphors for treatment that will help increase compliance with the plan for rehabilitation or maintenance. It is important to work with family members regarding their reactions to the intentions, motives, and behavior of the identified patient. Structural family therapy has been found to be a culturally syntonic approach for families that have experienced role disruption as a result of immigration, racism, underemployment, or the fact of serious mental illness itself (Minuchin, 1976). It is a technique that explores, clarifies, and reinforces hierarchical family roles. Working with families, whether or not the client lives with them, is an important part of strengthening the support system of the client. Periodic brief supportive psychotherapy and individual counseling are an integral part of clinical case management for long-term psychiatric clients. Prolonged psychodynamic therapy is generally considered to be ineffective, particularly for clients with chronic schizophrenia (McGlashan, 1982) The nature of the disorder, rather than the client's ethnicity, is what seems to be related to this ineffectiveness. This does not mean that the parameters of psychotherapy are not to be considered. Transference, where the client has a regressed sense of self, should be managed at a non-threatening level. Culturally competent psychotherapy requires that the case manager examine, in an ongoing way, the following questions related to countertransference: Who am I? Who do others (particularly the client and family) think I am? What are my own attitudes and beliefs about mental illness? about spirituality? about psychiatry? and, particularly, about the client's race/ethnicity? The clinician should assess his or her own degree of biculturality. Valle (1986, p. 137) speaks of bicultural individuals as persons "who reintegrate their cultural past at the lifestyle and the language/group interaction/group values identification level, but also represent a fusion of cultures though not at the expense of (each) other."

In addition to the attention to countertransference issues mentioned above, culturally competent counseling or psychotherapy requires that the practitioner demonstrate certain knowledge about the client's specific culture. Valle (1986) sees these broad knowledge areas as a working understanding of (1) the clients' symbolic/ linguistic systems, (2) the clients' naturalistic-interactional patterns, and (3) the values and beliefs held by the target ethnic group population. Culturally competent practice requires the ability to incorporate these elements into any planned intervention with members of the ethnic group in question.

THE CULTURE BROKER

From the above examination of the tasks a clinical case manager must perform with the seriously mentally ill, it becomes evident that such practitioners fill a variety of roles, sometimes concomitantly. They are at times caseworkers, advisors, therapists, friends, teachers, and advocates. How are we, then, to conceive of the pervasive role of the case manager, which encompasses the considerable cultural bridging described in these pages? The term *culture broker,* adopted from the field of anthropology where it is used to describe a person who serves as a link between two or more cultures, is helpful in this regard.

Weidman (1982, p. 211) has adapted the term for use in health care by writing,

> The process of cultural brokerage includes the establishment and maintenance of a system of interaction, mutual support, and communication between cocultures expressed through the culture broker's role. The process of mediation protects the cultural values of the involved ethnic groups. . . . Change is toward increased cultural appropriateness, access to resources, better health, and more compliance with medical regimens.

One of the key functions a culture broker performs is to make the medical/psychiatric culture more aware of, and sensitive to, the role multiplicity and complexity inherent in a person's ethnic culture. The medical/psychiatric culture, by definition, usually only relates to the person's "sick" role. Schwab, Drake, and Burghardt (1988, p. 176) note that the perspective of the culture broker model reflects the view that beliefs and behavior often "make sense" when viewed in their natural social contexts and from the point of view of the people involved. They include "translation" as a function of culture brokering, and illustrate this with the following case:

> The client was a 26-year-old schizophrenic man who was extremely paranoid and suffered from almost constant auditory hallucinations. The man's mother took him to the hospital emergency room because of vomiting and stomach pain. A communication stalemate was broken when the case manager

served as a translator, helping the physician to understand that the demon in the patient's stomach was a sharp pain and assuring the client that he would not be harmed by the doctor. The case manager was able to translate because she understood the metaphors by both parties.

Clinical case managers must be effective communicators if they are to be successful in their roles as culture brokers. In this regard, appropriate cross-cultural usage of language is crucial.

LANGUAGE

Language can be thought of as saying *something,* whereas culture, via metaphorical representations, can be thought of as saying something that is meaningful and situationally appropriate. The role of language has been explored in the cognitive functioning of bilingual individuals (Javier and Alpert, 1986) and in personality development (Marcos and Alpert, 1976). There is no question that language is one of the basic tools used by case managers and other clinicians who have been described as interpersonal change agents, or "professional communicators." Case managers must be sensitive to the diversity of nonstandard English forms found in the United States. Valentine (1971) challenged the simplistic notion of "Black English" by noting that African-American English patterns have evolved out of the African diaspora cultures of the West Indies, Guyana, and Suriname. Contemporary immigration patterns in the U.S. would have to add Ethiopia, and several West African nations to this mix. African-American nonstandard English is but one category of nonstandard English dialects, with Louisiana Cajun, Hawaiian pidgin, Southern, New England, and Brooklynese as examples of others.

In addition to the various dialects found in the United States, case managers, depending upon the area of the country in which they practice, are sure to encounter bilingual individuals, as well as those who are monolingual in a language other than English. Javier (1989, p. 89) describes two major types of bilingual people. The compound bilingual is a person who is equally proficient in both languages and is thereby thought to maintain a unitary linguistic organization for both languages. The subordinate bilingual describes the person who is deficient in a second language and therefore relies on first language processing to communicate in the second language. Clinical case managers must assess which of these two classifications best describes the client and each of the family members involved. When a client is monolingual in a language other than English, it is the obligation of the case manager to work with an appropriate interpreter. The term *interpreter* is used as opposed to *translator,* the latter implying someone who changes the meaning of what the client has said. It can be problematic when this happens in the mental health field, as well-meaning interpreters sometimes tend to "normalize" in translation an utterance by the client that was otherwise nonsensical. This can lead to the underidentification of pathology.

Putsch (1985) has issued a comprehensive set of guidelines for clinicians working through translators, which is partially summarized here.

1. Avoid using family members wherever possible. This will alter the dynamics of the family structure and skew the clinician's assessment.
2. Become familiar with special terminology used by patients. Specific beliefs, practices, and traditions are often referenced by indirect language or special terms.
3. Meet with the interpreter prior to the session.
4. Allow the clients to bring their own interpreter if they so choose, especially where sensitive material may be involved.
5. Be patient. Careful interpretation often requires that the interpreter use long explanatory phrases.
6. Talk directly to the client, not the interpreter. This is with whom the clinical relationship should be.
7. Develop alternatives to direct, intrusive questioning. Some non-Western clients may respond better to a conversational style.
8. Rumors, jealousy, privacy, and reputation are crucial issues in closely knit communities. Acknowledge this fact and assure the client of confidentiality.

When judiciously used, with proper word and phrase choice, language can be a powerful therapeutic tool. An integral part of culturally appropriate language is the use of metaphors.

THE USE OF METAPHORS

Metaphorical expression is a common way of conceiving of and communicating human feelings and experiences that is used in many cultures. Lakoff and Johnson (1980, p. 22) observe that "The most fundamental values in a culture will be coherent with the metaphorical structure of the most fundamental concepts in the culture." Metaphors are powerful communication tools and can be very useful when attempting to structure the context of an experience or influence the behavior of another person. Metaphors are so integral to a culture that Lakoff and Johnson (1980, p. 19) write: "no metaphor can ever be comprehended or even adequately represented independently of its experiential basis." Lankton and Lankton (1989) note that metaphors infuse life with worth, purpose, and meaning, and see them as valuable in motivating people and allowing them to have new insights. Littman (1985) cites the indirect messages of metaphors as being useful in accessing affective aspects of the personality that are often too strongly defended to be directly reachable. Metaphor selection has profound clinical importance as well as being the key to effective cross-cultural communication. Zuniga (1992), for example, has explored the metaphoric power of *dichos* in clinical work with Latino clients.

Therapeutic communication with a schizophrenic person should be guided by the fact that the disorder fragments the self. The metaphors used by the clinical case manager should therefore be based on complete experience and avoid secondary abstractions such as "Money talks," and "The book says not to do it that way" (action by inanimate objects). Examples of other types of metaphors that are contraindicated are: "Life cheated you" (personification), and "She liked to read Kafka" (metonymy). Metaphors that fragment the mind and body and thus contribute to depersonalization should also be avoided. Examples of such metaphors are, "a broken heart," or "the emptiness inside." Creative metaphors, however, can impart new meaning (Lakoff and Johnson, 1980, p.139). Such new meaning can be integral to the cognitive restructuring process that is part of the therapy with clients and their families. The use of such metaphors can reframe issues, contextualize feelings, help mutual understanding, and instill hope and inspiration. Examples are: "Therapy is like an intricate dance between two or more people," and "A whole family often feels as one person." The effectiveness of the metaphor depends upon how culturally syntonic it is. With proper timing, it is usually possible to use phrases like "Life is . . . ," or "Love is . . . ." The case manager should choose metaphors that relate to the client's actual life experience. If we are sufficiently familiar with the family's culture, the use of the proper metaphor can be not only supportive, but can also ease emotional pain (a common metaphor itself) as well.

The right metaphor can help a client "see" a situation in a certain way that then permits action on the client's part as the following example illustrates:

> One local case manager reports having been the co-facilitator of a weekly group comprised primarily of middle-aged, depressed, African-American women, a number of whom had moved to the large urban setting from the rural South. One woman reported weekly, with much anguish, on the latest antics of her adult, drug-addicted daughter who still lived with her. Despite prolonged urging from the group that the woman put her daughter out of her home, the client was not able to do it. Conceptualizations from the case manager like "unhealthy," and "codependent" were distinctly unhelpful. One day, one of the other group members gazed into the air and mused, "You know, each pot's got to stand on its own bottom." The client's face lit up and that evening she went home and confronted her daughter about finding her own place to live.

Rhodes (1984) has written about the use of metaphors in attempting to increase client compliance with medication regimens. The most commonly used metaphors in this regard have been comparing psychiatric disorders to other illnesses. For example, in explaining to a schizophrenic client and his/her family why medication will be necessary for a long time, clinicians often use other medical metaphors such as "Schizophrenia is like diabetes: you cannot be cured from it, but as long as you take your medication, you can live a relatively normal life. You'll always have to be careful, though." Such metaphors are effective at times; in other instances, clinicians are amazed at the levels of "noncompliance" demonstrated by clients. This is not surprising insofar as metaphors are not used that relate to the client's *internal* subjective states such as feeling and thinking. The efficacy of psychotropic medication is generally judged by its effect on "symptoms," i.e., external observable behavior. When a client says that the medication makes him feel "dead" inside, it is not surprising that noncompliance with prescribed drugs follows along with subsequent attempts to ameliorate such feelings with alcohol or illicit drugs. The case manager must try to discover what metaphors are meaningful to the client in describing her or his experience. Illness is but one of these, however. To pursue the illness metaphor when it is not appropriate, and describe the client as "resistant" and "lacking insight" can result in unnecessary power struggles and be disempowering for the client. Using a different metaphor can result, paradoxically, in a greater degree of compliance with behaviors sought by the clinician. The case manager must pursue metaphors about the mind and spirit, and about body and body parts that correspond to the client's cultural beliefs. Only then can the clinician derive metaphors about what can affect these entities, such as "control the emotions," "change the personality," or "calm the nerves."

CULTURAL REFRAMING

A final technique that can be useful in the process of cultural brokering often uses both strategic language and metaphors. For this purpose, the introduction of the term *cultural reframing* is timely. Reframing is a technique used in psychotherapy whereby new meaning is given to an attitude, belief, or perception of an event by a change in context. It alters the way a person "sees" something and is closely related to the Gestalt phenomenon of field-ground perception, and somewhat related to what has been called insight. This new way of "seeing" often opens the door to different behavior. Cultural reframing can be used by a clinical case manager in either intra-cultural, or cross-cultural situations. Most often, it is appropriate to use a positive form of the cross-cultural reframe when the relationship between the client and the treatment environment is in question, as the following example illustrates:

> A case manager attended the team discharge planning meeting at a psychiatric inpatient unit. The case being discussed was a 17-year-old woman who was born in Hong Kong and whose family had moved to the U.S. when she was 11. She was admitted to the hospital with a diagnosis of schizophrenia and had recompensated to the point where she could be discharged. Team members commented on how "protective," "overinvolved," and "enmeshed" the family members seemed to be. These were seen as factors that were likely to contribute to a relapse for the patient. The team consensus therefore moved toward a community care home placement. The case manager was certain that the client would get lost in such an alien cultural environment. She reframed the family's involvement as a strong, positive support that the client was unlikely to get elsewhere. She suggested discharge to her home with family therapy as part of the discharge plan. The family therapy was to be with an Asian-American therapist with the goal of "positive individuation" for the client. The case manager knew this would take some time. The team finally agreed with the plan.

The *intra*-cultural reframe is used when a cultural belief, attitude, or tradition is acting as an obstacle to optimal functioning for the client or family. Traditional gender roles may fall into this category when they conflict with survival demands placed by a contemporary U.S. economy. The following is an example of the usage of intracultural reframe to get a family "unstuck" in its efforts to help the identified client.

> The client was the second eldest female in a Puerto Rican family of eight grown children, all of whom had their own families. She was divorced and had been hospitalized once for depression and polydrug abuse. She was now living with her elderly parents who were infirm and needed 24-hour assistance. The client was receiving compensation from the county as the official caregiver. A crisis came when the client called a

meeting of the siblings to say she needed some respite. There was a plan advanced whereby each of the siblings would rotate taking a weekend with the parents, allowing the client the weekend off. An obstacle was encountered when two of the three eldest males complained that such caregiving was the role of women, and that this sort of thing would not have happened back in Puerto Rico. The whole plan would therefore not work as the female siblings each had jobs and family responsibilities of their own. The case manager arranged individual meetings with each of these male siblings to "talk about your sister." In these meetings he reframed the one weekend every other month as an opportunity to have the parents all to themselves, something that rarely happened with eight children as they were growing up. Also, as the parents were quite old, the case manager argued that it would be an opportunity to spend some intense time with parents while they were still around. This reframing made sense to them. The plan was able to move forward, thus providing needed support to the client.

Each of these techniques of cultural reframing can be useful, along with strategic usage of language and metaphors, as clinical case managers execute their culture brokering roles.

CONCLUSION

Case management has emerged as a fundamental method of practice in public mental health. While some claim it is nothing more than good old-fashioned casework as social workers have always practiced it, key modifications need to be made to the casework model for the practice to be effective in public mental health in the 1990s. The specific nature of the psychiatric disability makes it imperative that clinical case managers be knowledgeable about these disabilities. In reality, the case manager is often the service provider who sustains the most therapeutic relationship with the client and is the person in the best position to do periodic psychotherapy using appropriate methodologies such as cognitive and behavioral approaches. While there is increasing agreement that clinical case management should be driven by the needs of the client rather than by the mental health system, little attention has been given to the implications this principle holds for the immensely culturally diverse groups of people constituting the consumers of public mental health services. Meeting the challenge presented by the fact that each of these consumers has her/his own ethnic culture while the "system" is driven by psychiatric and other environmental cultures often alien to the client lies very much within the domain of concerns belonging to clinical case management. The fact that public mental health clients are, willingly or not, socialized into the roles associated with the monolithic and often strange psychiatric culture no doubt accounts for a significant portion of poor treatment outcomes. Adding the role of culture broker to the complex roles already performed by case managers will not only provide an alternative to the "one size fits all" approach of mental health services, but will no doubt improve the outcomes of treatment/rehabilitation and help create a system that is truly client-driven.

REFERENCES

Acosta, F. X., Yamamoto, J., and Evans, L. A. (1982). *Effective Psychotherapy for Low Income and Minority Patients.* New York: Plenum.

Adebimpe, V. (1984). American Blacks and Psychiatry. *Transcultural Psychiatric Research Review, 21,* 83-111.

Anthony, W., Cohen, M., Farkas, M., and Cohen, B. (1988, Fall). Clinical Care Update: The Chronically Mentally Ill. Case Management–More Than a Response to a Dysfunctional System. *Community Mental Health Journal, 24*(3).

Bender, M. G. (1986). Young Adult Chronic Patients: Visibility and Style of Interaction in Treatment. *Hospital and Community Psychiatry, 37,* 265-268.

Berry, J. (1975). Ecology, Cultural Adaptation and Psychological Differentiation: Traditional Patterning and Acculturative Stress. In R. Breslin, S. Bochner, and W. Lonner (Eds.), *Cross-Cultural Perspectives on Learning* (207-231). New York: John Wiley and Sons.

Billig, N., and Levinson, C. (1989). Social Work Students as Case Managers. *Hospital and Community Psychiatry, 40*(4).

Bond, G. R., Miller, L. D., Krumweid, R. D., and Ward, S. (1988). Assertive Case Management in Three CMHCs: A Controlled Study. *Hospital and Community Psychiatry, 39,* 411-418.

Breslin, R., Lonner, W., and Thorndike, R. (1973). *Cross-Cultural Research Methods.* New York: John Wiley and Sons.

Cheung, F., and Snowden, L. (1990). Community Mental Health and Ethnic Minority Populations. *Community Mental Health Journal, 26*(3).

Comas-Diaz, L., and Griffith, E. (Eds.). (1988). *Clinical Guidelines in Cross-Cultural Mental Health.* New York: John Wiley and Sons.

D'Andrade, R. G. (1981). The Cultural Part of Cognition. *Cognitive Sciences, 5,* 179-195.

D'Andrade, R. G. (1984). Cultural Meaning Systems. In R. A. Shwedes and R. A. Levine (Eds.), *Cultural Theory: Essays on Mind, Self, and Emotion* (88-119). Cambridge, MA: Cambridge University Press.

Deitchman, W. S. (1980). How Many Case Managers Does It Take to Screw in a Light Bulb? *Hospital and Community Psychiatry, 31,* 788-789.

De La Cancela, V. (1990). Latino CMI Males: Social Therapy Approaches. *The Clinical Psychologist, 43*(5).

Draguns, J. G. (1977). Problems of Defining and Comparing Abnormal Behavior Across Culture. *Annals of the New York Academy of Sciences, 285,* 664-675.

Draguns, J. G. (1980). Psychological Disorders of Clinical Severity. In H. C. Triandis and J. G. Draguns (Eds.), *Handbook of Cross-Cultural Psychology: Vol. 6 Psychopathology.* Boston: Allyn and Bacon.

Dworkin, R. J., and Adams, G. (1987). Retention of Hispanics in Public Sector Mental Health Services. *Community Mental Health Journal, 23,* 204-216.

Elpers, J.R. (1989). Public Mental Health Funding in California, 1959 to 1989. *Hospital and Community Psychiatry,* 40(8), 799-804.

Estroff, S. (1981). Making It Crazy. Berkeley: University of California Press.

Fabrega, H. (1987). Psychiatric Diagnosis: A Cultural Perspective. *Journal of Nervous and Mental Disease, 175*(7).

Fabrega, H. (1989a). Cultural Relativism and Psychiatric Illness. *Journal of Nervous and Mental Disease, 177*(7).

Fabrega, H. (1989b). An Ethnomedical Perspective on Anglo-American Psychiatry. *American Journal of Psychiatry, 146,* 588-596.

Fabrega, H. (1989c). The Self and Schizophrenia: A Cultural Perspective. *Schizophrenia Bulletin, 15,* 277-290.

Fairweather, G. W. (Ed.). (1969). Community Life for the Mentally Ill. Chicago: Aldine.

Gerhart, U. (1990). *Caring for the Chronic Mentally Ill.* New York: F. E. Peacock Publishers, Inc.

Gibbs, J., and Huang, L. (Eds.). (1989). *Children of Color: Psychological Interventions with Minority Youth.* San Francisco: Jossey-Bass.

Goering, P. N., Wasylenki, D., Farkas, M., and Ballentine, R. (1988) What Difference Does Case Management Make? *Hospital and Community Psychiatry,* 39, 272-276.

Goldman, H.H., Morrissey, J.P., and Bachrach, L.L. (1982). Deinstitutionalization in International Perspective: Variations on a Theme. *International Journal of Mental Health,* 11(4), 153-165.

Goldstrom, I., and Manderscheid, R. A. (1983). Descriptive Analysis of Community Support Program Case Managers Serving the Chronically Mentally Ill. *Community Mental Health Journal, 19,* 17-26.

Good, B. J., and Del Vecchio-Good, M. J. (1980). The Meaning of Symptoms. In L. Eisenberg and A. Kleinman (Eds.), *The Relevance of Social Science for Medicine* (165-196). Boston: D. Reidel Publishing Co.

Harding, C. M., Zubin, J., and Strauss, J. S. (1987). Chronicity in Schizophrenia: Fact, Partial Fact, or Artifact? *Hospital and Community Psychiatry, 38,* 477-486.

Harris, M., and Bachrach, L. L. (1988). *Clinical Case Management. New Directions for Mental Health Services.* No. 40, San Francisco: Jossey-Bass.

Harris, M., and Bergman, L. I. (1988). Case Management and Continuity of Care for the "Revolving-Door" Patient. In M. Harris and L. L. Bachrach (Eds.), *Clinical Case Management. New Directions for Mental Health Services.* No. 40, Winter.

Harrod, J. (1986). Defining Case Management in Community Support Systems. *Psychosocial Rehabilitation Journal, 9*(3), 56-61.

Harsch, H., and Holt, R. (1988). Use of Antidepressants in Attempted Suicide. *Hospital and Community Psychiatry, 39,* 990-992.

Intagliata, J. (1982). Improving the Quality of Community Care for the Chronically Mentally Disabled: The Role of Case Management. *Schizophrenia Bulletin, 8*(4).

Javier, R.A. (1989). Linguistic Considerations in the Treatment of Bilinguals. *Psychoanalytic Psychology, 6*(1), 87-96.

Javier, R.A., and Alpert, M. (1986). The Effects of Stress on the Linguistic Generalization of Bilingual Individuals. *Journal of Pyscholinguistic Research, 15*(5), 419-435.

Johnson, P. J., and Rubin, A. (1983). Case Management in Mental Health: A Social Work Domain? *Social Work, 28*(1), 49-55.

Jones, E., and Korchin, S. (Eds.). (1982). *Minority Mental Health.* New York: Praeger.

Kanter, J. (1988). Clinical Issues in the Case Management Relationship. In M. Harris and L. L. Bachrach (Eds.), *Clinical Case Management. New Directions for Mental Health Services.* No. 40, San Francisco: Jossey-Bass.

Kanter, J. (1989). Clinical Case Management: Definition, Principles, Components. *Hospital and Community Psychiatry, 40*(4).

Kanter, J. (1991). Integrating Case Management and Psychiatric Hospitalization. *Health and Social Work, 16*(1).

Keltner, N., and Folks, D. (1992). Culture as a Variable in Drug Therapy. *Perspectives in Pyschiatric Care, 28*(1), 33-36.

Kinzie, J. D., Leung, P., Bui, A., and Ben, R. (1988). Group Therapy with Southeast Asian Refugees. *Community Mental Health Journal, 24,* 157-166.

Kirmayer, L. J. (1984). Cultural Affect and Somatization. *Transcultural Research Review, 21,* 159-188.

Kleinman, A., and Good, B. (1985). *Culture and Depression: Studies in the Anthropology and Cross-Cultural Psychiatry of Affect and Disorders.* Berkeley: University of California Press.

Koegel, P., Burnham, M.A., and Farr, R. (1990). Subsistence Adaptation Among Homeless Adults in the Inner City of Los Angeles. *Journal of Social Issues, 46*(4), 83-107.

Lakoff, G., and Johnson, M. (1980). *Metaphors We Live By.* Chicago: University of Chicago Press.

Lamb, H. R. (1980). Therapist-Case Managers: More than Brokers of Service. *Hospital and Community Psychiatry, 31,* 762-764.

Lankton, C., and Lankton, S. (1989). *Tales of Enchantment: Goal-Oriented Metaphors for Adults and Children in Therapy.* New York: Brunner/Mazel.

Lawson, W. B. (1986). Racial and Ethnic Factors in Psychiatric Research. *Hospital and Community Psychiatry, 37,* 50-54.

Leavitt, S. S. (1983). Case Management: A Remedy for Problems of Community Care. In C. J. Sanborn (Ed.), *Case Management in Mental Health Services.* Binghamton, NY: The Haworth Press.

Lee, E., and Lu, F. (1989). Assessment and Therapy of Asian-American Survivors of Mass Violence. *Journal of Traumatic Stress,* 12, 93-120.

Lefley, H. (1990). Culture and Chronic Mental Illness. *Hospital and Community Psychiatry, 41*(3).

Leukefeld, C. G. (1990). Case Management: A Social Work Tradition. *Health and Social Work, 15*(3), 175-179.

Lin, T. (1986). Multiculturalism and Canadian Psychiatry: Opportunities and Challenges. *Canadian Journal of Psychiatry, 31*(7), 681-690.

Lin, K. M., and Kleinman, A. M. (1988). Psychopathology and Clinical Course of Schizophrenia: A Cross-Cultural Perspective. *Schizophrenia Bulletin, 15,* 555-567.

Littlewood, R., and Lipsedge, M. (1986). The Culture-Bound Syndromes of the Dominant Culture: Culture Psychopathology, and Biomedicine. In J. Cox (Ed.), *Transcultural Psychiatry* (253-273). London: Croom Helms.

Littlewood, R., and Lipsedge, M. (1987). The Butterfly and the Serpent: Culture Psychopathology and Biomedicine. *Culture, Medicine, and Psychiatry, 11*(3), 289-335.

Littman, S. K. (1985). Foreword. In P. Barker (Ed.), *Using Metaphors in Psychotherapy.* New York: Brunner/Mazel.

Lo, W. H., and Lo, T. (1977). A Ten Year Follow-Up Study of Chinese Schizophrenics in Hong Kong. *British Journal of Psychiatry, 131,* 63-66.

Loring, M., and Powell, B. (1988). Gender, Race, and DSM-III: A Study of the Objectivity of Psychiatric Diagnostic Behavior. *Journal of Health and Social Behavior, 29,* 1-22.

Marcos, L., and Cancro, R. (1982). Pharmacotherapy of Hispanic Depressed Patients: Clinical Observations. *American Journal of Psychotherapy, 36,* 505-512.

Marcos, L.R., and Alpert, M. (1976). Strategies and Risks in Psychotherapy with Bilingual Patients: The Phenomenon of Language Independence. *American Journal of Psychiatry, 133*(11), 1275-1278.

McCreath, J. (1984). The New Generation of Chronic Psychiatric Patients. *Social Work, 19,* 436-441.

McGlashan, T. H. (1982). DSM-III Schizophrenia and Individual Psychotherapy. *Journal of Nervous and Mental Disease, 170*(12), 752-757.

Minkoff, K. (1978). A Map of the Chronic Mental Patient. In J. A. Talbott (Ed.), *The Chronic Mental Patient* (11-38). Washington, DC: American Psychiatric Association.

Minuchin, S. (1976). Structural Family Therapy in Child and Adolescent Psychiatry: Sociocultural and Community Psychiatry. In G. Caplan (Ed.), *American Handbook of Psychiatry* (Vol. 2). New York: Basic Books.

Mirowsky, J., and Ross, C. (1989). Psychiatric Diagnosis As Reified Measurement. *Journal of Health and Social Behavior, 30*(1), 11-25.

Modrcin, M., Rapp, C. A., and Poertner, J. (1988). The Evaluation of Case Management Services with the Chronically Mentally Ill. *Evaluation and Program Planning, 11,* 307-314.

Morin, R. C., and Seidman, E. (1986). A Social Network Approach and the Revolving Door Patient. *Schizophrenia Bulletin, 12,* 262-273.

Murphy, H. M., and Raman, A. C. (1971). The Chronicity of Schizophrenia in Indigenous Tropical Peoples. *British Journal of Psychiatry, 118,* 489-497.

Pedersen, A., and Pedersen, P. (1989). The Cultural Grid: A Framework for Multicultural Counseling. *International Journal of the Advancement of Counseling, 12*(3).

Putsch, R.W. (1985). Cross-Cultural Communication: The Special Case of Interpreters in Health Care. *Journal of the American Medical Association, 254*(23).

Rapp, C. A., and Chamberlain, R. (1985). Case Management Services for the Chronically Mentally Ill. *Social Work, 30(5),* 417-422.

Rhodes, L.A. (1984). "This Will Clear Your Mind:" The Use of Metaphors for Medication in Pyschiatric Settings. *Culture, Medicine, and Psychiatry, 8*(1), 49-70.

Riffer, N., and Freedman, J. (1980). *Case Management in Community-Based Services: A Training Manual.* Albany: New York State Office of Mental Health.

Rivera, C. (1988). Culturally Sensitive Aftercare Services for Chronically Mentally Ill Hispanics: The Case of the Psychoeducational Treatment Model. *Fordham University Hispanic Research Center Research Bulletin,* Vol. 11.

Roberts, J. M. (1964). The Self Management of Cultures. In W. H. Goodenough (Ed.), *Explorations in Cultural Anthropology* (433-454). New York: McGraw-Hill.

Roll, S., Millen, L., and Martinez, R. (1980). Common Errors in Psychotherapy with Chicanos: Extrapolations from Research and Clinical Experience. *Psychotherapy: Theory, Research, and Practice, 17,* 158-168.

Romney, A. K., Weller, S. C., and Batchelder, W. H. (1986). Culture as Consensus: A Theory of Culture and Informant Accuracy. *American Anthropologist, 88,* 313-338.

Rose, S. M. (1992). *Case Management and Social Work Practice.* New York: Longman.

Sands, R. G. (1991). *Clinical Social Work Practice in Community Mental Health.* New York: Macmillan Publishing Co.

Sartorius, N. (1992). Prognosis for Schizophrenia in the Third World: A Revelation of Cross-Cultural Research: Commentary. *Culture, Medicine, and Psychiatry, 16*(1), 81-84.

Scheffler, R. M., and Miller, A. G. (1989). Demand Analysis of Mental Health Service Use Among Ethnic Subpopulations. *Inquiry, 26*, 202-215.

Schwab, B., Drake, R.E., and Burghardt, E. (1988). Health Care of the Chronically Mentally Ill: The Culture Broker Model. *Community Mental Health Journal, 24*(3), 174-184.

Segal, S., Silverman, C., and Baumohl, J. (1989). Seeking Person-Environment Fit in Community Care Placement. *Journal of Social Issues, 45*(3).

Shamis, S. (1976). Linguistic Relativity and the Diagnosis of Schizophrenia. *Schizophrenia Bulletin, 2*(4), 503-504.

Snowden, L., and Cheung, F. (1990). Use of Inpatient Mental Health Services by Members of Ethnic Minority Groups. *American Psychologist, 45*(3), 347-355.

Snowden, L., and Todman, P. (1982). The Psychological Assessment of Blacks: New and Needed Developments. In E. Jones and S. Korchin (Eds.), *Minority Mental Health* (193-226). New York: Praeger.

Spitz, B., and Abramson, J. (1987). Competition, Capitation, and Case Management: Barriers to Strategic Reform. *Milbank Quarterly, 65*, 348-370.

Staples, R. (1971). The Myth of the Impotent Black Male. *The Black Scholar, 2*(9).

Sue, D. W. (1981). *Counseling the Culturally Different: Theory and Practice.* New York: John Wiley and Sons.

Surber, R. (Ed.). (1994). *Clinical Case Management: A Guide to Comprehensive Treatment of Serious Mental Illness.* Thousand Oaks, CA: Sage Publications, Inc.

Turner, J. C., and TenHoor, W. J. (1978). The NIMH Community Support Program: Pilot Approach to a Needed Reform. *Schizophrenia Bulletin, 4*, 319-348.

Valentine, C. A. (1971). Deficit, Difference, and Bicultural Models of Afro-American Behavior. *Harvard Educational Review, 41*(2), 137-157.

Valle, R. (1986). Hispanic Social Networks and Prevention. In: Hough, R., Gongla, P., Brown, V., and Goldston, S. (Eds.), *Psychiatric Epidemiology and Prevention: The Possibilities.* Los Angeles: UCLA Neuropsychiatric Institute, 131-157.

Weidman, H. H. (1982). Research Strategies, Structural Alterations, and Clinically Applied Anthropology. In *Clinically Applied Anthropology: Anthropologies in Health Science Settings.* London: D. Reidel Publishing Co., 201-241.

Weidman, H. H. (1979). Falling-Out: A Diagnostic and Treatment Problem Viewed from a Transcultural Perspective. *Social Science and Medicine, 13*B, 95-112.

Westermeyer, J. (1985). Psychiatric Diagnosis Across Cultural Boundaries. *American Journal of Psychiatry, 142*(7).

Wilkinson, C. B. (Ed.). (1986). *Ethnic Psychiatry.* New York: Plenum.

Zeigler, V., and Biggs, J. (1977). Tricyclic Plasma Levels: Effect of Age, Race, Sex, and Smoking. *Journal of the American Medical Association,* 238, 2167-2169.

Zuniga, M. (1992). Using Metaphors in Therapy: Dichos and Latino Clients. *Social Work, 37*(1), 55-60.

Chapter 2

The Culture of Homelessness

Phillip Fellin

Our purpose in examining the culture of homelessness is to discover ways in which cultural perspectives can contribute to the practice of clinical case management with homeless mentally ill people. Homeless mentally ill persons constitute a significant client group within the public mental health system. Studies indicate that at least one-third of the homeless population suffers from a mental disorder (Leshner, 1992). A substantial proportion of these individuals are severely mentally ill (U.S. Dept. of Health and Human Services, 1991; Goldfinger, 1990; Koegel, Burnham, and Farr, 1988) with many suffering from a concurrent substance use disorder (Fischer and Breakey, 1991). Among the homeless, the mentally ill appear to have the greatest need for housing, health, mental health, and social services and to be the most underserved (Institute of Medicine, 1988; Leshner, 1992). As Levine and Rog (1990) have noted, "All too often homeless mentally ill persons are disenfranchised from their families, service providers, and communities" (p. 963).

A promising approach to serving homeless mentally ill clients is the practice of clinical case management (Dixon, Friedman, and Lehman, 1993b; Swayze, 1992). In order to engage in this practice effectively, the mental health professional must have knowledge in a number of areas. As Manoleas (1994) has noted, case management with the mentally ill requires an understanding of multiple subcultures, such as the mental health system and the social welfare system, as well as various other subcultures of the persons being served. When case management is used with the homeless mentally ill, the professional helper must understand the condition of homelessness and its cultural dimensions. The tasks of this chapter are

(1) to provide a framework for this understanding through the presentation of cultural perspectives and research findings about mentally ill homeless individuals, and (2) to illustrate how mental health professionals have modified models of case management in order to serve this special client group.

The concept of culture provides an important lens through which the characteristics, needs, and treatment of homeless mentally ill clients can be understood. Cultural dimensions of this client group are derived from a number of subcultures, such as membership in ethnic minority groups and health and welfare service systems (First, Roth, and Arewa, 1988; Gaw, 1993; Rossi, 1988; Welch and Toff, 1987). These subcultures overlap with the conditions of homelessness and mental illness. The intermix of these cultural dimensions with each other and with the dominant American culture has been characterized as "cross-cultural" relationships. For case management services to be effective, these relationships need to be understood and negotiated through a process of cultural bridging (Manoleas, 1994; Lefley and Bestman, 1991; Schwab, Drake, and Elisabeth, 1988). In serving the homeless mentally ill, cultural bridging involves taking into account the influence of a number of subcultures, but especially the cultural dimensions of homelessness. The identification of the mentally ill among the homeless population has been wrought with numerous conceptual and methodological problems (Susser, Goldfinger, and White, 1990; Bachrach, 1992a). Homeless mentally ill persons include those who suffer from mental disorders and have become homeless, as well as persons who become ill while they are homeless. Persons with severe and persistent mental illness, often labeled the chronically mentally ill, pose a set of special treatment and service needs (Bassuk, 1984a; Lefley, 1990; Leshner, 1992). This client group may be identified in terms of three major criteria: diagnosis, duration, and disability (Bachrach, 1988, 1992b; Levine and Haggard, 1989). These criteria are incorporated into the definition of severe mental illness as "a severe and persistent mental or emotional disorder (e.g., schizophrenia, schizoaffective disorders, and mood disorders) that disrupts functional capacities for such primary aspects of life as self-care, household management, interpersonal relationships, and work or school" (Levine and Rog, 1990, p. 963). It is this group of homeless mentally ill that is the most difficult to reach and to which case management services are increasingly directed.

Viewing homelessness from a cultural perspective is not a simple matter. For example, the homeless population is extremely heterogeneous, thereby raising questions as to whether or not homeless people share common cultural traits. There are differences in the amount of time persons endure homelessness and the extent to which they may be influenced by a homeless culture. Thus, the idea of culture has a somewhat different meaning for homeless people than for other groups, such as the majority American culture, ethnic minority cultures, or service delivery system cultures. Nevertheless, a cultural perspective provides a useful framework for understanding how homeless individuals differ from people who adhere to the culture of mainstream American society (Lefley, 1990; Toro et al., 1991). The meaning of homelessness for severely mentally ill persons is examined within this context. In focusing on homelessness, however, we "should not minimize psychiatric illness as a major variable in the lives of homeless mentally ill individuals" (Bachrach, 1984a, p. 16).

HOMELESSNESS AS CULTURE

The concepts of *homelessness* and *culture* are defined in a variety of ways. Rossi (1988) indicates some consensus around definitions that designate persons who do not have "customary and regular access" to a "conventional dwelling unit" as homeless. A similar definition is provided in the Stewart B. McKinney Homeless Assistance Act (1987), where homelessness is viewed as a condition under which persons lack "a fixed, regular, and adequate nighttime residence" or under which persons reside in temporary nighttime housing, such as shelters and welfare hotels. Our discussion of selected cultural dimensions of homelessness is guided by these definitions of homelessness.

A general framework for defining culture is presented by Manoleas (1994), with culture representing the passing from one generation to another of "ways of seeing, experiencing, interpreting and being," of "ways of coping and surviving in the world" (p. 11); and "learned systems of meaning" through which "groups of people adapt to their environment and structure interpersonal activities" (D'Andrade, 1984, p. 116). Terms used to define culture include customs, ways of life, ways of thinking, ways of defining the world, language and communication patterns, norms and values, behaviors, means of survival, and patterns of socialization (Newman,1989; Gilmore, 1992). Given these meanings, the condition of homelessness appears to be sufficiently different from life in mainstream American society to warrant the use of a cultural perspective for understanding the values, attitudes, and behaviors of homeless persons.

Cultural perspectives usually take into account the meaning of the concepts of culture and social structure and their interrelationship (Newman, 1989; Padilla, 1990). These concepts, as developed in the fields of anthropology and sociology, have been related to the construction of paradigms such as "culture of poverty" and "culture of the underclass" (Duncan, Hill, and Hoffman, 1988; Jencks and Peterson, 1991). From a culturalist point of view, culture guides and determines patterns of behavior. From this perspective, homeless people take on the attributes established within their group. In contrast, the structuralist perspective claims that social structure "determines patterns of social interaction and thought" (Gilmore, 1992, p. 405), and that "culture is driven by economic constraints or practical concerns" (Newman, 1989, p. 6). Applying these ideas to homelessness, the structural perspective treats "homelessness as a consequence of societal trends, including changes in the economy, mental health policy, and welfare provision" (Lee, 1992, p. 845).

As exemplified by discussions of poverty and the underclass, there is merit in incorporating both the cultural and structural perspectives into the study of homelessness. An example of this approach is found in Wilson's (1991) discussion of the urban underclass. Wilson suggests that not only does the economic structure place constraints and limited opportunities on poor people, but that these individuals are also influenced by the behaviors of other poor people– that is, by their culture. For example, Fiske (1991) suggests that homeless men "systematically reject the social values that have rejected them. Homelessness is not just their material condition; it saturates their 'whole way of life'" (p. 456).

Within the customary definitions of culture, the diversity of the homeless population, in terms of age, gender, health status, family composition, living arrangements, length of time homeless, and ethnicity, argues against the presence of a single culture of homelessness. Still, within this diversity, there appear to be some common cultural features of homelessness in current American society. In addition to lacking a home, homeless persons are likely to be involved in some kind of a subculture, that is, a "distinctive set of norms, values, and behavior setting them off from the dominant culture"(Adler and Adler, p. 328). Campbell and Reeves (1989) suggest that this is the case, noting how the media pictures the homeless as residing "outside the bounds of what it means to be a person in our society" (p. 28). As Fiske (1991) notes, "the loss of home signifies more or less invisibly, the loss of job, the loss of family, and the loss of a legitimate normalized relationship to the social order" (p. 473). Kozol (1988b) observes that this picture is especially likely to appear with regard to the homeless mentally ill: "Terming economic victims 'psychotic' or 'disordered' helps to place them at a distance. It says that they aren't quite like us–and, more important, that we could not be like them" (p. 155).

In order to pursue the question of culture among homeless persons, we focus on characteristics that may be viewed as cultural: (1) extreme poverty; (2) general lifestyles; (3) disaffiliation; (4) negative attitudes and behaviors in relation to treatment and social services; and (5) subcultures organized around place, such as streets, skid row, shelters. There may also be multiple subcultures organized around the "lifestyles" of different groups of homeless people and the ways in which they solve their problems. Thus, some cultural features may differ between and within such groups as young adults (Feitel et al, 1992), the elderly (Kutza and Keigher, 1991), men (First and Toomey, 1989), women (Harris and Bachrach, 1990; Milburn and D'Ercole, 1991), families (Rafferty and Shinn, 1991), individuals in the criminal justice system (Levine and Haggard, 1989), people with alcohol and drug disorders (Fischer, 1991; Levine and Huebner, 1991), and specific ethnic minority groups (Rossi, 1988).

While the concept of culture facilitates an understanding of the life conditions of homeless people, one must guard against creating cultural stereotypes or myths (Manoleas, 1994). Some generalizations from research findings are presented in our discussion, but in many instances the data are limited. Bachrach (1984b) has identified some concerns about interpretations of research on the mentally ill, especially when they result in stereotyping. Planners and service providers need to be aware of the bases for these reservations, such as the conceptual and operational issues in defining and measuring homelessness and mental illness, and the complexity and diversity of the homeless mentally ill population. These issues are apparent in our discussion of major research approaches to the study of homelessness–that is, social survey, ethnographic, and social program evaluation research.

THE STUDY OF HOMELESS PEOPLE

Information about homeless people comes from a variety of sources, ranging from the findings generated by social research to news features and video presentations by the mass media (Bachrach, 1990; Morrisey, 1986; National Institute of Mental Health, 1991). Social survey methods have been used to obtain information on such questions as: How many homeless people are there? What are the causes of homelessness? What are the needs of homeless persons? Major limitations to this information have been identified in the professional literature, such as biases from the sampling designs and the validity and reliability of the measurements (Rossi, 1989; Cowan, Breakey, and Fischer, 1988). Special concerns have been raised when studies focus on the mentally ill, since the identification of mental disorders among homeless persons presents difficult measurement problems (Breakey, 1987; Dennis, 1987; General Accounting Office, 1988; Susser, Conover, and Struening, 1989, 1990a).

Despite limitations of methodology, social surveys have provided useful data about the social and demographic characteristics of the homeless. An overriding contribution of this research has been the confirmation of the heterogeneity of the homeless population, an identification of who the "new homeless" are, and a demonstration of the fact that a significant proportion, but not a majority, of the homeless suffer from mental disorders (Koegel, 1987; Leshner, 1992), with many having dual diagnoses of mental illness and a concurrent drug and/or alcohol disorder (Fischer and Breakey, 1991). Researchers using survey methods have not focused on the question of whether or not there is a culture of homelessness. However, survey findings provide a basis for building profiles of various subgroups, such as homeless families, and for identifying cultural traits of homeless people (Bassuk, Rubin, and Lauriat, 1986; Rossi, 1989).

A strong argument has been made that information from ethnographic research is likely to be more useful than survey data in understanding homelessness. As Koegel (1987) points out, ethnography employs methods that may lead to more valid pictures of homelessness, methods that provide "myth exploding power." Proponents of ethnographic research highlight the benefits of participant observation and an "emic" point of view, that is, a concern with "the meanings which behavior and social life have for the people under study" (Koegel, p. 8). A number of studies based on ethnography provide pictures of "subcultures" of homeless people, such as the study of homeless mentally ill people in the skid row area of Los Angeles by Farr, Koegel, and Burnham (1986); homeless adults in the streets of New York City by Baxter and Hopper (1981); the homeless in the Bowery (Giamo, 1989); homeless families and their children by Kozol (1988a, 1988c); "shelterization" in New York City shelters for men (Gounis and Susser, 1990); and studies of homeless mentally ill women (Koegel, 1987).

Research studies can be used to identify cultural traits associated with homelessness and to discuss selected subcultures of homeless people. Most studies of homeless people have been carried out in local communities that vary in terms of size, demographic, social class, ethnic, and racial composition; resources of their economic, political, health, mental health, and social service subsystems; geographic location, and physical environment. While this variability limits the kinds of generalizations that can be made, these studies still provide a cumulative picture of the homeless mentally ill, and insights into what kinds of social interventions might be effective for these individuals (Bachrach, 1984a, 1984b; Dennis et al., 1991; Morrissey and Levine, 1987; Lamb, Bachrach, and Kass, 1992). Thus, community studies provide a basis for service planning and service delivery at the local level.

Social program evaluation represents another form of research that contributes to the delivery of services to the homeless mentally ill. The focus of this research is an assessment of the effectiveness of various models of intervention. Evaluation studies may use survey, ethnographic, or experimental designs in order to describe the efforts and efficiency of a model of intervention and to assess whether or not the program reaches its goals. Findings from evaluative studies of case management interventions with homeless mentally ill persons are presented toward the end of this chapter.

CULTURAL TRAITS

Definitions of culture often include one or more of the following dimensions: lifestyles, ways of life; bonds of attachment and integration of members; and systems of meaning and ways of thinking. The literature on homelessness reveals a number of indicators of these three cultural dimensions, as well as some overlap between them. Ways of life are described in terms of: culture of poverty, underclass culture, lack of adequate housing, lack of employment, lack of income, lack of personal hygiene, vulnerability to stress, difficulties with tasks of daily living, involvement with alcohol and/or drugs, criminal activity, and poor physical health (Drake, Osher, and Wallach, 1991). The dimension of social bonds and social integration is characterized by disaffiliation, uprootedness, lack of social networks and social supports, social isolation, lack of sense of community, and detachment from community and society. Ways of thinking are described in such terms as lack of trust, lack of motivation, desire for independence and autonomy, suspiciousness of bureaucracies, and treatment resistance. These dimensions of culture provide a way of organizing the examination of how homeless people differ from other poor people and from mainstream society.

POVERTY AND HOMELESSNESS

Extreme poverty is at the root of homelessness (Rossi, 1989). Also, as Belle (1990) notes, "Decades of research find poverty to be a correlate of psychological distress and diagnosable mental disorder" (p. 385). Poverty has an especially devastating effect on the mental health of women and ethnic minorities, especially in terms of increase in stress, decrease in ability to perform social roles, decrease in social support systems and social networks, and constraints on coping strategies (Belle, 1990; Milburn and D'Ercole, 1991). The homeless mentally ill are particularly disadvantaged economically, due to their low utilization of programs and entitlements for which they are eligible, and to their weak or nonexistent participation in the labor force (Leshner, 1992). Most homeless mentally ill persons live in a state of persistent unemployment, or with extremely low and/or irregular income. In his study of homeless people in Chicago, Rossi (1988) found the homeless "had been without steady employment for much longer periods of time than they had been homeless" and had "lived on inadequate personal incomes literally for years before becoming homeless" (p. 99).

Tienda and Stier (1991) provide some useful distinctions with regard to the labor force, noting that the unemployed are a diverse group: the unemployed, e.g., people out of work and actively seeking a job; the discouraged, without work and thinking no work is available; the constrained, out of work but limited by disabilities, etc.; and the shiftless, "those who are idle and do not want to work . . ." (p. 137). The homeless population includes all of these types of unemployed people. In regard to the first group, Sosin, Colson, and Grossman (1988) found in their study of homeless people in Chicago, that some 41 percent of the currently homeless were actively seeking employment (p. 284). Even so, unemployment remains a major problem for most homeless people. For example, First and Toomey (1989) found that almost one quarter of the homeless men in their Ohio study could be labeled "long-term needs group" by virtue of their having a mental disorder and other restrictions on work. Their prospects for employment were viewed as very limited. A "moderate needs" group of men, about half of whom had mild psychiatric impairments, were seen as having the potential to benefit from rehabilitation programs. Some 43 percent of the study sample were labeled "short-term needs group," as these men had positive work histories and had good potential for employment.

There are special problems for homeless mentally ill persons and employment. It is clear that many people with mental disorders have a need for social and job skills, and that habilitation and rehabilitation efforts can lead to work (Blau, 1989). At the same time, stigmatization is a barrier to employment, with employers often rejecting people with past or current histories of mental illness. This may be rectified to some extent with the passage of The Americans with Disabilities Act of 1990. Under this Act employers are prohibited from asking questions about past history of mental illness. After a person is employed, the law protects only individuals who are able to meet the basic job requirements of the assigned position. However, extra support and accommodation on the job is required if the person needs this assistance (Freudenheim, 1991).

In short, mentally ill persons who are homeless have little or no income and limited income sources, such as job opportunities, public assistance, or other welfare entitlements. The combination of poverty and mental illness creates strong demands on the capability of these individuals to survive. Not unlike people described as underclass, the homeless may be viewed as responding rationally to "an ungenerous social structure that imposes constraints and limited opportunities" (Greenstone, 1991, p. 400). As Wilson (1987) contends, some people live in poverty because the economic structure of society does not present opportunities for meaningful work. Homeless mentally ill people in particular may have limited capacity to take advantage of improved circumstances and health as a way of moving out of homelessness. Thus, without outside intervention to help negotiate the culture of the employment and service systems of mainstream society, homeless mentally ill individuals are likely to suffer in ways similar to other people in poverty, becoming at high risk for chronic homelessness (Jencks and Peterson, 1991).

GENERAL LIFESTYLES

Lifestyles, or life circumstances, of the homeless are apparent through observation of the daily living activities they engage in to assure survival (Baxter and Hopper, 1982; Segal and VanderVoort, 1993; Gory, Ritchey, and Mullis, 1990). Among the most important tasks is the search for shelter, bathroom facilities, and food. Temporary shelter is not always accessible and available for homeless persons, especially if they are mentally ill and/or abuse alcohol and other drugs. While many communities have programs where meals are served, lunch and/or evening meals are not usually offered in temporary shelters, but in separate locations. Generally, nutritional needs of the homeless are not met by these programs, resulting in serious undernourishment.

Many homeless people experience an ongoing sense of danger. Studies of public shelter users substantiate a lack of safety, leading Holloway (1991) to state, "Homeless people live in constant fear for their physical safety" (p. 592). This is especially true for homeless women, in terms of abuse and victimization, and even more true for mentally ill women. One of the characteristics of homeless mentally ill people is the fact that they "often come into contact with the criminal justice system, both as offenders and victims" (Leshner, 1992, p. 11). Problems of daily living seem to be less problematic for homeless people in "transitional" housing/shelters than for those living in the "streets" or in temporary shelters. Sosin, Colson, and Grossman (1988) report that these individuals, mostly women, report a lifestyle considerably different from other homeless people, that is, more feeling of safety, and fewer problems in receiving adequate nourishment.

Observers of the homeless often describe the personal appearance of these individuals as "disheveled and dirty." The lifestyle of many homeless people appears to include lack of personal hygiene and lack of adequate clothing. Rossi (1989) notes that in Chicago, homeless women over forty often fit the stereotype of the "bag lady," while "homeless men, whether young or old, were most likely to look like the stereotyped Skid Row inhabitant" (p. 141). Breakey et al. (1992) present a contrasting view in their study of homeless people in Baltimore. They found that "The common views that most homeless people are dirty, bizarrely dressed, unkempt, and infested with lice or other parasites are . . . shown to be untrue" (p. 107).

The lifestyle of homeless persons involves spending most of their time on the streets, in parks, and in public places. This factor has implications for mental health service delivery, as clients are often not easy to find. This problem is exacerbated when homeless persons are involved in various types of geographic mobility. Some move in and out of homelessness, in and out of shelters, in and out of neighborhoods or communities, as well as moving over wide geographic areas. All in all, there is a considerable amount of mobility, including local residential instability, seasonal movement, and migratory movement, which affects the provision of outreach case management services to the homeless (Bachrach, 1987).

DISAFFILIATION

Shared cultural experiences of the general population create the ties that people have to each other and to their local communities. These social ties are developed with family, friends, and neighbors, as well as through links to formal organizations such as workplaces, social welfare organizations, churches, schools, and voluntary associations. Homeless persons are described as lacking in these bonds and social ties, and hence not in a position to benefit from needed social supports. Homeless people are often characterized as "disaffiliated," "isolated," or "alienated" (Rossi, 1989; Chafetz, 1990; Segal and Baumohl, 1980; Rollinson, 1991). In fact, the Alcohol, Drug Abuse, and Mental Health Administration (1983) has defined homelessness as "both (the) lack of adequate and permanent shelter and (the) absence of community and social ties" (p. 1).

A number of studies report that homeless people have limited social networks, and hence low levels of social support (Sosin, Colson, and Grossman, 1988; Lipton and Sabatini, 1984; Levine and Haggard, 1989). Brown and Ziefert (1990) have observed that chronically homeless women "have become so isolated and alienated by their experiences that life revolves around their daily survival" (p. 9). These authors emphasize the significance of the losses by homeless women of personal relationships, financial security, possessions, safety, privacy, and sometimes their children. Other studies have found homeless mothers to be quite isolated and lacking in supportive relationships, and homeless families to have fragmented support networks (McChesney, 1986; Bassuk, Rubin, and Lauriat, 1986). Studies of skid row residents show a picture of "social disaffiliation, tenuous or absent ties to family and kin, with few or no friends" (Rossi, 1990, p. 955).

A lack of social ties is found to be even more prevalent among the homeless mentally ill (Bassuk, Rubin, and Lauriat, 1984; Roth and

Bean, 1986). Some of these individuals are said to be "drifters," "in search of autonomy, as a way of denying their dependency, and out of a desire for an isolated lifestyle" (Lamb, 1984, p. 65). Many of these persons avoid contact with the mental health system. There is some recognition of variation in the extent to which homeless people become disaffiliated. Thus, of the three groups identified by Arce et al. (1983) that is, street people, episodic homeless, and situationally homeless, the latter group may have the least amount of disaffiliation.

In contrast to this picture of disaffiliation, there is evidence to support the idea that for some homeless people, the condition of disaffiliation and isolation may be exaggerated. For example, Sosin, Colson, and Grossman (1988) found in a study of homeless people in Chicago that some 66 percent claimed to have some contact with their relatives. Homeless women have been found to be more affiliated than the general homeless population. One conclusion from a conference on homeless mentally ill women suggested that total isolation of homeless women is a myth (Koegel, 1987). It was recognized that some homeless women, e.g., "severe mentally ill isolates," are disaffiliated, but that this group is "only one highly visible slice of the homeless women population as a whole" (Koegel, 1987, p. 26). Toro et al. (1991) cite studies which suggest that most homeless people remain in contact with their families while homeless (Farr, Koegel, and Burnham, 1986; Toro, 1991a). While it appears that disaffiliation may be exaggerated in regard to some populations, most research findings still support the fact that many homeless individuals are disaffiliated from family, relatives, friends, and the community, with a weak system of social supports (Leshner, 1992).

TREATMENT/SERVICE RESISTANCE

Homeless people are often described as being unwilling to accept health, mental health, and social services. The terms used to label persons with this trait include "treatment resistant client" and/or "service resistant client." In considering the attitudes and behaviors of persons who are severely mentally ill and homeless, it is important to define the nature of mental health services for this population. These services are sometimes defined as including activities "provided for the purpose of the identification, diagnosis, and treatment of mental health problems" (George, 1989, p. 306). However, a broader definition that includes supportive services such as housing, job training, psychosocial club services, and other social or human services may be more appropriate in relation to the needs of mentally ill homeless persons (Morrissey, 1989).

Research findings on the attitudes of homeless people toward treatment and supportive services and their use of these services are mixed. There is some support for the idea of treatment resistance, especially among the mentally ill homeless, but there are also findings that suggest that many homeless people do accept treatment and other services. These findings lead to the question, under what conditions are homeless people unwilling or willing to use services? In one review of utilization of services by the homeless, Rossi (1989) found that "almost all the research on the homeless in the 1980's has shown that few of them participate in the welfare programs they appear to be eligible for by virtue of their financial plight and their disabilities" (p. 196). In contrast to this position, Sosin, Colson, and Grossman (1988) found that a majority of homeless people in their Chicago study made use of welfare programs. At the same time, these investigators note that "some minority of the homeless does appear to prefer independence to welfare . . ." (p. 233).

Resistance to help has been attributed to various groups of homeless people, but especially to the mentally ill. Johnson (1990) notes that "many of the homeless mentally ill have made it clear that they prefer life on the streets to life in an institution" (p. 154). Sosin, Colson, and Grossman (1988) provide some evidence that homeless mentally ill individuals "have become detached from community mental health centers" (p. 372). The literature on young severely mentally ill people suggests that a growing number exhibit antisocial, rebellious behavior and refuse to participate in structured, traditional mental health programs (Levine, Lezak, and Goldman, 1986; Bachrach, 1982; Pepper, Ryglewicz, and Kirschner, 1981). These "young chronic adults" are regarded as not being motivated to seek treatment or other services (Ridgely, Osher, and Talbott, 1987). In short, homeless mentally ill persons are often referred to as "noncompliant," "service resistant," and "difficult to serve," leading to a well-founded concern on the part of professional mental health practitioners as to how to engage this population in treatment (Rog, 1988; Cohen, 1989).

There is a contrasting and more positive view about use of services and treatment by homeless people. Some research studies support the idea that "the majority of homeless mentally ill individuals may be willing to receive a variety of services" (Rog, 1988). Martin (1990) has noted that "Individuals with severe, persistent and disabling mental illness who have become homeless almost always want help. All of the research efforts supported by N.I.M.H. found this to be true" (p. 441). For those who do not seek services, Rog (1988) identifies a number of factors which may influence this decision, such as fears of involuntary hospitalization, the stigma of being labeled mentally ill, and the nature of the mental health system.

In their report on homelessness as a public mental health problem, Levine and Haggard (1989) review research findings which indicate that "homeless mentally ill persons are usually willing to accept assistance" (p. 288). However, these individuals may place high priority on social services and housing needs, while mental health providers often emphasize mental health interventions (Sargent, 1989). Given the disparity in priorities, it may just seem that the homeless are rejecting services or are unmotivated. Bachrach (1984a) calls this situation one of "social distance" between the providers' expectations and the capabilities and interests of the homeless. Martin's (1986) review of research findings from NIMH projects on ethnic and racial minorities emphasizes that differences in perceptions of needs and services are particularly problematic for these individuals, and hence the service delivery system is not responsive to them.

The strongest argument that homeless people are willing to accept services comes from discussions about homeless women, with some researchers suggesting that "treatment resistance" is a myth (Koegel, 1987). Some research findings suggest that women generally do not refuse services. Rather, the services often do not fit their needs or are not delivered in an acceptable manner. Thus, in the area of help-seeking, Koegel's (1987) review indicates that "setting and service provider related characteristics . . . were every bit as important as client-related characteristics" (p. 43). This leads to a concept of treatment-resistant service providers and service settings.

A critical dimension of help-seeking for many homeless people appears to be the culture of the service providers, that is, the extent to which the culture of the service delivery system conflicts with the "ways of thinking" or "belief systems" of a homeless person. In the case of the homeless mentally ill, they are likely to be viewed by the mental health system as a dependent group in need of certain services and interventions. This service perspective will usually be in conflict with the belief systems of the homeless (Lamb, 1992). The homeless tend to focus on freedom and independence and the need for concrete services, such as food, clothing, and housing. As Cohen (1989) has noted, services need to be offered in a way that meets the perceptions of the homeless client, otherwise the services will not be utilized. This is due to the fact that mentally ill homeless persons have often had what are perceived as negative encounters with the traditional mental health system. This proposition is suggested in research by Moxley and Freddolino (1991) in which clients with psychiatric problems were interviewed about their self-perceived needs. These clients described the welfare and social security bureaucracy as overwhelming and they expressed a need for assistance in negotiating with these organizations. One of the arguments supporting the position that homeless people resist services is based on the fact that some individuals choose to live out-of-doors, in parks, public buildings, and streets. While there are some homeless people who prefer not to stay overnight in shelters, the majority seem willing to do so (Baxter and Hopper, 1982). In fact, many of the homeless have positive views of some types of emergency shelters (Rossi, 1989). There remain, however, a number of homeless people who perceive shelters in a negative way due to the institutional nature of the shelters, loss of independence, a lack of safety, rigid rules, overcrowding, and crime.

This discussion of cultural traits of homeless, and homeless mentally ill persons, has been organized around three dimensions: ways of life (poverty and general lifestyles), social bonds and integration (disaffiliation), and systems of meaning/ways of thinking (treatment/service resistance). Knowledge about these areas provides a cultural context for understanding homeless mentally ill clients. A complementary perspective on the culture of homelessness comes from the examination of subcultures based on location, that is, where homeless people live. Subcultures of skid row, streets, and shelters are used to illustrate cultural dimensions of place of residence.

SUBCULTURES OF HOMELESSNESS

Subcultures are often created by virtue of the particular location where homeless people reside, such as in skid row housing, the streets, or emergency shelters. Studies of skid row neighborhoods describe residents of SROs and missions as belonging to a subculture. The exemplar of skid rows has been the Bowery, described by authors such as Giamo (1989), Cohen and Sokolovsky (1989), Bogue (1963), Wallace (1965), Bahr and Caplow (1973), Rossi (1989), Baxter and Hopper (1981), and Hopper and Hamburg (1984). For example, Giamo (1989) describes the Bowery "as a well-established sense of place . . . a street and section of New York City . . . as an 'embodiment' of urban poverty and homelessness as well" (p. xiii). Bowery homelessness is characterized as a way of life, with "the radical estrangement of this subculture from the norm-governed ideology and political and economic framework of American society . . ." (p. xvii). Giamo (1989) found the homeless Bowery men to belong to an ordered community, with an identity, structure, and affiliative network of supports (p. 30).

A number of authors propose that with urban renewal, gentrification, and removal of many single room occupancy hotels, there is no longer a skid row culture of homelessness (Giamo, 1989; Hopper and Hamburg, 1984; Johnson, 1990). On the one hand, it is argued that contemporary homelessness involves an "uprootedness" from places like the Bowery and a "lack of involvement in any identifiable subculture" (Giamo, 1989, p. 200). The new homeless, particularly the deinstitutionalized mentally ill, are said to lack the support system of anything like the old skid row subculture.

A contrasting view is presented by Hopper and Hamburg (1984), who claim that "No longer geographically confined, skid row as a way of life is turning up everywhere" (p. 9). It is clear that the composition of the homeless has changed from predominantly white men in skid row neighborhoods to a much more diverse population in dispersed geographical places, particularly "temporary" emergency shelters. Under these changed conditions, many individuals living on the streets, in public parks, subways, bus and train stations, in emergency shelters, SROs, and missions may belong to a skid row-like subculture.

Many homeless people do not use shelters, missions, or other institutional housing arrangements, but "choose" to live in public places, "on the streets." Other homeless people, even when sheltered on a temporary basis, spend most of the daylight hours on the streets. When people are homeless for a period of time, they appear to handle day-to-day living in ways which might be termed a "street culture," that is, "a loose sense of cohesiveness and an irregular but often effective communication network" (Sosin, Colson, Grossman, 1988, p. 300). In their study of homeless adults on the streets of New York City, Baxter and Hopper (1981) found that a number of ex-mental patients "choose this means of survival over the 'available' alternatives" (p. 7). These individuals handled their daily sustenance problems within a "fragile balance, subject to the whims of those who control access to public spaces, the caprice of casual strangers, and the hazards of rain and cold weather" (p. 104).

The difficulties of providing mental health treatment to the homeless mentally ill who reside on the streets and in public places are illustrated by the activities of a number of programs in New York City. For example, Project HELP uses a mobile outreach interdisciplinary team approach to serving people living on the street (Barrow et al., 1989; Cohen, Putnam, and Sullivan, 1984; Cohen and Marcos, 1992). The Project staff has the legal authority to order individuals to an emergency room for evaluation on an involuntary basis, based on criteria of dangerousness to self or others (Kaufman, 1988). Project HELP invoked this authority with Joyce Brown, a highly publicized homeless person living on the streets of New York City (Campbell and Reeves, 1989).

Joyce Brown, as a member of a street culture, has been described as a "professional street person" who was "dirty, disheveled, malodorous, hostile, and verbally abusive" (Cournos, 1989). Her street behaviors led to her involuntary hospitalization in Bellevue Hospital for the treatment of mental illness. She was subsequently released when she persisted in refusing medication. She moved into a shelter for homeless women in Midtown Manhattan after a 12-week stay in the hospital. Joyce Brown is an example of individuals referred to as bag ladies, women who openly display a "deviant" way of life (Kates, 1985; Rousseau, 1981). They commonly have the cultural traits of other homeless people, that is, they are in extreme poverty, are disaffiliated, and are resistant to institutional living arrangements or health and welfare services. Whether they have regular contacts with other street people, pedestrians, and merchants, or are "loners" and shy away from social relationships, over time they appear to become a part of a street culture.

The idea of a "shelter culture" has recently emerged in the literature, particularly through the writings of Grunberg and Eagle (1990), Gounis and Susser (1990), and Susser, Goldfinger, and White (1990). Grunberg and Eagle (1990) describe the development of "shelterization" as an adaptation to the shelter, "characterized by a decrease in interpersonal responsiveness, a neglect of personal hygiene, increasing passivity, and increasing dependency on others" (p. 521). Based on their study of the residents of a New York City shelter, Grunberg and Eagle note that some shelter residents begin to "attach and adapt" to shelter life in order to survive. They take on the vocabulary and ideals and beliefs of the shelter life. In another illustration of shelter culture, Fiske (1991) describes a shelter for homeless men in a small Midwestern city as a micro-environment. The shelter has physical features that "are packed with meanings of social marginalization, of alienation and of being castoffs or outcasts" (p. 457). These features include lounges with "cast off" furniture, decorated along the tastes of "volunteers," with a supervisor's office for constant monitoring. In short, some homeless people come into a shelter disaffiliated, but soon affiliate with shelter residents and become more isolated from the outside world.

Gounis and Susser (1990) also have studied shelterization and its implications for mental health services. These authors note that for some homeless people, an emergency shelter becomes a more permanent home, leading the residents to become shelter dependent rather than moving back into the community. This development is reinforced in large part by staff and client attitudes. A long stay in a shelter is found to promote "shelterization," defined as "patterns of behavior that are adaptive primarily for shelter-dependent life"

(p. 241). Clients become involved in shelter life and concerned about how to improve life within the shelter, rather than a concern with using the shelter as a bridge to permanent housing.

Susser, Goldfinger, and White (1990) have also examined the "subculture" of shelters in their consideration of clinical approaches to the homeless mentally ill. These authors emphasize the fact that an understanding of the attitudes of shelter clients toward treatment must be discovered and dealt with in efforts to deliver mental health services. There is a need to understand not only the subculture of shelter residents, but also the subculture of the staff. Perceptions about a shelter staff appear to lead some homeless people to prefer living on the streets to living in a shelter.

Since most nighttime shelters do not permit residents to remain during the day, a number of drop-in centers have been established for daytime use. These centers not only offer homeless people a "place out of the cold," but they often provide coffee and snacks and sometimes serve meals. One of the major functions of staff is to advocate for the guests and to link them to health and welfare services. These daytime shelters provide a location for mental health and physical health professionals to contact and provide services for the homeless. Some drop-in centers for women have taken on features of a subculture, as they have become places where "a sense of community is fostered" and where clients learn social competence (Stoner, 1983; Breton, 1984). Other locations where a shelter culture may be developed include welfare hotels (Kozol, 1988a; 1988c; Gewirtzman and Fodor, 1987) and family lodges (Hutchinson, Searight, and Stretch, 1986). In each of these instances there may be strong resistance on the part of the care providers as well as the other residents to having the mentally ill mixed in with other clients. One way to overcome such concerns has been suggested by The Federal Task Force on Homelessness and Severe Mental Illness (Leshner, 1992). The Task Force has recognized the special needs of homeless mentally ill persons by recommending the development of "safe havens" as a housing option. The culture of the safe haven focuses on a "low-cost environment that provides safety, security, supervision, and support . . . with opportunities for residents to establish ties to treatment, benefits, and other support services" (Leshner, 1992, p. xv).

CASE MANAGEMENT WITH HOMELESS CLIENTS

The use of case management in working with mentally ill persons has been extended into the service activities with the homeless population (Levine and Rog, 1990; Tessler and Dennis, 1989; Freddolino and Moxley, 1992; Swayze, 1992). From our review of the cultural dimensions of homelessness, it is clear that special adaptations to case management need to be made when serving homeless mentally ill persons. Case management is defined in numerous ways (Rose, 1992; Rothman, 1992). Its major focus on coordination of services as well as direct delivery of services with individual clients appears to make this approach particularly suitable for work with homeless mentally ill clients. Case management has been identified as one of the basic services of Community Support Systems, an approach developed by NIMH to serve severely mentally ill persons (Turner and TenHoor, 1978; National Institute of Mental Health, 1982). Most models of case management involve the following core functions: client identification and outreach, individual assessment, service planning, service linkage, service monitoring, and client advocacy (Rog, Andranovich, and Rosenblum, 1987; Levine and Haggard, 1989).

Several different models of case management are used within the mental health field (Bachrach, 1989; Dixon, Friedman, and Lehman, 1993a, 1993b). These models have been developed in programs serving the mentally ill in outreach street teams, drop-in centers, shelters, community centers, and student field practicum units (Ridgway, 1986; Billig and Levinson, 1987; Belcher and Ephross, 1989; Bond et al., 1991; Morse et al., 1992). Levine, Lezak, and Goldman (1986) have suggested ways in which the Community Support Program framework can be adapted on behalf of homeless mentally ill persons. This involves adaptations within the ten functions essential for a community support system. An understanding of cultural traits of homeless people is particularly useful in regard to the case management function. As Levine, Lezak, and Goldman (1986) note, the usual mode of the case manager needs to be adapted to the special needs of the homeless mentally ill. For example, the case manager needs to consider the extent to which "the client's need for autonomy, failure to trust, propensity for mobility, or resistance to change sometimes interferes with the making of choices about services" (p. 36). Given these client characteristics, a community support system serves homeless mentally ill persons most effectively when subcultures and cultural traits of the homeless are understood.

Knowledge about the cultural dimensions of homeless mentally ill persons and about subcultures is especially helpful in relation to intensive case management. Intensive case management has become a prevalent approach to serving homeless mentally ill persons (Rog, Andranovich, and Rosenblum, 1987; Borland, McRae, and Lycan, 1989). This service model "involves a comprehensive, aggressive approach to accessing and securing basic health, and mental health services for seriously mentally ill individuals who are 'most in need' . . . individuals considered at risk of hospitalization, who lack both an adequate support system and independent living skills, and who either cannot or will not access services on their own" (Rog, Andranovich, and Rosenblum, 1987, p. 8). Intensive case management involves the core functions of case management, but places an emphasis on assertive outreach, on "advocacy for clients' 'needs' as well as rights," on the provision of services *in vivo* (shelters, streets, day drop-in centers, etc.), and in accord with the client's wishes. This approach gives priority to housing needs and clinical treatment, with services delivered in a "non-time-bound" manner, not restricted by appointment schedules and extended over a long period of time, with continued follow-up (Rog, Andranovich, and Rosenblum, 1987).

An intensive case management model has a number of the features of the Program for Assertive Community Treatment (Test, 1981; Stein and Test, 1980; Thompson, Griffith, and Leaf, 1990). One example of the use of the PACT model with homeless mentally ill persons is found in the work of an interdisciplinary mobile outreach treatment team in Baltimore (Dixon, Friedman, and Lehman, 1993a). The team, consisting of a clinical case manager, psychiatrist, nurse, and consumer advocate, demonstrated that their intervention was successful in moving homeless patients into adequate housing.

One of the major features of intensive case management involves the attempt to overcome "service resistance." As Rog (1988) has noted, it is an intervention that seeks to "engage homeless persons with mental illness into treatment" and to utilize other existing services. Engagement "provides for the initial and continued involvement in services traditionally for non-help-seeking individuals" (Rog, 1988, p. 1). Cohen (1989) draws from recent research on social work services to homeless mentally ill persons to identify strategies of engaging these clients in the helping process. The special attention given to "engagement" in practice with homeless mentally ill clients is due to the perception that these clients are disaffiliated and avoid seeking services and contact with mental health professionals. The tasks of engagement include assurance of the voluntary nature of the services, the offering of services in keeping with the client's perception of need, and the use of group experiences to develop social relationships among clients.

Ideally, intensive case management becomes one part of an integrated service system. The Task Force on Homelessness and Severe Mental Illness (Leshner, 1992) has emphasized the need for a systems approach to servicing the homeless mentally ill. The case management component of the service system is referred to by the Task Force as "integrated care management," with the goals of "enhancing continuity of care, access to services, and efficiency and accountability of service provision and integration" (Leshner, 1992). A key feature of integrated care management is the focus on helping the client negotiate access to and utilization of a range of services, benefits, and entitlements. This type of case management seeks to overcome barriers to homeless persons who are eligible for entitlements due to their poverty and disability status. In another version of an "ideal" form of "intensive case management," Stein (1992) calls for the abolishment of the case manager, due to the complexity of the tasks needed to serve the severe and persistent mentally ill. Stein's proposal for a multidisciplinary continuous care team rather than a case manager to work with this population offers another approach to serving severely mentally ill homeless people.

EVALUATION OF CASE MANAGEMENT

There are a number of descriptions of the use of case management with homeless mentally ill persons, but few systematic research studies evaluating effectiveness are reported in the literature (Breakey, 1987). Most studies on case management with severely mentally ill people focus on services to clients who are not homeless (Modrcin, Rapp, and Poertner, 1988; Chamberlain and Rapp, 1991). Of special note are experimental studies that demonstrate that case management is effective in reaching selected outcomes with the severely mentally ill (Olfson, 1990). For example, an experimental study by Goering et al. (1988) demonstrated that a rehabilitation-oriented case management program improved the quality of life for clients; that is, it led to "improved occupational functioning, less social isolation, and more independent living" (p. 275). In another experimental study of intensive case management for the mentally ill, Bush et al. (1990) found that this intervention led to reduced hospitalizations and hospital days, less use of emergency services, and improved adherence to service plans and medication regimens. Somewhat different findings come from an experimental study by Franklin et al. (1987). In this study of the effectiveness of case management there was an increase in the utilization of services, but no improvement in the quality of life for mentally ill clients receiving case management services.

A different model of intervention with mentally ill people was evaluated in a field experiment conducted by Freddolino and Moxley (1992). This model included aspects of case management, but emphasized advocacy based on needs expressed by mentally ill people. Participants in the study were randomly assigned to one of three groups: an experimental group, contact-only group, and a control group. Although the findings comparing the three groups were mixed, individuals receiving the Client Support and Representation services demonstrated a high level of goal accomplishment and satisfaction with the intervention. As a result of the program, the authors used the evaluation findings to refine the model to meet the special needs of homeless mentally ill individuals. The new model for homeless mentally ill people focused on acceptability, calling for mental health professionals to join with the client in advocating for client-determined needs and goals.

The NIMH Community Support Program is providing sponsorship of studies of case management with the homeless mentally ill. A number of program evaluations are underway in the study of demonstration projects sponsored by funds from the McKinney Act. One of the completed assessments of case management with this population is described by Toomey et al. (1989), Rife et al. (1991), and First, Rife, and Kraus (1990). These authors report on a three-year NIMH project that used a mobile mental health case management team model to serve homeless mentally ill persons. The services were based in two community mental health centers. The program evaluation of this project resulted in three major findings. First, frequent monitoring of clients led to a continued engagement in services and less likelihood of becoming homeless again. Second, clients placed for housing for at least six months "perceived that their quality of life had improved in the areas of global well-being, living situation, leisure activities, finances, safety, and health" (Rife et al., 1991, p. 65). Third, at the finish of the three-year project, "only 54 percent of the clients were still in placement and actively participating in the case management efforts" (Toomey et al. 1989, p. 24). Staff turnover as well as client mobility during the project was believed to have had an influence on the lack of contact with clients. Data from this project identified some of the barriers to implementation of the intensive case management approach, such as "lack of intensity in client/worker contact" and "inadequate or limited community resources," and a failure of workers to keep in contact with clients (First, Rife, and Kraus, 1990, p. 90).

Another evaluation of case management with homeless mentally ill clients is described by Goering et al. (1992). The case management program being evaluated used an intensive, assertive, outreach approach to service clients in men's and women's hostels in Toronto. The program was designed to serve "difficult to serve" homeless mentally ill clients, using "outreach workers trained in psychiatric rehabilitation (to) provide intensive case management to small caseloads of eight to ten clients" (p. 161). The activities of staff members included engaging clients, crisis intervention, referrals of clients to community resources, and direct support. In the first nine months of the program, clients showed improvement in various aspects of social functioning, and in "housing stability, social networks, and psychiatric symptoms and disability . . ." (p. 160).

A very sophisticated study involving case management services for homeless mentally ill persons is found in the work by Morse et al. (1992). This study used an experimental design that compared the "effectiveness of three community-based treatment programs serving homeless mentally ill people: traditional outpatient treatment offered by a mental health clinic, a daytime drop-in center, and a continuous treatment team program that included assertive outreach, a high staff-to-client ratio, and intensive case management" (p. 1005). After 12 months in these programs, participants in all programs improved in terms of days homeless, fewer psychiatric symptoms, increased income, improved interpersonal adjustment, and self-esteem. At the same time, continuous treatment clients "had more contact with their treatment program, were more satisfied with their program, spent fewer days homeless, and used more community services and resources than clients in the other two programs" (p. 1005). While the most successful treatment program included features in addition to intensive case management, the results supported the significant role of case management in serving homeless mentally ill clients.

In another evaluation of service programs for mentally ill homeless persons, Barrow et al. (1989) investigated five innovative programs that focused on "intensive services" to this target population. All of the programs combined direct service provision with referral, advocacy, and case management services. The service strategies of these programs included four overlapping phases: engagement, assessment of needs and definition of goals, direct service provision, and linkage to other service providers. Study findings indicated that engagement, "the process of gaining the clients' trust and agreement to accept program services," was especially crucial in programs that used outreach to recruit clients (p. ix). Most of the goals dealt with service linkages regarding housing, psychiatric treatment, and financial support, goals service workers believed were not attainable during a six-month period. While case management was used to establish links to these services, completed referrals were more difficult to achieve than providing direct services to clients. The goal of obtaining housing was more likely to be achieved when income and access was improved, with housing serving to increase the likelihood of reaching treatment goals. The study findings had a number of implications for service delivery, such as a recognition of the diversity of the homeless population, the labor-intensive nature of outreach and engagement, the need for direct services as well as referrals, the need for modification of traditional services to reach these clients, and the importance of client participation in defining housing goals and selection of housing that supports treatment (Barrow et al., 1989).

These evaluations demonstrate the success of case management in reaching client service goals with mentally ill persons. These goals are related to the cultural dimensions of homelessness, including: improved occupational functioning, increased income; less social isolation, improved interpersonal adjustment; more independent living; continuing engagement in treatment; reduction of psychiatric symptoms; and increase in use of community services. Descriptions of these projects suggest that those delivering services to the homeless mentally ill incorporated an understanding of cultural dimensions of homelessness in carrying out their case management interventions.

CONCLUSION

It is our contention that the effectiveness of case management with homeless mentally ill persons can be enhanced through an understanding of the cultural dimensions of homelessness. In making any kind of generalizations about the "culture" of homelessness, it is necessary to recognize the heterogeneity of the homeless population, in terms of their social and demographic characteristics and nighttime housing arrangements. At the same time, there are some cultural traits that have come to be associated with homeless people. Our review of research studies on homelessness suggests that a large proportion of the homeless share cultural traits of extreme poverty and weak or no attachment to the workforce, lifestyles different from mainstream society, social disaffiliation, and resistance to health and welfare services. There is strong evidence that homeless people differ from each other in the extent to which they have these traits and in the ways in which they relate to subcultures organized around housing arrangements, such as emergency shelters, streets and public places, and skid row areas. Recognition and understanding of these differences within the mentally ill subgroup of homeless people is necessary for the practice of effective case management with this client group.

Research studies generally demonstrate the effectiveness of case management with the homeless, and with the homeless mentally ill. The literature suggests that "intensive case management," a modification of the traditional case management approach, is effective with severely mentally ill homeless people. With its emphasis on "intensity," this model of case management responds to the client's homeless culture and environment, as well as to the client's mental illness. With the further development of this case management model into integrated care management, renewed emphasis is given to the advantages of a comprehensive and integrated system of care for homeless mentally ill people.

A significant role that mental health professionals might play in serving the homeless mentally ill through case management was identified by Baxter and Hopper (1982) over a decade ago when they suggested that "clinicians could play a critical advocacy role for an approach that sees therapeutic and social needs as intimately linked" (p. 393). The research findings presented in this chapter support this recommendation, and lend confirmation to the following major principles offered by Baxter and Hopper (1982):

1. The homeless are not unreachable.
2. Shelter is the indispensable first step in reaching them.
3. Clinical needs can only be addressed in a setting that satisfies survival needs.
4. Clinicians, in particular, occupy a place of singular intimacy vis-à-vis the homeless. (pp. 405, 406)

These principles provide a foundation for the practice of case management with homeless mentally ill persons. Our review suggests that practice built on these principles will be enhanced by an understanding of the cultural dimensions of homelessness and the special burdens this condition places on the severely mentally ill. A major theme in service to this client group is a recognition that the traditional institutional service cultures, such as the culture of psychiatry, the culture of welfare services, and the culture of temporary shelters, are often in conflict with the cultural characteristics, practices, and interests of homeless mentally ill people. With an increased understanding of these cultures, there is promise that more effective services will be developed to improve the quality of life of homeless mentally ill persons.

REFERENCES

Adler, P. and Adler, P. (1992). Countercultures. In Borgatta, E.F., and Borgatta, M.L. (eds.). Encyclopedia of Sociology. New York: Macmillan.

Alcohol, Drug Abuse, and Mental Health Administration. (1983). Problems of the Homeless: Proceedings of a Roundtable. Rockville, Maryland: ADAMHA.

Arce, A., Tadlock, M., Vergare, M., and Shapiro, S. (1983). A psychiatric profile of street people admitted to an emergency shelter. *Hospital and Community Psychiatry, 34*(9), 812-817.

Bachrach, L.L. (1982). Program planning for young adult chronic patients. *New Directions for Mental Health Services, 14*, 99-109.

Bachrach, L.L. (1984a). Research on services for the mentally ill. *Hospital and Community Psychiatry, 35*(9), 910-913.

Bachrach, L.L. (1984b). Interpreting research on the homeless mentally ill: Some caveats. *Hospital and Community Psychiatry, 35*(9), 914-917.

Bachrach, L.L. (1987). Geographic mobility and the homeless mentally ill. *Hospital and Community Psychiatry, 38*(1), 27-28.

Bachrach, L.L. (1988). Defining chronic mental illness: A concept paper. *Hospital and Community Psychiatry, 39*(4), 383-388.

Bachrach, L.L. (1990). The media and homeless mentally ill persons. *Hospital and Community Psychiatry, 41*(9), 963-964.

Bachrach, L.L. (1992a). What we know about homelessness among mentally ill persons: An analytical review and commentary. *Hospital and Community Psychiatry, 43*(5), 453-464.

Bachrach, L.L. (1992b). Case management revisited. *Hospital and Community Psychiatry, 43*(3), 209-210.

Bahr, J.M. and Caplow, T. (1973). *Old Men Drunk and Sober*. New York: New York University Press.

Barrow, S.M., Hellman, F., Lovell, A., and Plapinger, J. (1989). Effectiveness of programs for the mentally ill homeless. New York State Psychiatric Institute.

Bassuk, E. (1984). Is homelessness a mental health problem? *American Journal of Psychiatry, 141*(12), 1546-1550.

Bassuk, E.L., Rubin, L., and Lauriat, A. (1984). Is homelessness a mental health problem? *American Journal of Psychiatry, 141*, 1546-1550.

Bassuk, E.L., Rubin, L., and Lauriat, A. (1986). Characteristics of sheltered homeless families. *American Journal of Public Health, 76*, September, 1097-1101.

Baxter, E. and Hopper, K. (1981). Private lives/public spaces: Homeless adults on the streets of New York City. Community Service Society, Institute for Social Welfare Research.

Baxter, E. and Hopper, K. (1982). The new mendicancy: Homeless in New York City. *American Journal of Orthopsychiatry, 52*(3), 393-408.

Belcher, J.R. and Ephross, P.H. (1989). Toward an effective practice model for the homeless mentally ill. *Social Casework,* September, 421-427.

Belle, D. (1990). Poverty and women's mental health. *American Psychologist, 45*(3), 385-389.

Billig, N.S. and Levinson, C. (1987). Homelessness and case management in Montgomery County, Maryland: A focus on chronic mental illness. *Psychosocial Rehabilitation Journal,* XI(1), 59-66.

Blau, J. (1989). The limits of the welfare state: New York City's response to homelessness. *Journal of Sociology and Social Welfare,* Vol. XVI(1), March.

Bogue, D.A. (1963). Skid row in American cities. Chicago: Community and Family Study Center, University of Chicago.

Bond, G.R., Pensec, M., Dietzen, L., and McCafferty, D. (1991). Intensive case management for frequent users of psychiatric hospitals in a large city: A comparison of team and individual caseloads. *Psychosocial Rehabilitation Journal, 15*(1), 90-98.

Borland, A., McRae, J., and Lycan, C. (1989). Outcomes of five years of continuous intensive case management. *Hospital and Community Psychiatry, 40*(4), 369-376.

Breakey, W.R. (1987). Recent empirical research on the homeless mentally ill. In Dennis, D.L. (ed.). Research methodologies concerning homeless persons with serious mental illness and/or substance abuse disorders. Proceedings. Albany, New York: New York State Office of Mental Health.

Breakey, W.R., Fischer, P.J., Nestadt, G., and Romanoski, A. (1992). Stigma and stereotype: Homeless mentally ill persons. In Fink, P.J. and Tasman, A. Stigma and Mental Illness. Washington: American Psychiatric Press.

Breton, M. (1984). A drop-in program for transient women: Promoting competence through the environment. *Social Work,* November/December, 542-546.

Brown, K.S. and Ziefert, M. (1990). A feminist approach to working with homeless women. *Affilia, 5*(1).

Bush, C.T., Langford, M.W., Rosen, P., and Gutt, W. (1990). Operation outreach: Intensive case management for severely psychiatrically disabled adults. *Hospital and Community Psychiatry, 41*(6), 647-649.

Campbell, R. and Reeves, J.L. (1989). Covering the homeless: The Joyce Brown story. *Critical Studies in Mass Communication,* March, 21-42.

Chafetz, L. (1990). Withdrawal from the homeless mentally ill. *Community Mental Health Journal, 26*(5).

Chamberlain, R. and Rapp, C.A. (1991). A decade of case management: A methodological review of outcome research. *Community Mental Health Journal, 27*(3), 171-188.

Cohen, M.B. (1989). Social work practice with homeless mentally ill people: Engaging the client. *Social Work, 34*(6).

Cohen, N.L. and Marcos, L.R. (1992). Outreach intervention models for the homeless mentally ill. In Lamb, H.R., Bachrach, L.L., and Kass, F.I. (1992). Treating the homeless mentally ill. Washington, DC: American Psychiatric Association.

Cohen, C.I. and Sokolovsky, J. (1989). Old men of the bowery. New York: Guilford Press.

Cohen, N.L., Putnam, J.F., and Sullivan, A.M. (1984). The mentally ill homeless: Isolation and adaptation. *Hospital and Community Psychiatry, 35*(9).

Cournos, F.C. (1989). Involuntary medication and the case of Joyce Brown. *Hospital and Community Psychiatry, 40*(7), 736-740.

Cowan, C.D., Breakey, P., and Fischer, P. (1988). The methodology of counting the homeless. Washington, DC: Institute of Medicine.

D'Andrade, R.G. (1984). Cultural Meaning Systems. In Shwedes, R.A. and Levine, R.A. (eds.). Cultural Theory: Essays on mind, self, and emotion. Cambridge, MA: Cambridge University Press.

Dennis, D.I., Buckner, J.C., Lipton, F.R., and Levine, I.S. (1991). A decade of research and services for homeless mentally ill persons. *American Psychologist, 46*(11), 1129-1138.

Dennis, D.L. (ed.) (1987). Research methodologies concerning homeless persons with serious mental illness and/or substance abuse disorders. Proceedings. Albany, NY: New York State Office of Mental Health.

Dixon, L., Friedman, N., and Lehman, A. (1993a). Housing patterns of homeless mentally ill persons receiving assertive treatment services. *Hospital and Community Psychiatry, 44*(3), 286-288.

Dixon, L., Friedman, N., and Lehman, A. (1993b). Compliance of homeless mentally ill persons with assertive community treatment. *Hospital and Community Psychiatry, 44*(6), 581-583.

Drake, R.E., Osher, F.C., and Wallach, M.A. (1991). Homelessness and dual diagnosis. *American Pyschologist, 46*(11), 1149-1158.

Duncan, G.J. , Hill, M.S., and Hoffman, S.D. (1988). Welfare dependence within and across generations. *Science, 239*, 467-471.

Farr, R., Koegel, P.L., and Burnham, A. (1986). A study of homelessness and mental illness in the skid row of Los Angeles. Los Angeles: County Department of Mental Health.

Feitel, B., Margetson, N., Chamas, J., and Lipman, C. (1992). Psychosocial background and behavioral and emotional disorders of homeless and runaway youth. *Hospital and Community Psychiatry, 43*(2), 155-159.

First, R.J. and Toomey, B.G. (1989). Homeless men and the work ethic. *Social Service Review,* March.

First, R.J., Roth, D., and Arewa, B.D. (1988). Homelessness: Understanding the dimensions of the problem of minorities. *Social Work,* March/April.

First, R.J., Rife, J.C., and Kraus, S. (1990). Case management with people who are homeless and mentally ill: Preliminary findings from an NIMH demonstration project. *Psychosocial Rehabilitation Journal, 14*(2), 87-91.

Fischer, P.J. (1991). Alcohol, drug abuse, and mental health problems among homeless persons: A review of the literature, 1980-1990. Rockville, MD: U.S. Department of Health and Human Services.

Fischer, P.J. and Breakey, W.R. (1991). The epidemiology of alcohol, drug, and mental disorders among homeless persons. *American Psychologist, 46*(11), 1115-1128.

Fiske, J. (1991). For cultural interpretation: A study of the culture of homelessness. *Critical Studies in Mass Communication, 8,* 455-474.

Franklin, J.L., Solovitz, B., Mason, M., Clemons, J.R., and Miller, G.E. (1987). An evaluation of case management. *American Journal of Public Health,* 77(6), 674-678.

Freddolino, P.P. and Moxley, D.P. (1992). Refining an advocacy model for homeless people coping with psychiatric disabilities. *Community Mental Health Journal, 28*(4), 337-352.

Freudenheim, M. (1991). New law to bring wider job rights for mentally ill. *The New York Times,* 9/23/91.

Gaw, A.C. (1993). Culture, ethnicity, and mental illness. Washington, DC: American Psychiatric Association.

General Accounting Office (GAO). (1988). Homeless mentally ill: Problems and options in estimating numbers and trends. PEMD-88-24.

George, L.K. (1989). Definition, classification, and measurement of mental health services. In Taube, C.A., Mechanic, D., and Hohman, A.A. (eds.). The future of mental health services research. NIMH. DHHS Pub. No. (ADM) 99-1600. Washington, DC: Supt. of Docs., U.S. Govt. Print. Off.

Gewirtzman, R. and Fodor, I. (1987). The homeless child at school from welfare hotel to classroom. *Child Welfare.* LXVI(3).

Giamo, B. (1989). On the Bowery. Confronting homelessness in American society. Iowa City: University of Iowa Press.

Gilmore, S. (1992). Culture. In Borgatta, E.F. and Borgatta, M.L. (eds.). Encyclopedia of Sociology. New York: Macmillan.

Goering, P.N., Wasylenki, D., Farkas, M., and Lancee, W.J. (1988). What difference does case management make? *Hospital and Community Psychiatry,* 39(3), 272-276.

Goering, P., Wasylenki, M., St. Onge, D., Paduchak, D., and Lancee, W. (1992). Gender differences among clients of a case management program for the homeless. *Hospital and Community Psychiatry, 43*(2), 160-165.

Goldfinger, S.M. (1990). Introduction: Perspectives on the homeless mentally ill. *Community Mental Health Journal, 26*(5).

Gory, M.L., Ritchey, F.J., and Mullis, J. (1990). Depression among the homeless. *Journal of Health and Social Behavior, 31,* 87-101.

Gounis, K. and Susser, E. (1990). Shelterization and its implications for mental health services. In Cohen, N. (ed.), Psychiatry takes to the streets. New York: Guilford Press.

Greenstone, J.D. (1991). Culture, rationality, and the underclass. In Jencks, C. and Peterson, P.E. (eds.), The urban underclass. Washington: The Brookings Institution.

Grunberg, J. and Eagle, P.F. (1990). Shelterization: How the homeless adapt to shelter living. *Hospital and Community Psychiatry, 41*(5).

Harris, M. and Bachrach, L.L. (1990). Perspectives on homeless mentally ill women. *Hospital and Community Psychiatry, 41*, 252-254.

Holloway, S. (1991). Homeless People. In Gitterman, A. (ed.), Handbook of social work practice with vulnerable populations. New York: Columbia University Press.

Hopper, K. and Hamburg, J. (1984). The making of America's homeless: From skid row to new poor, 1945-1984. Report prepared for the Institute of Social Welfare Research. New York City: Community Service Society.

Hutchinson, W.J., Searight, P., and Stretch, J. (1986). Multidimensional networking: A response to the needs of homeless families. *Social Work*, November/December, 427-430.

Institute of Medicine. (1988). Homelessness, health, and human needs. Washington: National Academy Press.

Jencks, C. and Peterson, P.E. (eds.). (1991). The urban underclass. Washington: The Brookings Institution.

Johnson, A.B. (1990). Out of Bedlam. The Truth about Deinstitutionalization. New York: Basic Books.

Kates, B. (1985). The murder of a shopping bag lady. New York: Harcourt Brace Jovanovich.

Kaufman, M.S. (1988). "Crazy" until proven innocent? Civil commitment of the mentally ill homeless. *Columbia Human Rights Law Review, 19*(2), 333-367.

Koegel, P. (1987). Ethnographic perspectives on homeless and homeless mentally ill women. Los Angeles: University of California.

Koegel, P., Burnham, M.A., and Farr, R.K. (1988). The prevalence of specific psychiatric disorders among homeless individuals in the inner city of Los Angeles. *Archives of General Psychiatry, 45*(12).

Kozol, J. (1988a). The homeless. *The New Yorker,* Jan. 25, Feb. 1.

Kozol, J. (1988b). Are the homeless crazy? *Harper's,* September, 17-19.

Kozol, J. (1988c). Rachel and her children. New York: Ballantine Books.

Kutza, E.A. and Keigher, S.M. (1991). The elderly new homeless: An emerging population at risk. *Social Work, 36*(4), 288-293.

Lamb, H.R. (ed.). (1984). The homeless mentally ill. Washington: American Psychiatric Association.

Lamb, H.R. (1992). Perspectives on effective advocacy for homeless mentally ill persons. *Hospital and Community Psychiatry, 43*(12), 1209-1212.

Lamb, H.R., Bachrach, L.L., and Kass, F.I. (1992). Treating the homeless mentally ill. Washington, DC: American Psychiatric Association.

Lee, B.A. (1992) Homelessness. In Borgatta, E.F. and Borgatta, M.L. (eds.), Encyclopedia of Sociology. New York: Macmillan.

Lefley, H.P. (1990). Culture and chronic mental illness. *Hospital and Community Psychiatry, 41*(3), 277-286.

Lefley, H.P. and Bestman, E.W. (1991). Public-academic linkages for culturally sensistive community mental health. *Community Mental Health Journal, 27*(6), 473-488.

Leshner, A.I. (1992). Outcasts on main street. Report of the federal task force on homelessness and severe mental illness. Washington: Interagency Council on the Homeless (ADM) 92-1904.

Levine, I.S. and Haggard, L.K. (1989). Homelessness as a public mental health problem. In Rochefort, D.A. (ed.), Handbook on Mental Health Policy. New York: Greenwood Press.

Levine, I.S. and Huebner, R.B. (1991). Homeless persons with alcohol, drug, and mental disorders. *American Psychologist, 46*(11), 1113-1114.

Levine, I.S. and Rog, D.J. (1990). Mental health services for homeless mentally ill persons. *American Psychologist, 45*(8), 963-968.

Levine, I.S., Lezak, A.D., and Goldman, H.H. (1986). Community support systems for the homeless mentally ill. In Bassuk, E.I. (ed.), The mental health needs of homeless persons. San Francisco: Jossey-Bass.

Lipton, F.R. and Sabatini, A. (1984). Constructing support systems for homeless chronic patients. In Lamb, H.R. (ed.), The homeless mentally ill. Washington, DC: American Psychiatric Association.

Manoleas, P. (1994). The cross-cultural practice of clinical case management in mental health. Berkeley, CA: University of California at Berkeley.

Martin, M.A. (1986). The implications of NIMH-supported research for homeless mentally ill racial and ethnic minority persons. New York: Hunter College School of Social Work.

Martin, M.A. (1990). The homeless mentally ill and community-based care: Changing a mindset. *Community Mental Health Journal, 26*(5).

McChesney, K.Y. (1986). New findings on homeless families. *Family Professional, 1*(2).

Milburn, N. and D'Ercole, A. (1991). Homeless women. *American Psychologist, 46*(11), 1161-1169.

Modrcin, M., Rapp, C.A., and Poertner, J. (1988). Evaluation of case management services with the chronically mentally ill. *Evaluation and Program Planning, 11*, 307-314.

Morrissey, J. (1986). NIMH funded research on the homeless mentally ill. Albany, NY: Bureau of Evaluation Research, NYS Office of Mental Health.

Morrissey, J.P. (1989). Commentary. In Taube et al. (eds.), The future of mental health services research. NIMH. DHHS Pub. No. (ADM) 89-1600. Washington, DC: Supt. of Docs., U.S. Govt. Print. Off.

Morrissey, J.P. and Levine, I.S. (1987). Researchers discuss latest findings, examine needs of homeless mentally ill persons. *Hospital and Community Psychiatry, 38*(8), 811-812.

Morse, G.A., Calsyn, R.J., Allen, G., and Tempelhoff, B. (1992). Experimental comparison of the effects of three treatment programs for homeless mentally ill people. *Hospital and Community Psychiatry, 43*(10), 1005-1023.

Moxley, D.P. and Freddolino, P.P. (1991). Needs of homeless people coping with psychiatric problems: Findings from an innovative advocacy project. *Health and Social Work, 12*(1), 19-26.

National Institute of Mental Health. (1982). A Network for Caring: The community support program of the National Institute of Mental Health. U.S. Dept. of Health and Human Services (ADM) 81-1063.

National Institute of Mental Health. (1991). Caring for people with severe mental disorders: A national plan of research to improve services. DHHS Pub. No. (ADM) 19-1762. Washington, DC: Sup. of Docs., U.S. Govt. Print. Off.

Newman, K.S. (1989). Culture and structure in the truly disadvantaged: An anthropological perspective. Columbia University.

Olfson, M. (1990). Assertive community treatment: An evaluation of the experimental evidence. *Hospital and Community Psychiatry, 41*(6), 634-641.

Padilla, Y.C. (1990). Social science theory on the Mexican-American experience. *Social Service Review,* June.

Pepper, B., Ryglewicz, H., and Kirschner, M.C. (1981). The young adult chronic patient: overview of a population. *Hospital and Community Psychiatry, 32,* 463-469.

Rafferty, Y. and Shinn, M. (1991). The impact of homelessness on children. *American Psychologist, 46*(11), 1170-1179.

Ridgely, M.S., Osher, F.C., and Talbott, J.A. (1987). Chronic mentally ill young adults with substance abuse problems: Treatment and training issues. Baltimore: University of Maryland School of Medicine.

Ridgway, P. (1986). Case management services for persons who are homeless and mentally ill: Report from an NIMH workshop. Boston: Center for Psychiatric Rehabilitation, Boston University.

Rife, J.C., First, R.J., Greenlee, R., and Miller, L.D. (1991). Case management with homeless mentally ill people. *Health and Social Work, 16*(1), 59-67.

Rog, D.J. (1988). Engaging homeless persons with mental illnesses into treatment. Alexandria, VA: National Mental Health Association.

Rog, D.J., Andranovich, G.D., and Rosenblum, S. (1987). Intensive case management for persons who are homeless and mentally ill. Washington, DC: COSMOS corporation.

Rollinson, P.A. (1991). Elderly single room occupancy (SRO) hotel tenants: Still alone. *Social Work, 36*(4).

Rose, S.M. (1992). Case management and social work practice. New York: Longman.

Rossi, P. H. (1988). Minorities and homelessness. In Sandefur, G.D. and Tienda, M. (eds.), *Divided Opportunities.* New York: Plenum Press.

Rossi, P.H. (1989). *Down and Out in America.* Chicago: University of Chicago Press.

Rossi, P.H. (1990). The old homeless and the new homelessness in historical perspective. *American Psychologist, 45*(8), 954-959.

Roth, D. and Bean, G.J. (1986). New perspectives on homelessness: Findings from a statewide epidemiological study. *Hospital and Community Psychiatry, 37*(7), 712-719.

Rothman, J. (1992). *Guidelines for Case Management.* Itaska, IL: Peacock Publishers.

Rousseau, A.M. (1981). Shopping *Bag Ladies: Homeless Women Speak about Their Lives.* New York: Pilgrim Press.

Sargent, M. (1989). Update on programs for the homeless mentally ill. *Hospital and Community Psychiatry, 40*(10), 1015-1016.

Schwab, B., Drake, R.E., and Elisabeth, M. (1988). Health care of the chronically mentally ill: The culture broker model. *Community Mental Health Journal, 24*(3), 174-184.

Segal, S.P. and Baumohl, J. (1980). Engaging the disengaged: Proposals on madness and vagrancy. *Social Work,* September.

Segal, S.P. and VanderVoort, D.J. (1993). Daily hassles of persons with severe mental illness. *Hospital and Community Psychiatry, 44*(3), 276-277.

Segal, S.P., Bauhmohl, J., and Johnson, E. (1977). Falling through the cracks: Mental disorder and social margin in a young vagrant population. *Social Problems, 24*, 387-400.

Sosin, M.R., Colson, P., and Grossman, S. (1988). Homelessness in Chicago. Chicago: The Chicago Community Trust.

Stein, L.I. (1992). On the abolishment of the case manager. *Health Affairs,* Fall, 172-177.

Stein, L.I. and Test, M.A. (1980). Alternative to mental hospital treatment. *Archives of General Psychiatry, 37*, 392-397.

Stewart B. McKinney Homeless Assistance Act. (1987). Public Law 100-177.

Stoner, M.R. (1983). The plight of homeless women. *Social Service Review,* December.

Susser, E., Conover, S., and Struening, E.L. (1989). Problems of epidemiologic method in assessing the type and extent of mental illness among homeless adults. *Hospital and Community Psychiatry, 40*(3), 261-265.

Susser, E., Conover, S., and Struening, E.L. (1990). Mental illness in the homeless: Problems of epidemiologic method in surveys of the 1980s. *Community Mental Health Journal, 26*(5), October.

Susser, E., Goldfinger, S.M., and White, A. (1990). Some clinical approaches to the homeless mentally ill. *Community Mental Health Journal, 26*(5).

Swayze, F.V. (1992). Clinical case management with the homeless mentally ill. In Lamb, H.R., Bachrach, L.L., and Kass, F.I. (eds.), Treating the homeless mentally ill. Washington, DC: American Psychiatric Association.

Tessler, R.C. and Dennis, D.L. (1989). A synthesis of NIMH funded research covering persons who are homeless and mentally ill. Amherst, MA: University of Massachusetts.

Test, M.A. (1981). Effective community treatment of the chronically mentally ill: What is necessary? *Journal of Social Issues, 37*, 3.

Thompson, K.S., Griffith, E., and Leaf, P.J. (1990). A historical review of the Madison model of community care. *Hospital and Community Psychiatry, 41*(6), 625-633.

Tienda, M. and Stier, H. (1991). Joblessness and shiftlessness: Labor force activity in Chicago's inner city. In Jencks, C. and Peterson, P.E. (eds.), *The Urban Underclass.* Washington: The Brookings Institution.

Toomey, G.G., First, R.J., Rife, J.C., and Belcher, J.R. (1989). Evaluating community care for homeless mentally ill people. *Social Work Research and Abstracts,* December.

Toro, P.A. (1991a). Final evaluation report: Demonstration employment project. Unpublished report, U.S. Dept. of Labor, State University of New York at Buffalo, Dept. of Psychology.

Toro, P.A. and Wall, D.D. (in press). Research on homeless persons: Diagnostic comparisons and practice implications. Professional, Psychology: Research and Practice.

Toro, P.A., Trickett, E.J., Wall, D.D., and Salem, D.A. (1991). Homelessness in the United States: An ecological perspective. *American Psychologist, 46*(11), 1208-1218.

Turner, J.C. and TenHoor, W.J. (1978). The NIMH community support program: Pilot approach to a needed social reform. *Schizophrenia Bulletin, 4,* 319-343.

U.S. Department of Health and Human Services. (1991). Program Announcement PA 91-60. Mental Health Research on Homeless Persons.

Wallace, S.E. (1965). Skid row as a way of life. Totowa, NJ: Bedminster Press.

Welch, W.M. and Toff, G. (1987). Service needs of minority persons who are homeless and homeless mentally ill. George Washington University.

Wilson, W.J. (1987). *The Truly Disadvantaged.* Chicago: University of Chicago Press.

Wilson, W.J. (1991). Public policy research and the Truly Disadvantaged. In Jencks, C. and Peterson, E. (eds.), *The Urban Underclass.* Washington, DC: The Brookings Institution.

Chapter 3

Demoralization: A Useful Concept for Case Management with Native Americans

Felicia Schanche Hodge
Patricia Kipnis

INTRODUCTION

Certain problems have been paid a great deal of attention in the mental health literature on Native Americans. This literature has tended to focus on problems associated with *behaviors*. Examples of this are the work on alcoholism (Lewis, 1982; Health, 1983; Leland, 1976), suicide (Grossman and Mulligan, 1991; May, 1987), and domestic violence (*Regional Differences in Indian Health*, 1993) among Native Americans. This focused attention on problematic behaviors can tend to paint an incomplete clinical picture that may also be *ahistorical* in terms of the colonial experiences of Native Americans. It also can tend to encourage/allow a "victim blaming" view of American Indian problems among dominant culture clinicians and researchers.

Part of the reason for the above may be due, in part, to the limiting and Eurocentric nature of the current categories in the DSM III-R. Though the diagnostic category of depression may go a step further than the above in helping us understand the clinical, subjective, and internal realities of Native American clients, it is still a limiting construct. Responses to diagnostic scales and tools may be culturally defined and may indeed identify a separate measure. The appropriate use of the DSM III-R to diagnose depression is questionable and is in need of further validation.

NATIVE AMERICANS AND DEPRESSION: AN OVERVIEW

It has been said that a positive self-concept is both essential for and indicative of healthy psychological functioning (Lefley, 1982). Low self-concept is associated with depression, demoralization, and other psychological problems. Promotion of positive self-concept is both a preventive strategy and a treatment outcome. How one defines such areas of concern as self-concept, depression, and demoralization, and particularly, how one assesses these concepts, remains problematic.

Depression is reportedly one of the most prevalent psychiatric disorders among Native Americans (Vega and Rumbaut, 1991; Manson et al., 1990; Beals et al., 1991). Studies investigating depression among Native Americans have reported lower self-concept in Natives than in whites or other comparison groups (Corrigan, 1970; Mason, 1969; Rosenthal, 1974; Thornburg, 1974; Zirkel, 1971). These studies, however, have had some difficulty in identifying a standard measure for depression. The validity of these instruments has been questioned (Dohrenwend et al., 1980; Link and Dohrenwend, 1980; Kipnis et al., 1994), and further, it has been suggested that these instruments actually measure a condition Frank (1973) labeled "demoralization." This condition features low self-esteem, helplessness-hopelessness, sadness, and anxiety. The interchange between depression and demoralization may be slight. For the purpose of this chapter, we have chosen to define those areas of depression, low self-concept, and anxiety as demoralization.

Even though researchers have generally found high rates of depression or "demoralization" among Native Americans, and studies on risk factors for depression for the general population or for other ethnic minorities are plentiful, research on the risks associated with it among Native Americans is limited. The purpose of this chapter is to report the risk factors for depression/demoralization among Native Americans in 18 northern California health clinics. Some of these risk factors have also been shown to be risk factors for clinical depression. Given the strong relationship between both psychological phenomena mentioned above, demoralization and clinical depression, the findings reported in this chapter could apply for clinical depression to some extent.

PROBLEM DEFINITION AND PREVIOUS RESEARCH

Research on the use of various depression scales with ethnic minorities, in particular Native Americans, is fairly recent. Vega and Rumbaut (1991) presented a summary of current knowledge about minority mental health, comparing research on depressive symptomology among blacks, Hispanics, Asians, and Native Americans. Their review of studies on the subject found reports of high levels of depressive symptoms among Native Americans using standard depression scales, in particular the Center for Epidemiologic Studies Depression Scale (CES-D).

Most papers examining depression assessment in the Native American community have concentrated on adolescents. Davis, Hoffmann, and Nelson (1990) studied depression in Native American adults by comparing Native and white applicants' performance on the California Psychological Inventory (CPI), using a sample of employment applicants at a gambling casino in northern Minnesota. He found Native Americans scoring significantly lower than the equivalent white sample on several of the CPI scales. The ethnic differences found are attributed primarily to gender.

A number of instruments have been developed for the population to measure depression. The use of these instruments to measure levels of depressive symptoms among Native Americans has been controversial (Link and Dohrenwend, 1980; Kipnis et al., 1994). A review of the literature indicates significant concern over the universality of symptoms associated with depression, the cultural differences in symptom presentation, and the cross-cultural reliability and validity of diagnostic systems used. The large number of heterogeneous tribes (over 500) and the challenge of obtaining representative samples of Native American and Alaska Native populations has also brought into question the interpretation of results (Somervell et al., 1993).

Some authors (Dohrenwend et al., 1980; Link and Dohrenwend, 1980; Kipnis et al., 1994) have suggested that these instruments measure what Frank (1973) labeled "demoralization." This condition features low self-esteem, helplessness-hopelessness, sadness, and anxiety. Frank postulates that this condition is a major factor leading people to seek help and is also the condition that psychotherapy attempts to relieve. Dohrenwend et al. (1980) argues that demoralization is a condition that is likely

> . . . to be experienced in association with a variety of problems, including severe physical illness, particularly chronic illness, stressful life events, psychiatric disorders, and perhaps conditions of social marginality as experienced by minority groups and persons such as housewives and the poor whose social positions block them from mainstream strivings.

The relationship between demoralization and clinical depression is important in terms of measurement issues and epidemiology. It is equally important in terms of depression prevention and case management. The extent to which demoralized individuals become clinically depressed, and the extent to which the clinically depressed remain demoralized once not clinically depressed, has been examined by some authors. Link and Dohrenwend (1980) suggest that about half of those who are demoralized are also impaired clinically. Other data suggests that a majority of these individuals are suffering from clinical depression. Whether demoralization increases the risk of clinical depression and, if so, in whom and under what circumstances is still not clear. However, given the high rate of demoralization and depressive symptomology generally found in studies of Native American populations and its strong association with other psychiatric disorders and diseases, identifying and understanding factors contributing to this phenomenon is essential.

Psychiatric disorders, particularly depression, are among the most prevalent chronic diseases. Specific causes for these diseases are largely unknown. However, certain factors are known to increase the risk of depression. These factors include stress, major life events, and socio-economic status.

Primary prevention of depression must focus on the identification of population groups in the community that have a higher incidence and prevalence of depressive diseases and those population subgroups within them. Because of their exposure to or risk of exposure to stressful factors in the psycho-social environment, these groups are believed to be at greater risk of developing clinical depression.

UTILIZATION OF THE CES-D SCALE
IN A NATIVE AMERICAN POPULATION

The Center for Epidemiologic Studies Depression Scale (CES-D) is an instrument designed to screen for depressive symptomology and to establish relationships between depression and other variables across subgroups. Knowledge about the theory and epidemiology of depressive symptoms (Radloff, 1977) was the basis for its construct validity. It is important to note that the scale was not designed as a clinical diagnostic tool. The scale does not measure rates of illness but levels of symptoms that usually accompany clinical depression. This information is useful to identify subgroups at a *high risk* of depression.

The CES-D scale is a 20-symptom checklist representing major components of depressive symptoms as defined in the clinical literature. Items cover depressed mood, including feeling of guilt, worthlessness, helplessness, and hopelessness; as well as psycho-physical manifestations such as loss of appetite, psychomotor retardation, and sleep disturbance. (A sample of the CES-D scale is appended at the end of the chapter.) The scale has four components of depression interpreted as:

- *Depressed Affect:* such as loss of appetite, sleepiness, etc.

- *Positive Affect:* such as general well-being

- *Somatic/Retarded Activity Affect:* such as excessive sleeping, general malaise

- *Interpersonal Affect:* such as lack of interest, low response, etc.

The CES-D may be an indicator of demoralization *in addition* to being sensitive to specific depressive syndromes. Further, it may be useful as an adjunct to case management and treatment programs where counseling and referral of services is indicated.

THE STUDY

The data presented in this chapter was collected as part of an intervention research project funded by the National Cancer Institute. The Native American Cancer Control Project (AICCP) is a five-year program designed to promote smoking cessation among Native Americans living in Northern California. This study reports on the results of depression screening using the CES-D scale in the smoking prevalence study conducted in the first phase of the project.

Questionnaire data was collected from a sample of 1,369 adult Native American patients at 18 Native health clinics in northern California. Fourteen clinics were located in rural/reservation sites and four were urban Native clinics. All northern California Native clinics participated in the survey.

Each participant was asked to complete a self-administered questionnaire along with their clinic intake forms. The questionnaire was designed to assess smoking rates, patterns, and attitudes as well as health status, including mental health. Demographic information such as gender, age, employment status, marital status, and social status was also included in the questionnaire.

Each item on the CES-D scale has a range of four responses, indicating how often the respondent had experienced the symptom during the past week, ranging from 0 to 3 where:

$0 \rightarrow$ rarely or never (< 1 day)
$1 \rightarrow$ sometimes (1-2 days)
$2 \rightarrow$ occasionally (3-4 days)
$3 \rightarrow$ most or all the time (5-7 days)

The coded values for all 20 items (with positively worded items reverse-scored) are summed into a total CES-D score, which may range from 0 to 60. Note that there is no measure of severity of symptom. Some authors have suggested summing only those items occurring occasionally or most of the time to measure persistence of symptoms (Schoenback et al., 1982).

Scores of 16 or higher are interpreted to mean high levels of depressive symptomatology, or *caseness*. They represent roughly the 80th percentile of score from the sample on which the CES-D instrument was originally validated by the National Institute of Mental Health. Scores of 28 or higher have been interpreted to signify symptoms of severe depression.

In the present study, caseness rates using 16 and 28 cutoff scores were computed. Mean CES-D scores and caseness using both a 16 and a 28 cutoff score were obtained by various risk factors such as gender, age, cultural background, employment, marital, health, smoking, and socio-economic status. *Age* was divided into seven groups ranging from less than 20 years to 70 or more. *Employment status* was measured as unemployed/welfare (welfare, disabled, ill, unemployed) or employed. *Marital status* was classified into married/living together, widowed, divorced/separated, or single. A set of 20 questions was used to estimate the prevalence of specific illness such as heart disease, stroke, and obesity, among others. Participants also rated their *general health* as excellent/good or fair/poor. Participants were classified as current and former or non-smokers. *Socio-economic status* was measured by questions on monetary problems and unsafe living arrangements in our study.

Since no satisfactory acculturation scale for Native Americans was found, a set of questions intended to measure acculturation included in the questionnaire was used for this purpose. These are questions on religious affiliation, cultural/traditional gatherings, participation, knowledge and use of native language, and residence at a Native Reservation/Rancheria.

The relation between the above-mentioned risk factors and depressive symptoms was examined using logistic regression analysis. The result of this analysis is presented below.

STUDY RESULTS

A total of 1,369 adult Native American patients completed the prevalence survey. Ninety-one percent of these completed the CES-D with four or fewer items left blank. A total of N=1,249 cases were used for the analysis.

Table 3.1 shows a summary of demographic characteristics measured. The sample was young and mostly female (65 percent). Fifty-four percent of the sample was between 20 and 39 years of age. Seventy-five percent of the sample used one of the fourteen rural Indian clinics and 25 percent were patients in four urban Indian clinics. Thirty-three percent of respondents were either unemployed, disabled, on welfare, or ill. Sixty-nine percent evaluated their health as either excellent or good and 31 percent as fair or poor. Forty-one percent of survey participants were classified as current smokers and 59 percent as either former or non-smokers. Forty-five

Table 3.1. Sample Characteristics

	Percent	n
Gender		
Male	35%	434
Female	65%	805
Age		
Less than 20	7%	80
20-29	26%	315
30-39	29%	359
40-49	19%	230
50-59	10%	127
60-69	6%	80
Over 70	3%	36
Site		
Urban	25%	336
Rural	75%	943
Employment		
Employed	67%	816
Unemployed/Welfare	33%	409
Marital Status		
Married/Living together	45%	551
Divorced/Separated	21%	257
Widowed	6%	59
Single	29%	358
General Health		
Excellent/Good	69%	800
Fair/Poor	31%	363
Smoking Status		
Current	41%	493
Former or non-smoker	59%	721

percent were married or living as married, 21 percent divorced or separated, 29 percent single, and 6 percent widowed. Forty-seven percent of respondents complained about financial and family problems. Twenty-eight percent reported being concerned about living in an unsafe area.

Internal reliability for the CES-D scale was estimated using Cronbach's coefficient alpha. An alpha coefficient of .87 was found in this study. This finding is comparable to reliability coefficients found in similar studies (Zich, Attkisson, and Greenfield, 1990; Manson et al., 1990; Radloff, 1977; Roberts, Rhoades, and Vernon, 1990). The caseness rate for the sample as a whole with a 16 cutoff was 42 percent (95 percent $ci=39.3,44.7$), much higher than the 19 percent caseness rate found by Radloff (1977) for the general population. When we applied a cutoff score of 28, we found a caseness rate of 15 percent (95 percent $ci=13,17$) compared to 5 percent in Radloff's study. Mean CES-D score for the sample was 15.2 (95 percent $ci=14.62,15.8$), also much higher than the 9.52 found by Radloff and quite close to 16, the cutoff score.

Analysis was conducted using both the 16 and 28 cutoff scores and similar results were obtained. Table 3.2 compares crude mean CES-D scores and caseness rates. Native American women scored generally higher than Native American men. Urban Native clinic users scored higher than rural. Those reported as unemployed or on welfare scored higher than those employed. Single, divorced, or separated participants scored higher than married or widowed. Those rating their health as excellent or good scored much lower than those rating their health as fair or poor. Current smokers scored higher than former or non-smokers.

Participants who complained about monetary problems and unsafe living environment had a mean CES-D score of 21.2 compared to 12.6 of those with no such complaints. This group also had a higher caseness rate, as would be expected.

Mean CES-D and caseness were examined across the various acculturation questions included in the questionnaire. No significant relation (using chi-square multiple tests) was found between caseness rate and acculturation questions.

Table 3.3 shows both crude and adjusted odds ratios for these risk factors using both cutoff scores. Females were at a higher risk for

Table 3.2. CES-D and Sample Characteristics

	Mean	**%>=16**	**%>=28**
Gender			
Male	14.8	40%	13%
Female	15.5	44%	15%
Age			
Less than 20	17.7	5%	16%
20-29	17.0	48%	19%
30-39	14.5	38%	13%
40-49	14.9	42%	16%
50-59	13.6	42%	9%
60-69	12.5	30%	9%
Over 70	14.3	36%	8%
Site			
Urban	16.7	46%	17%
Rural	14.7	41%	14%
Employment			
Employed	13.8	36%	11%
Unemployed/Welfare	17.9	53%	21%
Marital Status			
Married/Living together	13.2	32%	10%
Divorced/Separated	17.4	51%	22%
Widowed	14.4	31%	12%
Single	16.7	47%	16%
General health			
Excellent/Good	13.6	35%	11%
Fair/Poor	18.7	56%	24%
Smoking status			
Current	16.5	46%	18%
Former or non-smoker	14.1	38%	12%
Enough money last 3 months			
Yes	13.2	30%	10%
No	17.6	49%	20%
Family trouble last 3 months			
Yes	18.2	51%	21%
No	12.7	32%	9%
Living in unsafe area last 3 months			
Yes	19.6	55%	26%
No	13.5	32%	10%

Table 3.3. Crude and Adjusted Odds Ratios for Experiencing Depressive Symptoms

Factor	16 cutoff		28 cutoff	
	Crude odds ratio (95% CI)	Adjusted odds ratio (95% CI)	Crude odds ratio (95% CI)	Adjusted odds ratio (95% CI)
Sex[1]	1.15 (.92, 1.39)	1.17 (.88, 1.56)	1.19 (.86, 1.53)	1.1 (.74, 1.62)
Site[2]	1.23 (.97, 1.49)	1 (.74, 1.38)	1.31 (.96, 1.66)	1.05 (.70, 1.58)
General health[3]	2.30 (2.05, 2.56)	2.20 (1.64, 2.95)	2.48 (2.01, 2.66)	1.43 (.97, 2.13)
Not enough money	2.14 (1.56, 2.37)	1.56 (1.18, 2.07)	2.34 (2.01, 2.66)	1.43 (.97, 2.13)
Family trouble	2.38 (2.15, 2.61)	1.63 (1.24, 2.16)	2.78 (2.45, 3.11)	1.83 (1.24, 2.70)
Live in unsafe area	2.59 (2.33, 2.84)	1.70 (1.25, 2.31)	3.13 (2.81, 3.45)	2.11 (1.43, 3.10)
Smoking	1.36 (1.13, 1.60)	1.22 (.93, 1.6)	1.67 (1.35, 2)	1.39 (.97, 2)
Unemployed	1.98 (1.74, 2.22)	1.35 (1.02, 1.80)	2.07 (1.75, 2.39)	1.48 (1.02, 2.15)
Married[4]	1.00	1.00	1.00	1.00
Widowed	1.18 (.63, 1.74)	.87 (.42, 1.79)	1.17 (.33, 2)	1.18 (.42, 3.31)
Single	1.91 (1.63, 2.18)	1.53 (1.10, 2.13)	1.67 (1.28, 2.07)	1.28 (.81, 2.04)
Divorced	2.24 (1.94, 2.54)	1.88 (1.33, 2.65)	2.41 (2.01, 2.82)	2.11 (1.34, 3.33)

1 Female to male ratio
2 Urban to rural ratio
3 Fair/poor to good/excellent ratio
4 Reference point
Note: p = .0001 with 7 degrees of freedom.

depressive symptoms than males but not significantly. Urban residents were at a higher risk for depressive symptoms than rural residents but not significantly. Odds ratios for all factors decreased when adjusted for gender, age, and site.

Native Americans with poor or fair general health showed a higher risk for depressive symptoms than those with good or excellent general health. Native Americans experiencing financial or housing problems were at a higher risk for depressive symptoms. Similarly, the unemployed, single, and divorced had higher odds of experiencing depressive symptoms. Smokers had a higher risk for depressive symptoms than former or never smokers but not significantly so when adjusted for gender, age, and site. Odds ratios using the 28 cutoff score were larger than odds ratios obtained using the 16 cutoff score. The effects of health, employment, smoking, financial and housing problems, and marital status adjusted for gender, site, and age were also found to be significant in predicting depressive symptoms.

DISCUSSION

The Native American population studied in this sample was found to have a high risk profile for depression. Certain demographic characteristics, such as gender, health status, and socio-economic status, and other suggested risk factors were analyzed.

This study also raised questions with regard to subgroup analyses, and appropriate application of the CES-D scale in ethnic populations. The high caseness rate found in this population group is discussed, with recommendations for further research.

Depression Risk Factors

Several studies show females to be at a higher risk of depression than males (Link and Dohrenwend, 1980; Frerichs, Aneshensel, and Clark, 1981; Radloff and Rae, 1979). However, there are also a number of studies that have found no significant differences in demoralization rates between men and women in the general population (Roberts and Roberts, 1982). This suggests that gender differences might actually be due to symptom presentation differences, item-specific biases (such as crying), or some unadjusted socio-economic or demographic factor. There was no greater risk for demoralization for women in this study controlling for certain socio-demographic variables such as age and acculturation.

An increased risk of demoralization found for individuals reporting fair or poor health is consistent with findings for the general population. However, given that the CES-D does not measure physical symptoms, these could actually be manifesting themselves as psychological distress.

Socio-economic factors such as unemployment, lack of money, unsafe living arrangements, divorce, and family trouble are highly correlated with depressive symptoms. This study's population over-representation of the lower socio-economic class might explain to a large extent the high prevalence of depressive symptoms found.

Smoking and Depression

Cigarette smoking is a significant problem among Native American populations, particularly in the northern states. Research in California has documented a smoking rate of 40 percent, double the California and U.S. general population.

When we examined cigarette smokers in the study, we found that smokers were at a higher risk of depression than non-smokers. This increased risk is not consistent in similar studies. Although Perez-Stable et al. (1990) found Latino smokers at a significantly higher risk for depressive symptoms than non-smokers after controlling for gender, acculturation, education, age, and employment, others have found the opposite. Frerichs et al. (1981) reported in a general community study that none of the smoking status variables contributed significantly in explaining the variance of the CES-D score when adjusting for the effects of income, age, employment status, and sex. These different findings may be a result of application of the instrument in ethnic versus non-ethnic or mixed populations.

CES-D Across Subgroups

Differences in average CES-D scores and caseness across gender, age, and employment status were similar to those found in similar studies on Native Americans (Manson et al., 1990; 1991). Women scored higher than men, unemployed scored higher than employed, and age exhibited a curvilinear effect with higher rates found in late adolescence and early adulthood. However, these differences were not significant across gender and age.

High Caseness Rate

This study found an extremely high caseness rate for depression (42 percent). Some likely explanations for the high caseness rate found in this study could be the following.

1. What Is the CES-D Measuring?

Historically, defining mental health, as well as knowing how to measure it satisfactorily, has been controversial. The items on the CES-D scale were created to tap depressed affect, psychological distress, and some level of dysfunction–including social role performance. Link and Dohrenwend (1980) noted that these short scales seem to cover a constellation of symptoms that typify psychological distress in its most common expression in the United States, and that these symptoms are commonly associated with low socio-economic status, stress, and physical health problems. These symptoms fit the concept of "demoralization" rather than a clinical diagnosis of "major depression." The feelings of inferiority and self-doubt that come with feeling disenfranchised could be falsely representing depression by Western standards. This notion could be one of the explanations for the high caseness rate obtained in the Native American health clinic population in our study. Individuals who do not have health insurance are more likely to receive care through these clinics than are those with medical coverage. Therefore, the study population overrepresents the low-income, unemployed, or underemployed. Thirty-four percent of the sample reported being on welfare, unemployed, ill, or disabled. This figure is much higher than the 5.6 percent California unemployment rate in 1990 (Fay and Fay, 1991).

Fifty-five percent reported not having had enough money for food, clothing, housing, or other necessities of life or being concerned about living in an unsafe area. Therefore, this population is considered to be at high risk of psychological distress because of low socio-economic status, health problems, and stress and its average CES-D score is likely to be high to begin with. When caseness rates were calculated controlling for poor health and low socio-economic status, caseness rates were only slightly higher than Radloff's and increased significantly as sub-samples with poor health, monetary or unsafe housing problems, and unemployed were also included.

2. Cutoff Score

The 16 cutoff score has been a controversial point in many papers on the subject, particularly regarding its validity in populations with a different cultural background, language, and race, and among adolescents. The CES-D produces a high percentage of false positive scores when applied to more varied subgroups. Some authors have shown that raising the cutoff score to 28 for certain groups, such as Native Americans and clinic population, improves the scale's specificity without affecting its sensitivity (Zich, Attkisson, and Greenfield, 1990; Manson et al, 1990).

The CES-D instrument was not developed to measure depressive symptoms for a specific minority population. It is unclear how patient symptom presentation varies across cultures and how cultural expectations might affect performance. Thus, a specific threshold value might not be reasonable for groups with different cultural backgrounds. The scale has been shown by other authors to have a high number of false positives in general. A cutoff score of 28 has been investigated by various researchers in the field. In our study, a cutoff score of 16 yielded an unreasonably high caseness rate.

3. Symptom Expression

The projected reliability of the CES-D across subgroups was based upon the notion that each subgroup would express depressive symptoms lightly in equal amounts of each component, or the majority in one component. The discrepancies of complaints would be different for each subgroup but the differences would be compensated for by the fact that the means of each subgroup would be somewhat equal to each other after the final tally. Note that if a particular subgroup expresses symptoms liberally in each component, that subgroup might be off the scale as a whole. This would account for a high average score for such a group.

It has been documented that certain subgroups may manifest different types of symptoms; in particular, lower socio-economic status individuals report more somatic symptoms while higher socio-economic status individuals complain of more depressed symptoms. The inclusion of both somatic and depressed components on the CES-D scale meant to account for differences between lower and upper socio-economic strata might be introducing a "loophole" by which certain subgroups are showing elevated scores.

4. Health Symptoms

The CES-D scale is not designed to measure health symptoms that might manifest themselves as depression. However, minorities disproportionately experience health problems because they are disproportionately of low socio-economical status and are more likely to experience depressive symptoms as a consequence. The CES-D might be measuring an overlap of Affective and Somatic complaints that are temporary results of a physical illness, especially considering this is a clinic population with a high percentage of individuals rating their health as fair or poor. This conclusion is supported by the factor analysis findings where items on the depressed and somatic/retarded activity affects are all loaded into the same factor.

5. Individual Scale Items

The four positive items on the scale were not highly correlated with the remaining 16 items. The literature on the subject shows some controversy regarding their presence in a depression scale. The amount of overt happiness and optimism may not be related to the level of distress in someone's life. The effect of positive questions about self-esteem on a depression scale could possibly be falsely labeling everyday introverts and pessimists in general as "high risk" for depressive symptoms.

The most often endorsed items on the scale were those on Somatic complaints and lack of Positive Affect. These same items did not correlate as well with the CES-D total score as those items intended to measure a Depressed Affect. This points again to the controversy regarding these items about their presence in a depression scale and what they really measure.

Another factor could be the lack of Positive Affect pertaining to Native American worldview, which emphasizes social homogeneity and does not hold self-glorification in high esteem. In fact, Native

Americans tend to be well aware of their faults and shortcomings, and tend to show more of a need and desire to grow, develop, and improve themselves rather than revel in present accomplishments. On psychological assessments, Native Americans have consistently judged themselves generally trustworthy and trusting of others, though not particularly smart or popular. Native Americans also have shown a greater concern for general happiness than for success. Results such as these have intrigued researchers and have raised "interesting questions about the personality and social characteristics, especially forgiveness, of many Indians" (Trimble, 1987). Although this information was discovered using a self-concept test and not a depression assessment, this information may pertain to the effect that worldview may have on the "I felt that I was just as good as other people" item on the CES-D.

A question raised is the effect that the history of U.S.-Native relations has on the present day mindset of Native Americans. They have rarely had control over their own destiny, and relationships between state and federal government agencies have always been strained. Eroded faith and trust in the government in the form of inconsistent treaty arrangements and shirked responsibilities are commonplace in Native American communities. The self-concept test by Trimble revealed a no more than moderate position in alienation subscales among Natives, but the effect of the generally widescale, evolving disenfranchisement of Native communities could have confounding effects on the "I feel hopeful about the future" item on the CES-D.

CONCLUSION

This study indicates high depression/demoralization risk factors for the Native American population in northern California using the CES-D instrument. Obtaining such information is extremely useful for counselors, social workers, and other health professionals responding to the elevated mental and health-related problems such as alcoholism, suicide, and accidents/violence evident in this population. Other studies have questioned the use of instruments originally designed for the general population such as the CES-D scale, and their reliability and validity for measurement in minority populations. This application factor has not been adequately addressed.

Identifying an appropriate depression screen for use on Native Americans, although desirable, is not without some difficulty. A less subjective instrument that distinguishes clearly between somatic symptoms, affective dimension, and satisfaction with different areas of life and life expectations would be more appropriate for use in ethnic groups. However, given that this is not the first study on depression among Native Americans where a high caseness rate is found, the possibility that this population is at a high risk of depressive symptoms cannot be ruled out. Further research needs to be done on the development of measures for depression, acculturation, and socio-economic status for minority populations.

While controversy surrounds the use of psychometric measures in minority populations, it is noteworthy that risk profiles for depression/demoralization found in our study are similar to other minority population studies. This justifies to some extent the use of the CES-D in Native American communities, at least until a reliable, culturally sensitive measurement is developed that more accurately measures depressive symptoms in this population.

This study has not only identified risk factors for depression among Native Americans based upon a rather large and diverse sample size, but also suggests that the concept of demoralization is more useful for culturally competent clinical interventions, since depression in this population seems to also entail deeper issues associated with acculturation and other factors related to adjustment for minority populations, such as low self-esteem and low socio-economic status.

Some of the risk factors identified in the study have direct implications for the practice of clinical case management with Native Americans. There is a strong suggestion that addressing problems of unemployment, unsafe living conditions, and relationship issues will have direct and positive clinical repercussions with Native American clients.

REFERENCES

Beals, J., Manson, S. M., Keane, E. M., and Dick, R. W. (1991). Factorial Structure of the Center for Epidemiological Studies-Depression Scale Among Native American College Students. *Psychological Assessment, 3(4)*, 623-627.
Corrigan, F. V. (1970). A Comparison of Self-Concepts of Native American

Students from Public or Federal School Backgrounds. Doctoral dissertation, George Washington University, 1970. Ann Arbor, MI: University Microfilms, No. 70-24, 959.

Davis, G. L., Hoffman, R. G., and Nelson K. S. (1990). Differences between Native Americans and Whites on the California Psychological Inventory. *Psychological Assessment, 2,* 3:238-242.

Dohrenwend, B. P., Shrout, P. E., Egri, G., and Mendelsohn, F. S. (1980). Non-specific Psychological Distress and Other Dimensions of Psychopathology. *Archives of General Psychiatry, 37,* 1229-1236.

Fay, J.S., and Fay, S.W. (1991). California Almanac (5th ed.). Santa Barbara, California: Pacific Data Resources.

Frank, J. D. (1973). *Persuasion and Healing.* New York: Schocken Books.

Frerichs, R. R., Aneshensel C. S., and Clark, V. A. (1981). Prevalence of Depression in Los Angeles County. *American Journal of Epidemiology, 113(6),* 691-699.

Frerichs, R. R., Aneshensel, C. S., Clark, V. A., and Yokopenic, P. (1981). Smoking and Depression: A Community Study. *American Journal of Public Health, 71(6),* 637-640.

Grossman, D. C. and Mulligan, B. C. (1991). Risk Factors for Suicide Attempts Among Navajo Adolescents. *American Journal of Public Health, 7,* 870-874.

Health, D. B. (1983). Alcohol Use Among North Native Americans: A Cross-Cultural Survey of Patterns and Problems. In R. G. Smart, F. B. Glaser, Y. Israel, H. Kaliant, R. E. Popham, and W. E. Schmidt, *Research Advances in Alcohol and Drug Problems.* New York: Plenun Publishing Co., 7:343-396.

Kipnis, P., Hodge F. S., Fredricks, L., and Teehee, K. (1994). Screening for Depression in Native American Clinics Using the CES-D Scale. (submitted).

Lefley, H. P. (1982). Self-Perception and Primary Prevention for Native Americans. In S. M. Manson (Ed.), *New Directions in Prevention Among Native American and Alaska Native Communities,* 65-90.

Leland, J. (1976). *Firewater Myths: North Native American Drinking and Alcohol Addiction.* Rutgers Center of Alcohol Studies Monograph No. 11. New Brunswick, NJ.

Lewis, R. G. (1982). Alcoholism and the Native American: A Review of the Literature. In *Alcohol and Health Monograph No. 4: Special Populations Issues,* U.S. Government Printing Office. Washington, DC, 315-328.

Link, B. and Dohrenwend, B. P. (1980). Formulation of Hypothesis of the True Prevalence of Demoralization in the United States. In B. P. Dohrenwend, B. S. Dohrenwend, M. S. Gould, B. Link, R. Neugebauer, and R. Wunsch-Hitzig (Eds.), *Mental Illness in the United States: Epidemiological Estimates.* New York: Praeger, 133-149.

Manson, S. M., Ackerson, L. M., Dick, R. W., Baron, A. E., and Fleming, C. M. (1990). Depressive Symptoms Among Native American Adolescents: Psychometric Properties of the CES-D. *Psychological Assessment, 2(3),* 231-237.

Mason, E. P. (1969). Cross-Validation Study of Personality Characteristics of Junior High School Students from Native American, Mexican, and Caucasian Ethnic Backgrounds. *Journal of Social Psychology, 77,* 15-24.

May, Phillip A. (1987). Suicide and Self-Destruction Among Native American Youth. *Native American and Alaska Native Mental Health Research, 1(1)*, 52-69.

Perez-Stable, E. J., Marin, G., Marin, B. V., and Katz, M. H. (1990). Depressive Symptoms and Cigarette Smoking Among Latinos in San Francisco. *American Journal of Public Health, 80(12)*, 1500-1502.

Radloff, L. S. (1977). The CES-D Scale: A Self-Report Depression Scale for Research in the General Population. *Applied Psychological Measurement, 1*, 385-401.

Radloff, L. S. and Rae, D. S. (1979). Susceptibility and Precipitating Factors in Depression: Sex Differences and Similarities. *Journal of Abnormal Psychology, 88*, 174-181.

Regional Differences in Indian Health (1993). U.S. DHHS, Public Health Service, Indian Health Service. U.S. Govt. Printing Office, 352-321-80427.

Roberts R. E., Rhoades, H. M., and Vernon, S. W. (1990). Using the CES-D Scale to Screen for Depression and Anxiety: Effects of Language and Ethnic Status. *Psychiatry Research, 31*, 69-83.

Roberts, R. E. and Roberts, C. R. (1982). Marriage, Work and Depressive Symptoms Among Mexican Americans. *Hispanic Journal of Behavioral Sciences, 4*, 199-221.

Rosenthal, B. G. (1974). Development of Self Identification in Relation to Attitudes Toward the Self in Chippewa Indians. *Genetic Psychology Monographs, 90*, 43-143.

Schoenbach, V. J., Kaplan, B. H., Grimson, R. C., and Wagner, E. H. (1982). Use of a Symptom Scale to Study the Prevalence of a Depressive Syndrome in Young Adolescents. *American Journal of Epidemiology, 116*, 791-800.

Somervell, P. D., Beals, J., Kinzie, D., Boehnlein, J., Leung, P., and Manson, S. M. (1993). Use of the CES-D in a Native American Village. *Culture, Medicine and Psychiatry, 16*, 503-517.

Thornburg, H. D. (1974). An Investigation of a Dropout Program Among Arizona's Minority Youth. *Education, 94*, 249-265.

Trimble, J.E. (1987). Self-perception and perceived alienation among Native Americans. *Journal of Community Psychology, 15(3)*, 316-333.

Vega, W. A. and Rumbaut, R. G. (1991). Ethnic Minorities and Mental Health. *Annu. Rev. Sociol. 17*, 351-383.

Zich J. M., Attkisson, C. C., and Greenfield, T. K. (1990). Screening for Depression in Primary Care Clinics: The CES-D and the BDI. *International Journal of Psychiatry in Medicine, 20(3)*, 259-277.

Zirkel, P.A. (1971). Self-Concept and the "Disadvantage" of Ethnic Group Membership, and the Mixture. *Review of Educational Research, 41*, 211-222.

Chapter 4

Crisis Intervention: An Essential Component of Culturally Competent Clinical Case Management

Rafael Herrera

INTRODUCTION

Comprehensive clinical case management can help public mental health clients maintain the necessary balance between managing external stressors and the intrapsychic reactions they face due to the nature of their illness, difficult socioeconomic conditions, and a sometimes unresponsive mental health system that does not adequately respond to their needs. Disruptions in this balance account for many of the situations requiring clinical intervention to alleviate symptoms and reduce external stress. Restoration of this balance forms one of the cornerstones of crisis intervention theory.

This chapter will argue that crisis intervention and other reality-based and present-focused models of brief therapy should form the foundation of mental health interventions, not only with the general population, but particularly with ethnic minorities facing serious mental illnesses. The positive role that crisis intervention and other brief intervention modalities can play in the provision of culturally competent clinical case management services to a diverse clientele will be examined. Although the chapter will utilize experience with Latinos[1], the issues considered are often applicable to other non-European ethnic minorities.

---

1. While Mexican Americans make up 60 percent of Hispanics, Puerto Ricans 12 percent, Cubans 5 percent, and other Hispanics 23 percent (U.S. Bureau of the Census, 1991), as Manoleas and Carrillo (1991) point out, "Latino" is the preferred term since "Hispanic" does not acknowledge the contributions indigenous and Afro-Latino cultures have made to the Americas.

This chapter also examines current thinking about the effectiveness of mental health interventions in general, and crisis and short-term interventions specifically. It contends that crisis intervention and other brief therapy intervention approaches are not only effective with the general population, but they incorporate elements associated with the cultural expectations of Latino and other ethnic mental health consumers. Meeting such expectations can result in greater and more useful utilization of services, reduce the need for involuntary services, and increase client "buy-in" and cooperation with voluntary treatment.

CASE MANAGEMENT

The never-ending search to improve service delivery to diverse populations has produced what has come to be known as case management. Case management is being utilized in a wide variety of settings, such as vocational rehabilitation, home-based care, developmental disabilities, and mental health (Roessler and Rubin, 1982; Sanborn, 1983; Steinberg and Carter, 1983; Zawadaski, 1984). This approach has become popular across human services because practitioners work with individuals whose needs are many and who require the services provided by the multitude of agencies that comprise the human service "system." These systems of care are, for the most part, unrelated to one another. Some are public and some are private, and receive funding from private, local, state, or federal sources. They have different priorities as to the populations they serve, subscribe to a wide range of "philosophies," and are guided by a variety of socio-political forces. Work with the seriously mentally ill, for example, requires the bringing together of many such systems of care.

Before the deinstitutionalization of the mentally ill, there was no need for case management as we understand it today. The institution was expected to provide most, if not all, of the services needed by those with serious mental illness. At the time of discharge, clients were given a list of community-based agencies and were expected to make contact with and arrangements for follow-up care on their own (Gerhart, 1990). This minimal type of "case management," consisting primarily of referrals to service providers, is still with us despite the fact that few discharged clients are, on their own, able to navigate through the bureaucratic maze to obtain the services they need.

By contrast, a comprehensive clinical case management model, such as the one proposed by Kanter (1989), identifies thirteen distinct activities, including engagement, client assessment, case planning, referral to service providers, consultation with families, advocacy, maintenance and expansion of social networks, and collaboration with other professionals. The case manager must be prepared to provide symptom management and other pertinent clinical interventions, such as crisis intervention, as the need for them arises. Given the difficult psychosocial circumstances faced by all consumers of public mental health services, especially minority consumers, crisis intervention and other brief therapy interventions are often needed. Such interventions, it will be argued, are also the type of interventions used by consumers more often than not.

LATINOS ARE A HIGH RISK POPULATION

Latinos, although they comprise one of the fastest-growing ethnic groups in the U.S. and are subject to a great deal of stress engendered by the social conditions in which they live, underutilize mental health services. In 1980 the Latino population in the U.S. stood at 14.6 million. By 1985 it had grown to almost 17 million, and by 1990 to approximately 22.4 million. This represents a 53 percent increase from the 1980 census (U.S. Bureau of the Census, 1991). It is estimated that by the year 2000 the number of Latinos in the U.S. will reach 30 to 35 million (Church, 1985) and will constitute the largest American minority (National Council of La Raza, 1991). Demographic data indicates that as a group, Latinos tend to be young, poor, have high fertility rates, and live in large families. While a majority reside in urban areas, a significant number live in rural areas. Educationally, Latinos have a higher dropout rate than whites or African Americans. In 1990, among 14- to 24-year-old Latinos, the dropout rate was 32.4 percent, compared to 13.2 percent for African Americans and 12.0 percent among whites (*Digest of Education Statistics*, 1991). This dismal statistic is reflected in Latinos' overrepresentation among the unemployed. While differences among Latinos occur, as a group they are likely to be employed in semi-skilled or unskilled occupations (Carrillo, 1982).

Keefe and Casas (1980) point out that "high stress indicators" such as poverty and language barriers place Latinos at risk of mental health problems. Rogler, Malgady, Constantino, and Blumenthal (1987) note that this grouping of factors render the population highly susceptible to developing mental health problems. It is critical, given their growing numbers and the risk factors Latinos (and other minority populations) face, that case managers and other mental health practitioners offer credible, practical, and culturally competent interventions.

UTILIZATION

Research over the years has documented the fact that Latinos neither seek nor receive mental health services in the numbers one would expect given the population (Atkinson, 1983; Casas, 1985; Flaskerud, 1990, Sue, 1977). Research conducted before 1980 (Jaco, 1959; Madsen, 1969), primarily with Mexican Americans, indicated that this group suffered a lower incidence of mental health problems than the population as a whole. Jaco (1959) hypothesized that because of strong family ties and stable support systems, Latinos suffered from fewer emotional problems, and consequently had less need for mental health services. This explanation of Latinos' underuse of mental health services was, of course, erroneous. More recent epidemiological surveys indicate that the frequency of psychological problems among Latinos is as high as in the general population, and, in some cases, higher (Padilla and Salgado De Snyder, 1985). In fact, while the emotional involvement, *respeto* (respect), affection, and mutual obligation enjoyed with extended family and friends can be a source of support during times of stress, at other times the same factors can cause great pressure and themselves be very stressful (Padilla and Salgado De Snyder, 1985). The following case illustrates one of the situations Latino students commonly encounter.

Leticia, a 22-year-old Latina, seeks help from a student health service. She presents with headaches, anxiety, poor appetite, and insomnia. She is about to complete a bachelor's degree in early childhood education, has received financial support from two aunts who operate a child care center, and has been accepted to the law school of her choice. Fearing their disapproval, she has not told her family of her desire to pursue a legal career. Her aunts expect her to take a job at the child care center upon graduation. Leticia finds herself under a great deal of pressure from her parents to take the job. They remind Leticia of her obligation to her aunts, who not only financed her education but also provided for the entire family when they moved here from San Salvador. Her therapist encourages her to assert herself and to follow her own wishes. Leticia feels her therapist does not understand her situation, and seeks services from a Latino-focused agency, but is put on a three-month waiting list.

Leticia is being served neither by the student health service therapist, who fails to recognize the strength of the cultural pressures on her, nor the Latino agency, which may understand her dilemma but cannot assist her with her current crisis because of heavy demand for services and a long-term treatment bias that creates interminable waiting lists for its few openings.

Sue et al. (1991) points out that 32 percent of Latinos have no health insurance. While this rate is the highest of any minority group, Latinos do manage to utilize mental health services. However, Atkinson (1983) and Casas (1985), in a study of Mexican Americans, found that they drop out of treatment faster and, on the average, attend fewer sessions than Caucasians and other ethnic groups. Sue (1977) found a 42 percent dropout rate among Mexican Americans, compared to 30 percent for Caucasians. He also found that the mean number of total sessions ranged from two to five for ethnic minorities, with a mean of eight sessions for Caucasians. A replication of the Sue utilization study done in the Seattle area for the year 1983 revealed that the failure-to-return rate for Latinos had gone down considerably, and that the number of sessions had increased to a range of 11 to 16 (O'Sullivan et al., 1989). This dramatic change was attributed to an increase in the number of Latino staff in the mental health centers, a ratio comparable to that of the Latino population the centers served.

BARRIERS

More recently, O'Sullivan and Lasso (1992) found that the ethnicity of the provider affects the utilization rates of Latinos. When Latinos were seen by a non-Latino mental health provider, the dropout rate was almost 18 percent as opposed to 7 percent when seen by a Latino provider. The multiple barriers to adequate mental health care have been documented by, among others, Atkinson (1983); Keefe and Casas (1980); and Sue and Sue (1977).

Sue (1981) has pointed out that linguistic inaccessibility is a fundamental barrier to the utilization of mental health services. Language is of extreme importance for an accurate psychiatric assessment. Marcos et al. (1973), for example, has shown how Spanish-speaking clients diagnosed with schizophrenia are judged to have more psychopathology when interviewed in English than when interviewed in Spanish. This was true even when the clients were relatively fluent in English. This study suggests that there are other cross-cultural factors at play. One possibility, advanced by Marcos et al., is that speaking in a somewhat unfamiliar language creates an additional burden to an individual whose subjective experience is already disorganized by his illness. Under these conditions, disturbances present themselves in English but not in Spanish. Lukianowicz (1962) found that bilingual psychotic patients report hearing aggressive and threatening voices in their second language, while what he called the "good" voices spoke in their native language. It is fair to assume that this phenomenon also occurs when the native language of clients is other than Spanish. Bilingual and monolingual clinicians must be aware of such linguistic factors if they are to provide competent evaluations, assessments, and interventions. Bilingual clinicians working with bilingual clients would best serve them if they performed the evaluations and assessments in their clients' native language.

Keefe and Casas (1980) cite as barriers to utilization: (1) geographical location and access to mental health services; (2) lack of Latino mental health professionals; and (3) providers' attachment to traditional intrapsychic intervention modalities and the exclusion of external causative factors. There are, to be sure, references in the literature to Latinos' positive responses to traditional treatment modalities. Karno and Morales (1971) make reference to such determining factors as familiarity with and acceptance of the language and culture. In other words, those with a strong orientation to the dominant culture (more acculturated) will have less difficulty adapting to the requirements of traditional introspective therapies. In contrast, Sanchez and Atkinson (1983) found that Mexican Americans with strong ties to their culture and traditions have difficulty being open and self-disclosing. Needless to say, attention to the level of acculturation will provide the clinician with useful information necessary to properly assess, plan, and deliver services. It is the blind attachment to conventional interventions, shared by many minority and non-minority mental health professionals, to the exclusion of viable and more advantageous modalities, to which we now turn.

MOST THERAPEUTIC ENCOUNTERS ARE BRIEF

While many factors determine whether or not mental health services will be sought in the first place and, once offered, for how long utilized, the fact is that, in general, most mental health interventions are brief. Talmon (1990), based on a study of 100,000 scheduled appointments over a five-year period, found that for over 50 percent of all clients, a single session is the norm. This is true regardless of the therapist's theoretical orientation, the treatment plan, or the client's insurance coverage.

Talmon's review of the literature shows that as early as 1975, studies revealed that a large percentage of clients, including ethnic minorities, did not return for services after the first session. Kogan (1957) found a 56 percent rate of "no return" after one interview. Spoerl (1975) reported a 39 percent dropout rate after one session, even though the almost 7,000 clients he studied had full coverage for 10 sessions.

It is often assumed that the public sector mental health system is more prone to "no shows" than the private system. However, neither Bloom (1975) nor Koss (1979) found any difference in the dropout rates between the public and private sectors. Given that most clients, whether they receive services in private or public settings, will be seen a few times only, mental health professionals must be prepared to seize the opportunity presented and provide the most effective intervention possible in the short number of sessions clients are likely to attend.

CRISIS AND BRIEF THERAPY ARE EFFECTIVE

It is commonly believed by mental health practitioners that what contributes most to high dropout rates are factors such as the client's "lack of motivation" or "resistance" (Steenbarger, 1992; Curtis, 1992). Some note that the client is "not psychologically minded," or offer some other explanation that preserves the integrity and validity of the clinician's favored orientation by placing the blame at the client's doorstep. Others (Budman and Armstrong, 1992) focus on the mental health "system," faulting "access," "utilization review restrictions," "emphasis on case management," "the paper work of managed care," or some other factor external to both the client and the chosen treatment modality to explain why they do not stay in treatment.

Against this background are the findings of Kogan (1957), Silverman and Beech (1979), and Talmon (1990), all of whom have reported 75 percent or better successful outcomes after a single session. For example, Silverman and Beech (1979) in a study of dropouts from a mental health center found that 80 percent of clients reported their problems had been resolved, 70 percent were satisfied with the services received, and the majority felt that the center had met their expectations. Based on these results, Silverman and Beech concluded that it is untenable to believe that dropouts reflect failure either "by the client or the intervention system" (p. 240).

WHAT IS CRISIS INTERVENTION?

Most individuals seek mental health services when some situation, problem, or "crisis" disrupts their lives. Unable to resolve the problem on their own, they seek the services of a mental health professional. As has been shown, most mental health services provided are of the brief variety in both the public and private sectors, with both clients and therapists reporting improvement and satisfaction with brief interventions.

Crisis intervention is by definition a form of brief therapy. The literature defines *crisis situations* as those lasting anywhere from one to six weeks (Aguilera and Messick, 1974; Burgess and Baldwin, 1981). Caplan (1964) reports six weeks as the typical time period for a crisis situation to be resolved. Since mental health interventions are typically provided weekly, the time periods reported correspond closely with the two to five mean number of sessions for ethnic minorities, and eight for Caucasians noted by Sue (1977). This also corresponds with the between six to eight average number of sessions reported from a number of studies of patients in outpatient therapy in a variety of settings (Garfield, 1986).

The term *crisis* has many different meanings and definitions. Caplan (1961) referred to a crisis state as a problematic situation where an individual's usual methods of problem solving do not result in its resolution. Carkuff and Berenson (1977) refer to crisis as a situation where a person knows no response to deal with it, while Brammer (1985) calls crisis a state of disorganization that disrupts not only the clients' lives, but also their normal methods of coping with stressors. Brammer (1985) along with Taplin (1971) stress that it is the individual's response and feeling about an event that creates a crisis, not the event itself.

CULTURAL VARIATIONS IN THE DEFINITIONS OF CRISIS

Worldviews vary significantly from one culture to another and correlate highly with a person's experiences and cultural upbringing (Ibrahim, 1985). It follows then, that a person's culture and worldview play an important role in determining whether or not a specific event or situation becomes a crisis. According to Sue and Sue (1990) "world views are not only composed of our attitudes, values, opinions, and concepts, but also they may effect how we think, make decisions, behave, and define events" (p. 137). Culture can influence how a given event is perceived and can prescribe culturally sanctioned ways of behaving.

The variation in bereavement practices across cultures serves to illustrate the point. In some Latin-American countries, following the death of their husbands widows are expected to be *de luto* (a state of mourning) for up to a year or longer. This not only involves dressing in black, but the society also expects that, at least in public, widows behave and appear solemn and sad whether or not they subjectively feel that way. Consequently, widows forgo make-up, most socializing, listening to "happy music," or dancing. They are not supposed to laugh or do anything that may indicate they are enjoying themselves. Widows are expected to be "in crisis," and the resolution of this crisis will take significantly longer than the six weeks referred to in the crisis intervention literature.

Just as cultural norms can influence whether or not an event will trigger a crisis for an individual, culturally sensitive interventions can assist in their resolution.

> Carmen, a 62-year-old Puerto Rican woman whose husband of 30 years had died six months prior, was referred by her doctor to a Latino-focused mental health clinic because of severe depression manifested by withdrawal from family and friends, weight loss, insomnia, and loss of interest in usual activities. A devout Catholic, she had participated in and arranged for her husband's burial according to the practices of her religion. Her husband had died at age 72 after a long and painful illness, and she was relieved he was no longer suffering. Her husband had died before she had the opportunity to tell him something very important and she believed, as do many Puerto Ricans, that this would prevent her spirit from joining her husband's in the hereafter when her time came. (See Hardwood, 1981, for the importance of this belief among Puerto Ricans.) She had not been able to tell her husband, nor anyone else, about having had a brief affair with another man before ever meeting him. She had considered confession, but wanted to tell her husband first. After much discussion among staff, the following "treatment plan" was developed:

Carmen was told a priest had been consulted regarding a similar situation (this was true), and that he had recommended confession. She was urged to do so by mental health staff. Since it was learned from her relatives that she would only go to confession with her own parish priest, he was presented with a hypothetical situation (to preserve confidentiality) and was asked to cooperate with the plan. The parish priest, who was Mexican American, was "educated" about Puerto Rican beliefs about the consequences of dying without having spoken about things of importance. He was asked to include, as part of the penance, that Carmen assume responsibility for designing and supervising the making of a rather large new white mantelpiece for the altar of the church, with the cost of materials to be paid by the church. She was known to be an accomplished seamstress and had a reputation for her embroidery skills. Staff counted on the symbolism of the white or "clean" mantelpiece and on the fact that because the priest saw no contradiction between Carmen's belief about her spirit and his own belief in the soul, he could assure her that the penance would permit her "spirit" to join her husband's. The penance would also cause her to get out of the house to shop for materials, to interact with others, and would involve her in meaningful activities. Her depression lifted and, because she received so many compliments on her embroidery work, she decided to start a small business out of her home. This was something she had wanted to do for years, but had lacked confidence.

Carmen's case serves to underline a key concept in crisis intervention theory, that is, the notion that a crisis event presents both danger and opportunity: danger in that the consequences of an event may lead to further difficulties, opportunity in the sense that a crisis situation may force an individual to confront a situation in a new manner, resulting in improvement. Also important in crisis intervention work is the notion of what Halpern (1973) referred to as "reduced defensiveness." Confused and unable to cope, an individual may be open to new ideas or suggestions as to how to resolve the crisis. It is this vulnerability and suggestibility during times of crisis, Tyhurst (1958) suggests, that provides the possibility for change.

Caplan (1964) has outlined the sequence of crisis events as follows:

1. Increase in tension as a result of the stressful event results in the activation of usual problem-solving responses.
2. The problem-solving responses fail, while the stressful situation continues, resulting in an increase in tension.
3. Other problem-solving resources are put into play. If the cause

of the stressor diminishes or if the new problem-solving approach works, the crisis may be avoided.
4. If none of the above occurs, tension increases to a "breaking point" and results in emotional disorganization.

There are several models and theories of crisis intervention. Crisis situations or crisis states can be viewed as situational or developmental and not as pathological. The psychosocial transition model considers the person in relationship to others and the social surroundings. This model proposes that individuals have certain inherited legacies that are combined with what has been learned from the environment. Because individuals are always changing and their social circumstances are in a constant state of flux, crisis states may be related to psychological, social, or environmental difficulties (Dorn, 1986). This model views problems or events leading to crisis as not necessarily intrapsychic, but looks to peers, family, friends, and community as possibly responsible for the crisis and/or as allies in its resolution. It recognizes that system change is not always possible. According to this model, the goal of crisis intervention is to assist clients with their external or internal difficulties by looking for intervention strategies in areas that may be psychological, social, or environmental.

ECLECTIC CRISIS INTERVENTION THEORY

Eclectic crisis intervention theory refers to the incorporation of all valid and available approaches to helping clients. Given the current state of knowledge about what kind of intervention is best, for what kind of problem, and for whom, there is no viable alternative. Eclectic crisis intervention requires keeping an open mind and becoming skillful in a variety of intervention approaches. As we have seen, the difficulties facing individuals with mental health problems do not lend themselves to solutions found in any one theoretical approach. Eclectic crisis theory operates from a task orientation and has few major concepts. Some of the most significant tasks consist of the following (Gilliland, James, and Bowman, 1989):

1. Identify valid elements in all systems and integrate them into a consistent whole.

2. Consider all pertinent theories for evaluating and manipulating data according to the most advanced knowledge.
3. No identification with any one specific theory and continue to try to experiment with strategies that produce positive outcomes (Gilliland, James, and Bowman, 1989).

It is important to note that the goal of crisis intervention is not the development of insight, but rather the successful resolution or restoration of the equilibrium disrupted by a stressful event. Crisis intervention approaches do not ignore the external stressors such as employment, housing, immigration status, and economic survival that are so much a part of many minorities' daily experience. Several mental health professionals (Ponterotto, 1987; Ruiz and Casas, 1981; Yamamoto and Acosta, 1982) are of the opinion that when counseling Latinos, it is best to utilize techniques that are concrete, active, practical, and oriented toward problem solving. Pragmatic approaches meet the culturally based expectations of Latinos and other ethnic minorities, making crisis intervention an invaluable case management tool.

CULTURAL KNOWLEDGE AND HELP-SEEKING PATTERNS

One of the most important aspects for the success of any therapeutic encounter is the therapeutic alliance (Luborsky, Singer, and Luborsky, 1975), in which clients will accept and depend for help on a competent and caring therapist (Gurman, 1977). Under what circumstances are cultural knowledge or culture specific interventions required for successful interventions with minority clients? Sue and Zane (1987) present the notion of credibility (the client's belief that the therapist is effective and trustworthy) as an important consideration when working with minority clients. They argue that neither cultural knowledge nor culture-specific interventions are related to "particular processes that result in effective psychotherapy" (p. 39). Cultural knowledge is helpful only to the extent that it serves to enhance the therapist's credibility.

Beliefs and practices related to health and illness are a reflection of the worldview of the particular cultural group (Helman, 1990; Johnson and Sargent, 1990). These beliefs are enduring and carried with them even when they are seeking services from the majority culture. It follows that intervention approaches that take into consideration a client's culture, language, and worldview, and that are provided by sensitive and credible clinicians who take into account a client's expectations about what is to occur, are more likely to be effective.

The case of Carmen illustrates how cultural knowledge and the utilization of natural support systems can be a very powerful tool. While their utilization is rare in traditional mental health interventions, crisis intervention approaches, such as the psychosocial transition model mentioned earlier, utilize natural support systems such as family, friends, church, and natural healers.

Natural supports are defined by Valle (1980) as primary group networks, which he describes as relational-interactional systems that are part of the everyday life of Latinos and other cultural groups. He notes that these natural networks persist as a "first tier of coping-survival behaviors" (p. 36) for members of the group. Natural supports can be a most important asset to minority and non-minority mental health practitioners. The identification and mobilization of support systems can sometimes be the intervention that proves to be crucial in the resolution of a problem.

In many Latino communities, there are natural helpers such as curanderos (folk curer), espiritistas (spiritists), espiritualistas (spiritual healers), yerberas (herbalists), and sobadoras (masseuses), who are very much a part of the system of care. They are consulted regarding health, mental health, and "problemas de la vida" (problems of life) issues. Their clients expect to be provided with practical advice and a quick resolution to the presenting problem. For example, a Mexican woman worried that her young son's high temperature and skin rash were caused by someone with "strong vision" and who had admired him recently, would consult a curandero. The curandero might advise her that her son was the victim of the "evil eye," and would prescribe a definite course of treatment, one easily undertaken by his client. For example, he might counsel her to locate the person who had placed the "mal ojo" on her child and encourage that person to pat the child on the head, thus neutralizing the spell. The point here is that the curandero would not prescribe a lengthy course of treatment utilizing alien methodologies and promising only uncertain and unspecified results.

Awareness and understanding of the help-seeking patterns of minority communities is essential for culturally competent interventions. It is useful, and sometimes essential, to enlist the assistance and collaboration of natural helpers when working with clients whose "worldview" includes them and their theories of causality. All ethnic groups view and interpret their life situations through the window of their particular culture. Initially, efforts will be made to solve the problem on their own or with the assistance of others within their culturally accepted social network. It is when cultural-specific remedies fail that the mental health system may be approached. The provision of culturally competent clinical case management services requires interventions that are compatible with the cultural expectations and beliefs of their clients. But the clinician must guard against ignoring those cultural behaviors that are harmful and detrimental to their clients.

SUMMARY AND CONCLUSIONS

This chapter has argued that, whether by design or not, most mental health interventions are of the brief variety. These interventions are provided, more often than not, in response to events or situations that clients find disruptive. Drawing upon the Latino experience, barriers to care, underutilization, language, the importance of cultural knowledge, and other material pertinent to the provision of clinical case management services to ethnic minorities were explored.

Crisis intervention and other reality-based models of intervention embrace, or can incorporate, many of the elements that have been identified as necessary when working with ethnic minorities. These include a problem-solving and present orientation, more activity on the part of the counselor, and the utilization of natural support systems and natural healers.

For these and other reasons, brief treatment modalities are the treatment of choice for Latinos and other ethnic minorities. Rather than utilizing these modalities grudgingly, as a "managed care" mandated substitute for the preferred long-term treatments, mental health professionals should avail themselves of the many opportunities currently available to learn brief intervention modalities. Professional schools should adapt their curricula to reflect these teachings and actively encourage their students to adopt this highly successful treatment method.

REFERENCES

Aguilera, D. and Messick, J.M. (1974). *Crisis Intervention: Theory and Methodology.* St. Louis: Mosby.

Atkinson, D.R. (1983). "Ethnic Similarity in Counseling Psychology: A Review of Research." *The Counseling Psychologist, 11*, 79-92.

Bloom, B.L. (1975). *Changing Patterns of Psychiatric Care.* New York: Human Sciences Press.

Brammer, L.M. (1985). *The Helping Relationship: Process and Skills* (3rd ed). Englewood Cliffs, NJ: Prentice Hall.

Budman, S.H. and Armstrong, E. (1992). "Training for Managed Care Settings. How to Make It Happen." *Psychotherapy, 29*, 416-421.

Burgess, A.W. and Balwin, B.A. (1981). *Crisis Intervention Theory and Practice: A Clinical Handbook.* Englewood Cliffs, NJ: Prentice Hall.

Caplan, G. (1961). *An Approach to Community Mental Health.* New York: Grune and Stratton.

Caplan, G. (1964). *Principles of Preventive Psychiatry.* New York: Basic Books.

Carkuff, R.R. and Berenson, B.G. (1977). *Beyond Counseling and Therapy* (2nd ed.). New York: Holt, Rinehart & Winston.

Carrillo, C. (1982). "Changing Norms of Hispanic Families: Implications for Treatment." In E. Jones and S. Korchin (Eds.), *Minority Mental Health,* 251-265, New York: Prager.

Casas, J.M. (1985). "A Reflection on the Status of Racial/Ethnic Minority Research." *The Counseling Psychologist, 13*, 581-598.

Church, G.J. (1985). "A Melding of Cultures." *Time,* July 8, 36-39.

Curtis, H.C. (1992). "Impasses in Psychotherapy." *Psychiatric Annals, 22*, 500-501.

Digest of Education Statistics (1991). Washington, DC: National Center for Education Statistics.

Dorn, F.J. (Ed.) (1986). *The Social Influence Process in Counseling and Psychotherapy.* Springfield, IL: Charles C Thomas.

Flaskerud, J.H. (1990). "Matching Client and Therapist Ethnicity, Language and Gender: A Review of Research." *Issues in Mental Health Nursing, 11*, 321-336.

Frank, J.D. and Frank, J.B. (1991). *Persuasion and Healing: A Comparative Study of Psychotherapy* (3rd ed.). Baltimore: Johns Hopkins University Press.

Garfield, S.L. (1986). "Research on Client Variables in Psychotherapy." In S.L. Garfield and A.E. Bergin (Eds.), *Handbook of Psychotherapy and Behavior Change* (3rd ed.), 213-256, New York: Wiley.

Gerhart, U.C. (1990). *Caring for the Chronic Mentally Ill.* Itasca, IL: F.E. Peacock.

Gilliland, B. E., James, R.K., & Bowman, J. T. (1989). *Theories and Strategies in Counseling and Psychotherapy.* (2nd ed). Englewood Cliffs, NJ: Prentice Hall.

Gurman, A.S. (1977). Therapist and patient factors influencing the patient's perception of facilitative therapeutic conditions. *Psychiatry, 40*(3), 218-231.

Halpern, H.A. (1973). "Crisis Theory: A Definitional Study." *Community Mental Health Journal, 9,* 342-349.

Hardwood, A. (1981). "Mainland Puerto Ricans." In A. Hardwood (Ed.), *Ethnicity and Medical Care.* Cambridge: Cambridge University Press.

Helman, C.G. (1990). *Culture, Health and Illness: An Introduction for Health Professionals.* London: Wright.

Ibrahim, F.A. (1985). Effective cross-cultural counseling and psychotherapy: A framework. *Counseling Psychologist, 13*(4), 625-638.

Jaco, E.G. (1959). "Mental Health of the Spanish-American in Texas." In M.K. Opler (Ed.), *Culture and Mental Health: Cross-Cultural Studies,* 467-485, New York: Macmillan.

Janosick, E.H. (1984) *Crisis Counseling: A Contemporary Approach.* Monterey, California: Wadsworth Health Sciences Division.

Johnson, T.M. and Sargent, C.F. (Eds.) (1990). *Medical Anthropology: A Handbook of Theory and Method.* New York: Greenwood Press.

Kanfer, F.H. and Goldstein, A.P. (Eds.) (1975). *Helping People Change: A Textbook of Methods.* New York: Pergamon Press.

Kanter, J. (1989). "Clinical Case Management: Definition, Principles, Components." *Hospital and Community Psychiatry, 40,* 361-368.

Karno, M. and Morales, A. (1971). A Community Mental Health Service for Mexican-Americans in a Metropolis. *Comprehensive Psychiatry, 12,* 116-121.

Keefe, S.E. and Casas, J.M. (1980). "Mexican-Americans and Mental Health: A Selected Review and Recommendations for Mental Health Service Delivery." *American Journal of Community Psychology, 8,* 303-326.

Kogan, L.S. (1957). " The Short-Term Case in a Family Agency. Part III. Further Results and Conclusions." *Social Casework, 38,* 366-374.

Koss, M.P. (1979). "Length of Psychotherapy for Clients Seen in Private Practice." *Journal of Consulting Psychology, 47,* 210-212.

Luborsky, L., Singer, B., and Luborsky, L. (1975). Is it true that, "Everyone has won and all must have prizes?" *Archives of General Psychiatry, 32*(8), 995-1008.

Lukianowicz, N. (1962). "Auditory Hallucinations in Polyglot Subjects." *Psychiatria et Neurologia, 143,* 274-294.

Madsen, W. (1969). "Mexican Americans and Anglo Americans: A Comparative Study of Mental Health in Texas." In S.C. Plog and R.B. Edgerton (Eds.),

Changing Perspectives in Mental Illness, 217-241. New York: Holt, Rinehart & Winston.

Manoleas, P. and Carrillo, C. (1991). "A Culturally Syntonic Approach to the Field Education of Latino Students." *Journal of Social Work Education, 27,* 135-144.

Marcos, L.R., Urcuyo, L., Kesselman, M., and Alpert, M. (1973). "The Language Barrier in Evaluating Spanish-American Patients." *Archives of General Psychiatry, 29,* 655-659.

National Council of La Raza. (1991). *State of Hispanic America 1991: An Overview.* Washington, DC: National Council of La Raza.

O'Sullivan, M.J. and Lasso, B. (1992). Community mental health services for hispanics: A test of the culture compatibility hypothesis. *Hispanic Journal of Behavioral Sciences, 14*(4), 455-468.

O'Sullivan, M.J., Peterson, P.D., Cox, G.B., and Kirkeby, J. (1989). "Ethnic Populations: Community Mental Health Services Ten Years Later." *American Journal of Community Psychology, 17,* 17-30.

Padilla, A.M. and De Snyder, N.S. (1985). "Counseling Hispanics: Strategies for Effective Intervention." In P. B. Pederson (Ed.), *Handbook of Cross-Cultural Counseling and Therapy,* 157-164, Westport, CT: Greenwood Press.

Ponterotto, J.G. (1987). "Counseling Mexican Americans: A Multimodal Approach." *Journal of Counseling and Development, 65,* 308-312.

Roessler, R.T. and Rubin, S.E. (1982). *Case Management and Rehabilitation Counseling.* Baltimore: University Park Press.

Rogler, L.H., Malgady, R.G., Constantino, G., and Blumenthal, R. (1987). "What Do Culturally Sensitive Mental Health Services Mean? The Case of Hispanics." *American Psychologist, 42,* 565-570.

Ruiz, R.A. and Casas, J.M. (1981). "Culturally Relevant and Behavioristic Counseling for Chicano College Students." In P.B. Pedersen, J.G. Draguns, W. J. Looner, and J. E. Timble (Eds.), *Counseling Across Cultures.* Honolulu: University of Hawaii Press.

Sanborn, C.J. (Ed.) (1983). *Case Management in Mental Health Services.* Binghamton, NY: The Haworth Press, Inc.

Sanchez, A.R. and Atkinson, D.R. (1983). "Mexican American Cultural Commitment, Preference for Counselor Ethnicity, and Willingness to Use Counseling." *Journal of Counseling Psychology, 30,* 215-220.

Silverman, W.H. and Beech, R.P. (1979). "Are Dropouts Dropouts?" *Journal of Community Psychology, 7,* 236-242.

Spoerl, O.H. (1975). "Single Session Psychotherapy." *Diseases of the Nervous System, 36,* 283-285.

Steenbarger, B.N. (1992). "Intentionalizing Brief College Student Psychotherapy." *Journal of College Student Psychotherapy, 7,* 47-61.

Steinberg, R.M. and Carter, G.W. (1983). *Case Management and the Elderly.* Lexington, MA: Lexington Books.

Sue, S. (1977). "Community Mental Health Services to Minority Groups: Some Optimism, Some Pessimism." *American Psychologist, 32,* 616-624.

Sue, D.W. (1981). *Counseling the Culturally-Different: Theory and Practice*. New York: John Wiley.

Sue, D.W. and Sue, D. (1977). Barriers to effective cross-cultural counseling. *Journal of Counseling Psychology, 24*(5), 420-429.

Sue, D.W. and Sue, D. (1990). *Counseling the Culturally Different: Theory and Practice* (2nd ed.). New York: John Wiley.

Sue, S. and Zane, N. (1987). "The Role of Culture and Cultural Techniques in Psychotherapy: A Critique and Reformulation." *American Psychologist, 42*, 37-45.

Sue, S., Fujino, D.C., Hu, L., Takeuchi, D.J., and Zane, N.W.S. (1991). Community mental health services for ethnic minority groups: A test of the cultural responsiveness hypothesis. *Journal of Consulting and Clinical Psychology, 59*(4), 533-540.

Talmon, M. (1990). *Single-Session Therapy*, San Francisco: Jossey-Bass.

Taplin, J.R. (1971). "Crisis Theory: Critique and Reformulation." *Community Mental Health Journal, 2*, 13-23.

Tyhurst, J.S. (1958). "The Role of Transition States Including Disasters in Mental Illness." In *Symposium of Preventive and Social Psychiatry*, Washington, DC: Walter Reed Army Institute of Research.

U.S. Bureau of the Census. (1991). The Hispanic Population of the United States: March 1991. Current Population Reports Population Characteristics Series P-20, No. 455. Washington, DC: U.S. Government Printing Office.

Valle, R. (1980). "A Natural Resource System for Health-Mental Health Promotion to Latino/Hispano Populations." In R. Valle and W. Vega (Eds.), *Hispanic Natural Support Systems*. State of California, Dept. of Mental Health.

Yamamoto, J. and Acosta, F.X. (1982). "Treatment of Asian-Americans and Hispanic-Americans: Similarities and Differences." *Journal of the Academy of Psychoanalysis, 10*, 585-607.

Zawadaski, R.T. (Ed.) (1984). *Community-Based Systems of Long Term Care*. Binghamton, NY: The Haworth Press, Inc.

Chapter 5

Clinical Case Management and Cognitive-Behavioral Therapy: Integrated Psychosocial Services for Depressed Latino Primary Care Patients

Kurt C. Organista
Eleanor Valdes Dwyer

DEPRESSION IN PRIMARY CARE

While prevalence rates of major depression in the general population range from 2.1 to 3.5 percent, rates in primary care settings are now between 6 and 10 percent (Katon, 1982). Indeed, depression is now considered to be one of the most common problems seen in general medicine (Kamerow, 1989), and numerous guidelines for detecting and treating depression in primary care are currently being disseminated by national professional organizations such as the Agency for Health Care Policy and Research (AHCPR) (Depression Guideline Panel, 1993a, 1993b) and the American Psychiatric Association (APA, 1993). These guidelines are a welcomed response to the traditionally low detection and treatment of depression in medical settings (Katon, 1987) and to emerging evidence that depression may be more debilitating than many chronic medical conditions. For example, Wells et al. (1989) found that the impaired social functioning associated with depressive symptoms was generally worse than impaired functioning associated with eight major chronic medical conditions such as hypertension, diabetes, and arthritis. In fact, the only medical condition that proved comparable to depression in terms of functional impairment was heart disease.

For comorbid patients, Wells et al. (1989) found that the combined effects of depressive symptoms and medical conditions on impairment were additive (e.g., the combination of heart disease and depression was associated with twice the reduction in social functioning associated with either condition alone). Thus, the need to detect and treat depression in primary care is critical. Although AHCPR and APA guidelines are to be praised for addressing the magnitude of the problem and for educating both physicians and the general public, these guidelines have recently been criticized by the professions of social work (NASW, 1993) and psychology (Muñoz et al., 1994) for their biomedical bias and lack of attention to psychosocial stressors, economic factors, and the role of ethnicity and gender in the treatment of depression. These criticisms have important implications for exploring ways to respond to the problem of depression in primary care as it affects low income and ethnic minority patients.

RELEVANCE OF THE PROBLEM TO LATINOS

The problem of depression in primary care is highly relevant to Latinos for two significant reasons. First, there is evidence to suggest that Latinos may be at higher risk for depression than the general population. With regard to current diagnosable affective disorders, results from the National Comorbidity Survey (Kessler et al., 1994), which are based on a national probability sample, show that Latinos now have significantly higher rates than non-Hispanic whites. This finding is alarmingly inconsistent with past findings from the Epidemiologic Catchment Area Study which showed no differences between races in current affective disorders (Weissman et al., 1991).

With regard to depression, Roberts' (1987) review of the epidemiological literature showed that Latinos had higher rates of depression symptoms than non-Hispanic whites in four separate studies. When SES was controlled for in these studies, Latino-White differences disappeared, highlighting the powerful role that economic factors play in the higher rates of depression in Latinos.

A second reason for targeting depressed Latinos in primary care has to do with their distinctive service utilization patterns. While it is well known that Latinos underutilize mental health services (Acosta, 1979; Barrera, 1978; Sue et al., 1991), it is also well know that Latinos are likely to see medical doctors for emotional and psychological problems (Karno, Ross, and Caper, 1969; Padilla, Carlos, and Keefe, 1976). Hence, Latino service utilization patterns suggest that in addition to decreasing barriers to mental health services, medical staff also need to be actively involved in outreach to depressed Latinos in hospital settings.

DECREASING TRADITIONAL BARRIERS TO MENTAL HEALTH UTILIZATION

More than 15 years ago the *President's Commission on Mental Health* studied and summarized the four main reasons why ethnic minorities underutilize mental health services: (1) availability (i.e., too few services); (2) accessibility (too distant and unaffordable); (3) acceptability (too few culturally acceptable services consistent with patient cultural needs and expectations); and (4) accountability (lack of consultation with minority groups regarding services desired) (Parron, 1982). Decreasing these barriers is the first major step in providing culturally responsive services to Latinos and other ethnic minority groups. The next step involves directly responding to psychosocial stressors outside the realm of traditional psychotherapy.

ADDRESSING PSYCHOSOCIAL STRESSORS IN LOW INCOME AND MINORITY CLIENTS

In their book *Effective Psychotherapy for Low-Income and Minority Patients,* Acosta, Yamamoto, and Evans (1982) state that problems in living should be considered "co-equal" with emotional problems and that therapists need to help patients deal with individuals and agencies in their social environment. These authors emphasize the "double neediness" of low income and minority patients manifested in emotional and environmental stressors such as crowded living conditions, domestic violence, and lack of money for bills following injury and illness. In addition to urging psychotherapists to advocate for client rights, they also encourage consulting caseworkers as needed.

Although such a dual role for psychotherapists seems responsive to the psychological and social problems of low income patients, it probably is not widely practiced in contemporary psychotherapy with its traditional, individual focus on the client while in session.

An obvious and often overlooked strategy for dealing with the "double neediness" of low income clients is clinical case management (CCM), which blends psychotherapy with traditional case management services in order to address psychosocial problems. The remainder of this chapter will describe culturally responsive efforts to address depression in Latino primary care patients by integrating short-term CCM and cognitive-behavior therapy (CBT).

RESPONDING TO DEPRESSED LATINOS IN PRIMARY CARE

Hospital-Based Depression Clinic

The University of California, San Francisco (UCSF) Depression Clinic at San Francisco General Hospital (SFGH) was founded in 1985 to meet a need documented while conducting a depression prevention research project (Muñoz et al., 1987). Primary care patients at SFGH that were screened for the project were found to have current rates of major depression of 16.5 percent among the English-speaking patients and 20 percent among the Spanish-speaking patients. In addition, primary care physicians had only recognized 36 percent of cases with diagnosable depression in this patient population (Pérez-Stable et al., 19990).

Barriers to mental health service utilization are decreased in the clinic by providing free (affordable), hospital-based (available, accessible) mental health and case management services by linguistically and ethnically matched therapists (acceptability). In terms of outreach, primary care physicians and medical staff have been trained to recognize and refer patients suspected of depression (e.g., presenting with sad affect or multiple somatic complaints with little organic basis or in excess of what would be expected from their medical conditions).

The clinic director teaches primary care providers to recognize and refer patients to the clinic by meeting with them twice a year and by conducting grand rounds on Depression Clinic progress on an annual basis. She also spends one afternoon a week seeing patients with primary care staff to help them recognize depression and other psychiatric symptoms. Referral forms containing a checklist of DSM III-R (APA, 1987) criteria for major depression are used by primary care staff to screen patients for a referral to the clinic.

Referrals sent to the clinic are distributed to social workers and therapists who call or write patients and offer them an evaluation for depression based on their physician's recommendation, which facilitates the acceptance of mental health services. The clinic receives over 200 referrals a year and about half are Spanish-speaking Latino primary care patients.

Services are offered to primary care patients that meet criteria for unipolar major depression without psychotic features. Persons with active substance abuse, organic brain disorders, or other Axis I psychiatric diagnoses are referred out for appropriate services. However, patients with concomitant anxiety disorders (e.g., generalized anxiety, post-traumatic stress disorder [PTSD], somatization, etc.) are not excluded.

Patients are offered 16 weeks of group CBT and six months of concurrent CCM. Services are provided to Latino patients by bilingual, bicultural Latino social workers and a clinical psychologist.

The Need for Clinical Case Management

Preliminary exploratory analyses (Organista, Muñoz, and González, 1994) conducted at the clinic indicated that CBT was only moderately successful at decreasing depression for primary care patients. At post-treatment, patients frequently attributed their continued depression to multiple life stressors. For this reason, CCM was integrated into existing CBT services.

It has been documented that acute life stressors such as loss of job or spouse (Lloyd, 1980a, 1980b; Hirschfeld and Cross, 1982; Paykel, 1982) and chronic life stressors such as chronic medical illness and poverty are associated with depression (Pearlin and Lieberman, 1979). Traditional case management functions such as linkage, advocacy, and service coordination aim to remedy life stressors associated with depression. In one outcome study on depression, social work interventions added to psychiatric services improved social functioning in English medical patients as compared to patients receiving only psychiatric treatment, and this gain was observed up to one year post-treatment (Shepard et al., 1979).

In addition, the greater prevalence of both depression and stressful events in low SES women (Brown and Harris, 1978) makes CCM especially indicated for our Latino patient population, which consists of predominantly low SES, first-generation, immigrant women.

According to Beck et al. (1979), depression is characterized as a vicious cycle of low mood, lack of activity, and negative perception of self, others, the world, and the future. For disadvantaged primary care patients, the social environment is stressful enough without having the added burden of major depression with its excessively negative perceptions. For example, most Americans will never know the frustration of the application process for entitlement (DiNitto, 1991). The clinical case manager facilitates the entitlement application while involving and empowering the client through the process. Successful experiences in negotiating the social environment are therapeutic in that they provide clients with tangible benefits and also help them to dispute the negative perceptions that characteristically accompany depression. The following vignette illustrates how chronic economic problems, exacerbating depression and medical problems, were immediately targeted by case management intervention.

> Sra. S. is a 56-year-old monolingual Spanish-speaking divorced woman who emigrated from Central America during her country's civil war. Sra. S. was employed as a supervisor in a government office in her country of origin. When she arrived in the United States, she was under-employed as a janitor for ten years because of her lack of English skills. She presented to the Depression Clinic anxious, tearful, and with the persistent negative thought, "I am a coward and can't better my life."

She had been unemployed for three years because of medical problems including a hypothyroid condition and gastritis. Both the patient and her 84-year-old mother were living on one general assistance check of $340 per month and the patient had not applied for SSI because she was fearful of being denied. She explained, "I do not have the face of a needy person and I am not an alcoholic or drug abuser. Besides, I am not accustomed to asking for help." The case manager recognized the patient's lack of knowledge about entitlements as reflecting her low level of acculturation. Time was spent educating the patient about this country's social policy and the SSI benefits. Next, Sra. S. was asked to examine her thoughts and their relation to her lack of help-seeking behavior. With the case manager's assistance, the patient applied for SSI, which she had avoided for two years, and the eventual acceptance of her application alleviated both her financial stress and symptoms of depression.

Beck et al. (1979) suggest that therapists use collateral contacts to test the validity of the client's negative thinking. At the Depression Clinic, clinical case managers routinely collaborate with primary care physicians given the high comorbidity of depression and medical illnesses in our patient population (Organista, Muñoz, and González, 1994). Hospital-based clinical case managers have direct access to medical information that facilitates reality testing with clients regarding their health concerns.

Clinical case managers also assess social supports and initiate collateral contacts with family, spouses and partners, friends, and social service providers. These contacts further help to test the validity of the patient's depressed thinking as well as strengthen the support system, which can be inadequate for low income minority groups.

The Case for CBT

There appear to be clear cultural and economic reasons for advocating CBT for traditionally oriented Latinos of low SES. According to Miranda (1976), the expectations of traditional Latino patients include immediate symptom relief, guidance and advice, and a problem-centered approach. Short-term, directive, problem-solving therapies are also more consistent with the expectations of low income groups whose pressing life circumstances frequently demand immediate attention and interfere with long-term treatment (Goldstein, 1971; Torres-Matrullo, 1982).

Unfortunately, no outcome research on the efficacy of CBT with Latinos has been conducted. Only one study by Comas-Diaz (1981) investigated the efficacy of cognitive therapy and behavior therapy in a small sample of depressed, Spanish-speaking, unmarried Puerto Rican mothers from low SES backgrounds (N=26). Results showed significant and comparable reductions in depression for both cognitive and behavioral treatments relative to a waiting list control group. More empirical and descriptive reports of cognitive and behavioral therapies alone and combined are needed with Latino samples.

A standardized model of CBT is used in the clinic that focuses on the role of thoughts, behaviors, and interpersonal interactions on mood. Patients are taught to monitor their mood, to discover those thoughts and behaviors related to depressed mood, and to change these behaviors to improve mood. The 16 weeks of group therapy cover three CBT modules that emphasize cognitive restructuring, activity schedules, and improving interpersonal relations, respectively. A treatment manual developed at the clinic (Muñoz, Aguilar-Gaxiola, and Guzman, 1986) is used to guide therapy. This manual was adapted from the book *Control Your Depression* (Lewinsohn et al., 1986) and cognitive therapy (Beck et al., 1979; Burns, 1980). Patients are given their own copy of the treatment manual that contains outlines of each session and forms for doing homework that is assigned and reviewed each week.

INTEGRATED CCM AND CBT: A CULTURALLY RESPONSIVE APPROACH TO DEPRESSION IN LATINO PRIMARY CARE PATIENTS

Prerequisites

Linguistic matching with monolingual or predominantly Spanish-speaking clients is obviously needed. Research also supports the effectiveness of matching traditionally oriented Latinos with ethnically similar psychotherapists. For example, Sue et al. (1991) found that ethnic matching predicted better treatment outcome, lower dropout rates, and a greater number of therapy sessions for non-English-speaking Mexican patients in a study that included the mental health records of 3,000 Mexican-descent patients in the Los Angeles County mental health system. The above finding suggests that a cultural match between Latino clinicians and Latino clients low in acculturation facilitates better service utilization and outcome. According to Surber (1994), case managers incorporate their understanding of culture automatically and largely unconsciously into their work. While this may be true, we must continue to explicate and evaluate the culturally responsive components of cross-cultural services beginning with self-examination.

Culturally competent service providers need to understand their own level of acculturation and the extent to which they subscribe to traditional versus modern-Western values and behaviors. For example, the use of social and mental health services automatically becomes part of the Latino client's acculturation process. While service providers are responsible for socializing clients to the process of service utilization (e.g., explaining client's role in the collaborative relationship), care must be taken not to devalue their traditional cultural orientation (e.g., the expectation to be told what to do by the service provider authority figures). The goal here is to help the client "biculturate" rather than assimilate, which historically has involved devaluing and replacing culture of origin with culture of host society (Berry, 1980).

Assessment

In addition to standard psychological and CCM assessment, a number of Latino experience domains are routinely explored in order to culturally contextualize client problems. These domains include: (1) level of acculturation; (2) country of origin and conditions of migration to U.S. (e.g., Central American "cross fire" refugee of the 1980s versus Mexican economic migrant versus Cuban refugee from the 1960s); (3) extended family relations (e.g., degree of intactness, family reunification issues) and degree of involvement in Latino community (utilizing available resources?).

While it is very helpful to be familiar with traditional Latino culture, it is equally important to recognize that different Latino clients will deviate to varying degrees from this traditional cultural frame of reference.

Problem Themes and Gender Issues

Problem themes that emerge in psychotherapy with Latino patients most often include interpersonal conflicts in marriage and family (Acosta, 1982; Comas-Diaz, 1985; Delgado and Humm-Delgado, 1984). For Latino primary care patients, relationship problems frequently interact with chronic medical conditions (e.g., diabetes, heart disease, hypertension, stroke, chronic pain, etc.) in ways that make adaptation difficult. In the case of our many Central American patients, family and medical problems frequently interact with war-related losses and PTSD.

Because our patients are predominantly women, traditional gender roles prescribing that Latinas be submissive, self-sacrificing, and enduring of suffering inflicted by men (Comas-Diaz, 1985) also complicate depression and health problems. As Torres-Matrullo (1982) noted in her work with depressed Puerto Rican women, their depressed thinking appeared related to unrealistic sex-role expectations with respect to prohibiting the expression of anger, remaining married despite the quality of the marriage, and the expectation to give help but not to request it. Problem themes and gender issues in our Latino primary care population provide consistent intervention targets.

Interventions

Components of CCM include: (1) an initial phase of engagement, assessment, and planning; (2) *environment-focused interventions* such as linkage with community resources, work with families, social network enhancement, and collaboration with treatment providers; and (3) *patient-focused interventions* such as coping skills training and education (Kanter, 1989). Clinical case management is defined as *hybridization* when practitioners combine the clinical sensitivity and interpersonal skill of the trained psychotherapist with the creativity and action orientation of the environmental architect (Harris and Bachrach, 1988).

The CCM program designed for the Depression Clinic blends elements from several models to produce a flexible and responsive intervention. The program incorporates objectives of the Full Support Model, which aims to optimize client functioning by emphasizing coping skills and providing whatever support is necessary, and objectives of the Personal Strengths Model, which includes the development of a partnership for identifying client strengths and creating environmental and personal situations in which client strengths can be enhanced (Robinson and Toff-Bergman, 1990).

More specifically, CCM services are broken into seven categories: (1) individual contact; (2) phone contact; (3) outreach; (4) home visits; (5) consultation with health care providers; (6) collateral contacts within the social support system; and (7) brokering, advocacy, and linkage. Outreach is designed to minimize dropout from the clinic, which is a substantial problem for ethnic minority patients in the mental health system (Sue, 1977) and with our patient population (Organista, Muñoz, and González, 1994). The case manager provides outreach for up to two months following intake with numerous phone calls, letters, and home visits. Clients are routinely engaged in active problem-solving to decrease potential barriers to treatment such as transportation problems, lack of child care, lack of family support, etc.

A flexible, individualized, case management plan is developed for each client, assessing areas such as social support network, housing, financial, legal, medical, and sexual functioning. Within these areas, strengths are reinforced and adaptive coping skills are identified. Next, problems are identified and prioritized. Concrete goals for the six-month CCM program are developed collaboratively and the case manager emphasizes that the plan is a flexible working guide subject to revision.

The integration of CCM and CBT is accomplished by having case managers work closely with group leaders and in many cases actually serve as group co-therapists. Hence, case managers are knowledgeable about the nature of depression and trained in the use of CBT to treat this problem. This dual role places the clinical case manager in the unique position of observing patient functioning both inside and outside of therapy sessions. In addition to group therapy interventions, the case manager constantly reinforces CBT work outside of sessions while addressing life stressors that can become serious obstacles to remaining in treatment.

The following example illustrates how a clinical case manager was able to quickly respond to a crisis situation involving financial, familial, and health-related stressors during the initial phase of treatment. Stabilization of life stressors enabled the client to focus on therapy and probably prevented dropout.

> Ms. S. is a 45-year-old, separated female who was unemployed for 18 months because of herniated discs in her neck and back. State Disability Insurance had expired and this single mother of four had no income. She was supporting her family with her children's college fund, which was quickly dwindling. She presented to the clinic with sad affect and vegetative symptoms of depression. Moreover, she was immobilized with pain. Feelings of worthlessness and guilt overwhelmed her as reflected in the thoughts, "I should not be sick. I should be able to work and take care of my family." The case manager immediately assisted this patient with her application for Aid to Families with Dependent Children (AFDC) and Medi-Cal, and food stamps and cash benefits were instituted within a couple of weeks. Once the case manager validated and addressed the patient's crisis, a collaborative therapeutic relationship was fostered. The patient also became more receptive to behavioral interventions such as increasing pleasant activities to help decrease her vegetative symptoms. Without clinical case management, the patient may have considered pleasant activities trivial and insensitive given the gravity of her situation. In addition, this client received concrete evidence to dispute her negative thoughts about being worthless and unable to care for her family.

Beginning Services

Special care is taken throughout both CBT and CCM contacts to follow a culturally sensitive relationship protocol that includes several salient Latino values. For example, *Respeto* is practiced by formally addressing patients as "Señora" and "Señor" along with their last names and by maintaining a humble "para servirle" ["to serve you"] attitude. *Personalismo* is practiced by taking time to engage in the kind of self-disclosure and small talk or *plática* advocated by cultural competence experts to build *confianza* or trust with Latino patients (Falicov, 1982; Lum, 1992). The goal is to be perceived by Latino clients as "bien educados," which literally translates to "well-educated" but which actually refers to being well-versed in social etiquette.

Consistent with Latino relationship protocol, group therapy begins with "presentaciones" in which group leaders and patients share background information about where they are from, their family, work that they have done, personal interests, and things about themselves they feel are important. These presentations also give group leaders the opportunity to convey their personal commitment to speaking Spanish and serving Latinos.

Whereas traditional psychotherapy is characterized by fairly rigid boundaries between therapists and patients, work with traditional Latinos requires more flexible boundaries that allow for recapitulations of familism as reflected in acts such as graciously accepting small gifts from patients (e.g., fruit, homemade foods, an article of clothing) and perhaps hugs upon termination. One patient requested a "despedida," or farewell party, for her last session, and volunteered to bring pastry. Group leaders responded to this request by volunteering to bring coffee.

Psychoeducation

The stigma attached to mental illness is pronounced in our patient population. Assessing treatment motivation includes asking clients what their spouses or family members think of them coming in for treatment. For many of our patients, the answer all too often is that they are considered "loco." Fortunately, the didactic style of CBT helps to quickly orient patients to treatment by educating them about depression, its diagnosis, and how CBT is used to treat the problem. Home visits by bilingual and bicultural Latino case managers also help to change misconceptions of treatment by personalizing the process in the client's language.

The fact that our patients are given therapy manuals and homework assignments, and that therapists use a chalkboard for teaching, results in many patients referring to CBT as "La clase de depresión," which alleviates the stigma attached to therapy. Patients claim that such stigma is very pronounced in their countries of origin where scarce mental health services are reserved almost exclusively for hospitalized patients with severe mental disorders.

Psychoeducation also includes information on how to negotiate the immediate social environment, including the hospital. For example, one patient complained that he felt confused about his severe back problems as a result of mixed messages he had received from different physicians. The case manager taught the patient about hospital procedures he could use for clarifying his medical condition (i.e., consulting a patient advocate to organize a meeting of the patient's doctors).

Cognitive Restructuring

Cognitive restructuring is used to teach patients the difference between depression-related and normal thinking (e.g., Burns' [1980] errors in thinking or common irrational thoughts as described by Ellis and Grieger [1977]). Teaching Latino patients how to restructure problematic thinking can be challenging in that they understand the basic idea of "good" and "bad" thoughts but rarely apply Ellis' A-B-C-D method, which is designed to help patients restructure thoughts by teaching them to identify the *A*ctivating event, *B*eliefs about the activating event, the emotional *C*onsequences of beliefs, and finally how to *D*ispute irrational beliefs related to emotional consequences (Ellis and Grieger, 1977).

In view of this continuing problem, we have streamlined cognitive restructuring by teaching a "Yes, but . . ." technique in which patients are taught that much of their depressed thinking amounts to half-truths about problems in need of completion. The "Yes, but . . ." technique is illustrated in the following vignettes, which deal with adaptation to medical illness and family reunification issues, respectively:

> A young South American woman with gastritis and an ulcer became very depressed, anxious, and physically symptomatic following a visit to her eye doctor, who informed her that she

had glaucoma and would need to begin applying daily eye drops to decrease eye pressure. Her automatic thought "I'm going to loose my eyesight and the doctors are not telling me the truth" was changed to *"Yes,* its disturbing to learn that I have glaucoma and have to take daily medication, *but* I'm not going to lose my vision if I take the medication as prescribed, and the doctors have no reason to hide the truth from me." This restructuring immediately relieved the patient's multiple symptoms.

A woman from Nicaragua was depressed that she had migrated to the U.S. without her children and had been unable to return or to send for her children over the past ten years. Now that her 12-year-old son was visiting with her for the first time, she feared that his quietness meant that he didn't love or want to be with her because of the years of separation. The patient began to feel better when she restructured her belief to say *"Yes,* my son probably does feel strange being with me after all those years apart, *but* this doesn't mean that we can't develop a loving relationship."

Religion is another cognitive-related domain in which therapists need to work with traditional Latino patients. We generally reinforce church-going and prayer as behavioral and cognitive activities, respectively, that help patients deal with stress and negative mood states. However, we have learned to explore and challenge forms of prayer that seem to lessen the probability of active problem-solving. For example, when patients report that they "just prayed" instead of doing the week's homework assignment, we ask them to share their prayers. They often reply that they asked God to take away their bad thoughts or to end their problems. In this case, we help patients to shift prayers in a more active direction with techniques like discussing the saying, "Ayudate para que Dios te ayude," which is the Spanish equivalent of "God helps those who help themselves."

Pleasant Activities

Pleasant activity schedules and personal contracts to increase activities are used to achieve an adequate number of pleasant activities for improving mood. Because Latino patients are disproportionately poor, care needs to be taken to generate discussions and lists of local activities that cost little or no money (e.g., free admission to museums and the zoo on the first Wednesday of the month, walks in the park or on the beach, having a cup of coffee in a charming cafe, etc.).

Depressed Latinos frequently report low involvement in activities that they normally enjoy, such as visiting with friends, crocheting, listening to music, going for walks, shopping, etc. At the same time, we find that our mostly female patients are usually over-extended with family responsibilities. Thus, the need to balance routine activities with simple pleasurable activities needs to be stressed.

One drawback with activity-oriented interventions is that the mainstream American value of "taking time out for one's self" is less emphasized in Latino culture, especially for women. However, Latino patients are usually willing to increase pleasurable activities for the purpose of "distraerse" or distracting themselves from worry and problems. The perception of pleasant activities as a way of temporarily escaping problems provides practitioners with an opening for emphasizing this effective intervention strategy. Another strategy is to help patients understand that by taking the time out to decrease their depression, they will be able to return to family responsibilities with more energy and fewer negative feelings.

> Señora M. is a 55-year-old widow from El Salvador with three adult children and several grandchildren. Although she lives on her own, her children would routinely and unexpectedly drop off the grandchildren for her to take care of. In the course of treatment, Señora M. learned to balance baby-sitting with pleasurable "distracciones" or distractions (e.g., walks, reading, volunteer work at a senior citizens center) by setting limits on her children. Limit-setting was facilitated by assertiveness training and cognitive work aimed at her discomfort with saying "no" to requests for favors.

Recent Latino immigrants often describe their experience of culture change as "total" and often feel overwhelmed by losses and issues of adaptation. Many need to secure housing, jobs, school, and employment skills and learn English. Another useful component of activity interventions is goal setting. Goal setting is discussed as less overwhelming and more motivating if broken down into clear, manageable steps. For example, the popular goal of learning English is broken down into steps that include locating classes in the area, calling the school to ask about schedule and materials needed, purchasing materials, enrolling, etc.

Assertiveness Training

Because of the considerable interaction between depression, medical problems, and interpersonal conflicts in our Latino patient population, much time is spent helping patients to cope better with family problems. Our patients commonly report a tendency to "guardar" or hold in anger rather than express it to spouses and family members with whom they are upset. This culture-based inhibition is especially prominent for Latinas (Soto and Shaver, 1982), who are also stressed by excessive family responsibilities such as caring for grandchildren and sick relatives in addition to household chores and even part-time work.

Encouraging descriptions of assertiveness training (AT) with Latinos have been reported (Acosta, 1982; Boulette, 1976; Herrera and Sanchez, 1976; Torres-Matrullo, 1982) as well as culturally sensitive guidelines for conducting AT with ethnic minorities in general (Wood and Mallinckrodt, 1990) and with Latinas in particular (Comas-Diaz and Duncan, 1985). Culturally sensitive guidelines are extremely important in view of recent recognition by experts that assertiveness is a modern, Western, and particularly North American concept and technology (e.g., Rakos, 1991). As such, assertiveness is extremely appropriate and adaptive in mainstream society, but can be inappropriate and problematic in traditional cultural contexts.

In traditional Latino culture, communication and behavior are more strongly governed by traditional institutions (e.g., family, community, and the church) and values (e.g., deference to authority based on age, gender, social position, etc.). Assertiveness can run contrary to the culture's emphasis on communication that is polite, personable, nonconfrontational, and deferential. This is especially true for women who are taught to be submissive to men and to subordinate their needs to those of the family (Comas-Diaz, 1985).

Despite this cultural dilemma, the argument to do AT with depressed, traditional Latino primary care patients is compelling. For example, Soto and Shaver (1982) found that sex-role traditionalism was inversely related to assertiveness, which in turn was inversely related to psychological distress in a sample of Puerto Rican women (N=278). The question that remains is how to conduct assertiveness training in a culturally sensitive manner.

Standard AT includes discussion of personal rights, modeling, and role-playing to improve interpersonal effectiveness. The manner in which assertiveness is introduced greatly influences the willingness of Latino patients to learn and apply this skill to their interpersonal problems. Clinical case managers "biculturate" patients by describing assertiveness as a popular skill that is quite effective in mainstream America in areas like work, school, agency settings, and interpersonal relationships. Care is taken to stress culturally compatible aspects of assertiveness such as the emphasis on communication that is not only direct but also honest and respectful. Assertiveness is also discussed more as a way of cultivating family relationships and not just individual independence and accomplishments.

Consistent with Comas-Diaz and Duncan's (1985) recommendations, Latino cultural factors that mitigate against developing assertiveness are discussed as well as strategies for dealing with negative reactions from spouses and other family members. For example, Comas-Dias and Duncan taught Puerto Rican women to preface assertive expressions with phrases like "With all due respect . . ." and to respond to negative reactions with explanations like "Expressing my feelings makes me less upset and better able to manage things."

An excellent way to motivate Latino primary care patients to consider assertiveness is to ask them what happens when they "guardar" or hold in negative feelings. Almost without exception patients describe the exacerbation of existing physical illness such as high blood pressure, diabetes, heart disease, and gastro-intestinal problems. For example, one woman who had survived a stroke became very motivated to become assertive as a way of decreasing the probability of a second stroke by not holding in anger and resentment toward a son who drank excessively and became belligerent when intoxicated. Another example of the need for AT is provided in the vignette below which again highlights the need to address economic and family problems in order to alleviate depression in Latino primary care patients.

> Sr. and Sra. C. are a Latino couple in their late 50s who were each sequentially referred to the Depression Clinic. Both met criteria for major depression. During the wife's initial assessment, the case manager discovered that the couple risked eviction from their home. The case manager immediately initiated an SSI application and worked closely with a social worker at a senior housing complex to expedite acceptance into this residential setting. As the housing crisis subsided, marital issues became apparent. During group therapy sessions with the husband, marital problems were identified as a significant obstacle to decreasing his depression. Recognizing the importance of familism in this immigrant couple, the case manager offered them eight couple sessions focusing primarily on assertive communication as taught in the CBT group. The case manager also helped the couple to dispute and restructure distorted thinking about each other's actions. For example, although Sr. C. had debilitating chronic back problems, he believed that his wife expected him to accompany her anywhere she went outside of the home. Often Sra C. reinforced this belief by requesting Sr. C.'s company, and he would agree to go because he thought it unmanly to share the extent of his pain and need to do less strenuous activities. Concurrent case management reinforced the CBT techniques in a culturally appropriate family context. As a result, the depression in both clients lessened as did couple conflict.

Termination

Termination in our clinic involves a titrated, two-stage process in which patients first terminate from CBT at 16 weeks and then begin termination from CCM which continues for two months beyond CBT. Within the group context, therapists and patients review treatment gains and continuing problem areas. Primary problem themes related to depression are reviewed (e.g., medical illness and family conflict) as well as their cognitive and behavioral solutions (e.g., specific counter-beliefs, activities, and assertive responses). The CBT termination session ends with a written "prescription" of techniques to continue using as well as personalized goodbyes between participants.

In CCM, termination begins weeks before the last session by reviewing the individualized treatment plan, stated goals, and accomplishments. This review process helps clients to recognize their strengths and to maintain motivation by reviewing and revising goals.

Because termination can provoke fear and even relapse, CBT techniques are again reinforced by their direct application to patient reactions to termination. For example, the "Yes, but . . ." technique is used to generate thoughts like, *"Yes,* it is frightening to end services, *but* I've made many gains and learned many techniques to help me continue managing my depression and other problems." Case managers also review both formal and informal sources of support to help patients maintain normal mood states and progress toward coping with life stressors and accomplishing personal goals. Specific community resources are identified and referrals made to others services if necessary (e.g., self-help and support groups). Linkages to referral agencies are facilitated by the case manager's expression of trust and confidence in the particular service.

Latino patients are especially grateful for services received. Presenting the case manager with small gifts or a hug demonstrate courtesy and good manners and should be accepted gracefully. Sometimes patients state that they wish they could continue using CCM indefinitely. Does such a statement indicate excessive dependency as we are often trained to think? Generally we find this not to be the case. The desire to continue working with service providers seems to more accurately reflect both cultural and social factors. Latino patients form personalized relationships that they are reluctant to leave behind simply because services have ended. In addition, the extreme scarcity of bilingual/bicultural services makes culturally responsive services attractive. Thus, desire to continue services, and occasional social visits, are not pathologized and are instead handled with social grace.

CONCLUSIONS

The problem of depression in primary care is especially relevant to Latinos who are now at higher risk for affective disorders in general (Kessler et al., 1994) and for depression in particular (Robins, 1987) as compared to non-Hispanic whites. In addition, the distinct tendency for Latinos to under-utilize mental health service and to over-utilize medical services for emotional problems further underscores the need to target depressed Latinos in primary care settings.

This chapter described the use of concurrent, short-term, and culturally responsive CBT and CCM to address the multiple physical and psychosocial problems of depressed Latino primary care patients. The active, directive, and problem-solving focus of these integrated services is responsive to the traditional cultural expectations of Latino patients as well as to their low SES backgrounds, where the combination of high stress and low resources demands timely, problem-focused attention.

Clinical case management is a flexible, comprehensive, and individualized service that diminishes many obstacles to the treatment of depression in Latino primary care patients. As group therapy leaders, case managers enjoy an informative dual role that allows them to more effectively address both acute and chronic life stressors and the frequently overwhelming psychological reactions to these stressors. With support for external problems and continuous reinforcement of CBT techniques, clients are probably better able to maintain long-term benefits of cognitive behavioral group therapy.

In CBT, streamlined methods of cognitive restructuring are recommended and even prayer is viewed as amenable to restructuring to promote active problem solving. Pleasant activities schedules help to decrease depression but persuasion is necessary to counter the self-sacrificing socialization of traditional Latinas. Assertiveness training is also helpful in addressing the central problem of interpersonal conflict and its negative impact on medical conditions, but assertiveness training with Latinos needs to follow culturally sensitive guidelines to overcome the cultural dilemma inherent in this intervention.

Several case management programs are described in the literature, yet empirical demonstration of their efficacy is limited. Data is currently being collected and analyzed to evaluate the efficacy of integrated CCM and CBT in terms of dropout and various indices of outcome, including depression and more effective coping with life stressors in depressed Latino primary care patients.

REFERENCES

Acosta, F. X. (1979). Barriers between mental health services and Mexican Americans: An examination of a paradox. *American Journal of Community Psychology, 7,* 503-520.

Acosta, F. X. (1982). Group psychotherapy with Spanish-speaking patients. In R. M. Becerra, M. Karno, and J. I. Escobar (Eds.), *Mental Health and Hispanic Americans* (183-197). New York: Grune and Stratton.

Acosta, F. X., Yamamoto, J., and Evans, L. A. (1982). *Effective psychotherapy for low-income and minority patients.* New York: Plenum Press.

American Psychiatric Association (1993). Practice guidelines for major depression disorder in adults. *American Journal of Psychiatry, 150* (Suppl. 4).

American Psychological Association (1987). *Diagnostic and Statistical Manual of Mental Disorders (3rd ed.).* Washington, DC: American Psychological Association.

Barrera, M., Jr. (1978). Mexican-American mental health service utilization: A critical examination of some proposed variables. *Community Mental Health Journal, 14,* 35-45.

Beck, A. T., Rush, J. R., Shaw, B. F., and Emery, G. (1979). *Cognitive Therapy for Depression.* New York: The Guilford Press.

Berry, J. W. (1980). Acculturation as varieties of adaptation. In A. M. Padilla (Ed.), *Acculturation: Theory, Models, and Some New Findings* (9-25). Boulder, CO: Westview Press.

Boulette, T. R. (1976). Assertion training with low income Mexican American women. In M. R. Miranda (Ed.), *Psychotherapy with the Spanish-Speaking: Issues in Research and Service Delivery (Monograph #3)* (16-71). Los Angeles: Spanish-Speaking Mental Health Research Center, University of California.

Brown, G. and Harris, T. (1978). *Social Origins of Depression: A Study of Psychiatric Disorder in Women.* London: Tavistock.

Burns, D. (1980). *Feeling Good: The New Mood Therapy.* New York: Signet.

Comas-Diaz, L. (1981). Effects of cognitive and behavioral group treatment on the depressive symptomatology of Puerto Rican women. *Journal of Consulting and Clinical Psychology, 49*(5), 627-632.

Comas-Diaz, L. (1985). Cognitive and behavioral group therapy with Puerto Rican women: A comparison of content themes. *Hispanic Journal of Behavioral Sciences, 7*(3), 273-283.

Comas-Diaz, L. and Duncan, J. W. (1985). The cultural context: A factor in assertiveness training with mainland Puerto Rican women. *Psychology of Women Quarterly, 9,* 463-476.

Delgado, M. and Humm-Delgado, D. (1984). Hispanics and group work: A review of the literature. *Ethnicity in Group Work Practice,* 85-96.

Depression Guideline Panel (1993a). *Depression in Primary Care: Vol 1. Diagnosis and Detection* (Clinical Practice Guideline No. 5, AHCPR Publication No. 93-0550). Rockville, MD: Department of Health and Human Services, Public Health Service, Agency for Health Care Policy and Research.

Depression Guideline Panel (1993b). *Depression in Primary Care: Vol 2. Treatment of Major Depression* (Clinical Practice Guideline No. 5, AHCPR Publication No. 93-0551). Rockville, MD: Department of Health and Human Services, Public Health Service, Agency for Health Care Policy and Research.

DiNitto, D. (1991). *Social Welfare: Politics and Public Policy.* Englewood Cliffs, NJ: Prentice Hall.

Ellis, A. and Grieger, R. (1977). *Handbook of Rational Emotive Therapy.* New York: Holt, Rinehart, and Winston.

Falicov, C. J. (1982). Mexican families. In M. McGoldrick, J. K. Pearce, and J. Giordano (Eds.), *Ethnicity and Family Therapy* (134-163). New York: The Guilford Press.

Goldstein, A. P. (1971). *Psychotherapeutic Attraction.* New York: Pergamon.

Harris, M. and Bachrach, L. (Eds.) (1988). *Clinical Case Management.* San Francisco: Jossey-Bass.

Herrera, A. E. and Sanchez, V. C. (1976). Behaviorally oriented group therapy: A successful application in the treatment of low income Spanish-speaking clients. In M. R. Miranda (Ed.), *Psychotherapy with the Spanish-speaking: Issues in Research and Service Delivery (Monograph #3)* (73-84). Los Angeles: Spanish-Speaking Mental Health Research Center, University of California.

Hirschfeld, R. and Cross, L. (1982). Epidemiology of affective disorders. *Archives of General Psychiatry, 39,* 35-46.

Kamerow, D. B. (1989). The management of depression in primary care: Introduction. *General Hospital Psychiatry, 11,* 187.

Kanter, J. S. (1989). Clinical case management: Definitions, principles, components. *Hospital and Community Psychiatry, 40,* 361-368.

Karno, M., Ross, R. N., and Caper, R. A. (1969). Mental health roles of physicians in a Mexican American community. *Community Mental Health Journal, 5,* 62-69.

Katon, W. (1982). Depression: Somatic symptoms and medical disorders in primary care. *Comprehensive Psychiatry, 23,* 274-275.

Katon, W. (1987). The epidemiology of depression in medical care. *International Journal in Medicine, 17,* 93-112.

Kessler, R. C., McGonagle, K. A., Zhao, S., Nelson, C. B., Hughes, M., Eshleman, S., Wittchen, H., and Kendler, K. S. (1994). Lifetime and 12-month prevalence of DSM-III-R psychiatric disorders in the United States. *Archives of General Psychiatry, 51,* 8-19.

Lewinsohn, P. M., Muñoz, R. F., Youngren, M. A., and Zeiss, A. M. (1986). *Control Your Depression* (Revised edition). New York: Prentice-Hall.

Lloyd, C. (1980a). Life events and depressive disorder reviewed: I. Events as predisposing factors. *Archives of General Psychiatry, 37,* 529-535.

Lloyd, C. (1980b). Life events and depressive disorder reviewed: II. Events as precipitating factors. *Archives of General Psychiatry, 37,* 542-548.

Lum, D. (1992). *Social Work Practice & People of Color: A Process Stage Approach (2nd ed.).* Monterey, CA: Brooks/Cole Publishing Company.

Miranda, M. R. (Ed.) (1976). Health Research Center, University of California. *Psychotherapy with the Spanish-Speaking: Issues in Research and Service Delivery (Monograph No. 3).* Los Angeles: Spanish-Speaking Mental Research Center.

Muñoz, R. F., Aguilar-Gaxiola, S., and Guzman, J. (1986). *Manual de terapia de grupo para el tratamiento cognitivo-conductual de depresion* [Group therapy manual for cognitive-behavioral treatment of depression]. Unpublished manual, San Francisco General Hospital, Depression Clinic, San Francisco.

Muñoz, R. F., Hollon, S. D., McGrath, E., Rehm, L. P., and VandenBos, G. R. (1994). On the AHCPR Depression in primary care guidelines: Further considerations for practitioners. *American Psychologist, 49*(1), 42-61.

Muñoz, R. F., Ying, Y. W., Armas, R., Chan, F., and Gurza, R. (1987). The San Francisco Depression Prevention Research Project: A randomized trial with medical outpatients. In R. F. Muñoz (Ed.), *Depression Prevention: Research Directions* (199-215). Washington, DC: Hemisphere.

National Association of Social Work (1993, June). Colleagues aid in guidelines on depression. *NASW News, 38,* 9.

Organista, K. C., Muñoz, R. F., and González, G. (1994). Cognitive behavioral therapy for depression in low-income and minority medical outpatients: Description of a program and exploratory analyses. *Cognitive Therapy and Researc, 18*(3), 241-259.

Padilla, A. M., Carlos, M. L., and Keefe, S. E. (1976). Mental health service utilization by Mexican Americans. In M. R. Miranda (Ed.), *Psychotherapy with the Spanish-speaking: Issues in Research and Service Delivery (Monograph No. 3).* Los Angeles: Spanish-Speaking Mental Health Research Center.

Parron, D. L. (1982). An overview of minority group mental health needs and issues as presented to the President's Commission on Mental Health. In F. V. Muñoz and R. Endo (Eds.), *Perspectives on Minority Group Mental Health* (3-22). Washington, DC: University Press of America.

Paykel, E. S. (1982). Life events and early environment. In E. Paykel (Ed.), *Handbook of Affective Disorders* (146-161). New York: The Guilford Press.

Pearlin, L. and Lieberman, M. (1979). Social sources of emotional distress. In R. Simmons (Ed.), *Research in Community and Mental Health* (Vol. 1, 217-248). Greenwich, CT: JAI Press.

Pérez-Stable, E. J., Miranda, J., Muñoz, R. F., and Ying, Y. W. (1990). Depression in medical outpatients: Underrecognition and misdiagnosis. *Archives of Internal Medicine, 150,* 1083-1088.

Rakos, R. F. (1991). *Assertive Behavior: Theory, Research, and Training.* New York: Routledge.

Roberts, R. E. (1987). Epidemiological issues in measuring preventive effects. In R. F. Muñoz (Ed.), *Depression Prevention: Research Directions* (45-75). San Francisco: Hemisphere Publishing Corporation.

Robins, L.N. (1987). The assessment of psychiatric diagnosis in epidemiological studies. In: Hales, R.E. and Frances, A.J., (Eds.), *American Psychiatric Association Annual Review.* Washington, DC: American Psychiatric Press, Inc., 589-609.

Robinson, G. K. and Toff-Bergman, G. (1990). *Choices in case management: Current knowledge & practice for mental health programs* (Institute of Mental Health Publication No. 278-87-0026). Rockville, MD: Department of Health and Human Services, Mental Health Policy Resource Center.

Shepard, M., Harwin, B., Delpa, C. and Cairns, V. (1979). Social work and the primary care of mental disorder. *Psychological Medicine, 9,* 661-669.

Soto, E. and Shaver, P. (1982). Sex-role traditionalism, assertiveness, and symptoms of Puerto Rican women living in the United States. *Hispanic Journal of Behavioral Sciences, 4*(1), 1-19.

Sue, S. (1977). Community mental health services to minority groups: Some optimism, some pessimism. *American Psychologist, 32,* 616-624.

Sue, S., Fujino, D. C., Hu, L., Takeuchi, D. T., and Zane, N. W. S. (1991). Community mental health services for ethnic minority groups: A test of the cultural responsiveness hypothesis. *Journal of Consulting and Clinical Psychology, 59*(4), 533-540.

Surber, R. (Ed.) (1994). *Clinical Case Management: A Guide to Comprehensive Treatment of Serious Mental Illness.* Thousand Oaks, CA: Sage Publications.

Torres-Matrullo, C. (1982). Cognitive therapy of depressive disorders in the Puerto Rican female. In R. M. Becerra, M. Karno, and J. I. Escobar (Eds.), *Mental Health and Hispanic Americans* (101-113). New York: Grune & Stratton.

Weissman, M. M., Bruce, M. L., Leaf, P. J., and Holzer, C., III. (1991). Affective disorders. In L. N. Robins and D. A. Regier (Eds.), *Psychiatric Disorders in America: The Epidemiologic Catchment Area Study* (53-80). New York: Free Press.

Wells, K. B., Stewart, A., Hays, R. D., Burnham, A., Rogers, W., Daniels, M., Berry, S., Greenfield, S., and Ware, J. (1989). The functioning and well-being of depressed patients: Results from the medical outcomes study. *Journal of the American Medical Association, 262,* 914-919.

Wood, P.S. and Mallinckrodt, B. (1990). Culturally sensitive training for ethnic minority clients. *Professional Psychology: Research and Practice,* 21(1), 5-11.

Chapter 6

Culturally Responsive Psychiatric Case Management with Southeast Asians

Yeunhee Joyce Kim
Birgitta Oey Snyder
Alice Y. Lai-Bitker

A DIVERSE POPULATION

The Asian-American population has grown dramatically in the past 20 years. From 1980 to 1989 alone, the growth was from 1.7 percent to 2.8 percent of the total U.S. population (O'Hare, 1990). Many of the more recent Asian arrivals are displaced individuals from countries disrupted by war, poverty, or political persecutions. These immigrants and refugees bring with them not only rich and diverse cultures, but also unique problems associated with the transition and their experiences with past traumas. In addition, they encounter new difficulties during their adjustment to the host country. It is a serious mistake to assume that due to phenotypic similarities, all Asians share the same heritage, values, and mannerisms. Such generalizations make therapeutic interventions ineffective and are often alienating to the client. More helpful is an attempt to understand and study the historical backgrounds and immigration patterns of Asians in the United States. Past circumstances under which they came to this country affect their current attempts to adjust, and also explain why difficulties frequently arise in the transculturation process. Casting all Asians as immigrants is misleading. The term implies a voluntary and planned act of moving from one country to another. The term *refugee*, however, implies that a person is fleeing involuntarily to escape an undesirable situation such as war or political oppression (Szule, 1980, p. 139). The method of leaving one's homeland directly affects the mental status of the individual. Williams (1985) discussed the psychological effects of refugee flight, and the increased risk for emotional problems that result from the disruption. Key questions are: Was the flight associated with fear and disorganization? Did they lose much in the process? Were they able to leave with relatives and some token pieces or reminders of their country? Or were they forced to flee immediately with nothing but what they could carry through forests and war zones?

ONE PROGRAM'S EXPERIENCE

Asian Community Mental Health Services (ACMHS) is a multiservice outpatient program located in Oakland, California, which serves the diverse Asian-American population of the East Bay area. Over the past ten years, our client population has become increasingly more predominated by refugees. Located in an urban setting, the clinic is situated in Oakland's Chinatown. For many in the community, this mental health clinic is the only language-accessible mental health agency available to them. Since its beginning 18 years ago, ACMHS has seen a dramatic shift in the ethnic groups it serves. Reflective of the surrounding communities, we noticed that from a previously predominately Chinese-American clientele, more than half of those currently served are from Southeast Asian countries. The problems presented have also shifted in focus: we find that apart from mental health issues, clinicians have had to increasingly address the case management aspects of clients' lives. Workers, finding few outside resources to which they could refer clients, have found the need to be responsible for all aspects of a client's case. Echoing this position, Miller (1983) has proposed that rather than being an option, comprehensive case management is an essential modality for the successful outcome of a client's case.

Many of the clients we serve depend on government assistance and live in poverty-stricken neighborhoods. Crime, violence, and illiteracy are common within these settings. Some recent studies have focused upon the adjustment difficulties encountered by Southeast Asian refugees. Strand and Jones (1985) discussed the problems confronted by the refugees when they attempt to obtain employment or to access necessary agencies. They found that the lack of English language skills is the foremost challenge faced by refugees. Our experience corroborates this. They arrive in this country with few Western skills and rarely speak English. Most came from rural, pre-industrial societies and find themselves abruptly placed in the midst of twentieth-century automation and Western ways of living. In addition to absorbing the complexities of the new society, the refugees must also cope with homesickness, depression, and disorders related to post-traumatic stress.

Among the refugees ACMHS serves are those who come from Vietnam, Cambodia, and Laos. These groups comprise 61 percent of ACMHS's client population. The immigration patterns of these three groups often reflect the emotional issues and psychiatric symptoms that they bring to their new environment. The first wave of refugees from Vietnam came in 1975 when Saigon fell to the Communists. This group was able to leave by a hasty, but relatively safe method in aircraft. Between 1977 and 1980 an estimated 500,000 Vietnamese and Chinese left Vietnam. They were the group of refugees known as the boat people. Of this large group, 200,000 people perished during the flight (Knoll, 1982). Vietnam subsequently invaded Cambodia, and those people fled across the border to Thailand where they settled into UN-sponsored refugee camps. Many Laotians also fled their country into Thailand in 1975 subsequent to the Pathet Lao takeover. Past affiliations with non-Communist regimes made many individuals and their families targets for persecution by the invading armies (Beiser, 1988).

It was under these circumstances that many Southeast Asians came to the U.S. Confused, many times illiterate, and unable to effectively work with the system, they nonetheless needed to find housing, income, and medical attention. Psychological traumas, while present, could not be addressed until these basic needs were met. Many times, the suppressing, denying or forgetting of past experiences is necessary to expedite the assimilation process. However, almost without exception, these refugees still suffer from emotional or psychological problems as a result of the disruption.

The refugees from Vietnam tended to come alone or in pairs, whereas those from Cambodia and Laos came with family members in one large group. McGoldrick (1982) noted that adjustment to the host country is directly related to the amount of familial support present. In addition, Kinzie et al. (1986) found that symptoms of major depression and/or post-traumatic stress syndrome were evident in almost all of the refugees from these countries. Cambodian refugees have been described as having the most severe psychological problems due to their experiences during the mass genocide program of the Pol Pot regime between 1975-1979 (Gong-Guy, 1987). All of these refugees face the trauma of being uprooted from the totality of that which was familiar to them. Their image of themselves as self-sufficient and able are constantly challenged by the new and alien environment they face. Appropriate resources, in addition, are scarce and difficult to find.

Once the basic necessities are secured, psychological problems remain for most of the refugees. The idea of psychotherapy, however, is threatening and very unlike the Asian philosophy of stoically conducting personal matters within a personal or familial context. Rozée and Boemel (1989) discussed how psychological problems are commonly manifested by somatic complaints. In their study, 30 Cambodian women were selected following complaints of loss of vision. The visual acuity loss was determined to be a direct emotional reaction to the atrocities they witnessed during the Pol Pot regime, rather than due to an organic component. They conclude that physical complaints for many Asian groups appear to be socially more acceptable than admitting one's emotional inability to cope with traumatic past experiences.

LACK OF SERVICE AVAILABILITY

Refugee clients come in with myriad problems. Financial difficulty, medical needs, psychological problems, social adjustment issues, housing, racism, and violence in the neighborhood are just a few. These problems are pressing survival issues, requiring immediate attention. Solving the problems presented by a refugee client requires a multi-prong approach involving different components of a service system.

Case management is a methodology that ensures a comprehensive program will meet an individual's need for care by coordinating and linking the components of service delivery. The functions of case management are suited to the refugee client's need for well-coordinated services to address his or her multi-layered problems. In actuality, however, services accessible to the refugee client are limited due to language and cultural barriers. Case management loses its efficacy when the services critical for a successful outcome are not accessible to the refugee client.

Some authors (Loo, Tong, and True, 1989; Snowden and Cheung, 1990; Sue et al., 1991) have observed that refugee clients tend to shy away from mental health services due to the lack of understanding of mental health and stigma attached to mental illnesses. Another study (Sue, 1977) contends that Asian clients tend to leave mental health programs prematurely. Our experience at ACMHS, however, indicates that the majority of the refugee clients admitted to the clinic stay in the program long-term. ACMHS delivers clinical mental health services and ancillary services through case management. A multi-service approach to dealing with mental health issues among the Southeast Asian refugees makes the services palatable and responsive to their needs. At the same time, due to the lack of accessibility of other services in the system, bilingual/bicultural mental health services at ACMHS are used as a way of gaining access to other services.

Southeast Asian clients are well represented at our outpatient clinic in Alameda County. The same group, however, is extremely underrepresented in the rest of the mental health system in the county or has never been served. This phenomenon is not indicative of the level of service needs among the refugees. Instead, it is more a reflection of the service accessibility of that system of care. When the local county hospital opened a new psychiatric facility, for example, and made extra efforts to increase accessibility by providing Southeast Asian languages, the clients from those groups began appearing at the psychiatric emergency service. As the program became more familiar, the Southeast Asian community, as well as mental health professionals, had increased confidence in the system's ability to serve the clients and there were increased referrals. In the past, those individuals could have benefited from psychiatric emergency services but had been kept in the community and inadequately served.

Another aim of case management is to achieve client empowerment through the process of identifying needs and goals and through the coordination of services and advocacy on behalf of the client. In order for case management to be successful, however, there must be a constellation of services that can be coordinated to fulfill the client's needs and desires. In most cases, though, there is a scarcity of resources for refugee groups and the existing services available to the refugees are often inadequate or limited in their scope.

The literature on the Southeast Asian groups reports underutilization of services due to cultural beliefs (Kinzie, 1985). We believe this underutilization is derived from lack of availability and accessibility of the service for refugee groups. Linguistic accessibility is easy to identify by the languages available. Cultural relevance of the program, however, is harder to identify but equally affects the effectiveness of the service. For example, a parenting education program by a school district that emphasizes equality of relationships and assertiveness among members in the family may not be relevant for the refugee parents who are struggling with rapidly acculturating children.

There is an absolute shortage of services for ethnic minority groups. As the demographics of our community change rapidly, there has to be a reprioritization and reallocation of resources. This change, however, comes very slowly and the refugee groups continue to suffer from grossly inadequate services. The shrinking economic resources for human services in recent years make it very difficult to advocate for more adequate services for this population.

SERVICE DELIVERY STRATEGIES FOR THE REFUGEE POPULATION

The remainder of this chapter will discuss culturally responsive service delivery strategies, derived from our experiences at ACMHS and supported by literature on this subject. Our experience and much of the concerned literature concur that it is most effective and efficient to provide services by bilingual and bicultural staff (Fox, 1985; Lorenzo and Adler, 1984). The purpose of case management is to help clients gain access to needed services. A large portion of case management service to monolingual clients in particular involves linkage services using the case manager's bilingual skills. Because of this, it is much more cost-efficient and effective to have a bilingual/bicultural case manager. If a bilingual and bicultural professional staff person is not available to deliver services, however, we strongly recommend that linguistic and cultural consultation be utilized. In this manner, a service provider will become familiarized with the background of the client for an accurate assessment and to develop appropriate service plans.

CASE MANAGEMENT ISSUES

Case management with Southeast Asian refugee clients is both challenging and rewarding. Acting as a "culture broker" between the client and community resources, the case worker can assist the refugee to access the needed services. Culturally sensitive case managers and social workers are crucial for these refugees. As is true with other ethnic and linguistic minority groups, they bring a unique set of political, cultural, and socio-economic backgrounds as well as values and expectations to the service provider. In order to serve Southeast Asian clients effectively, the service provider first must understand their life experiences and their presentation of needs and concerns. This understanding will assist in developing culturally attuned case management interventions. Often times, if the therapist also speaks the client's native language, a trusting relationship will be easier to develop. Some of the common case management issues important to Southeast Asian clients will be discussed in this section. Following, there will be an attempt to translate our understanding of the refugee experiences into effective service delivery strategies.

CULTURAL APPRECIATION AND ASSESSMENT OF SERVICE NEEDS

Southeast Asian groups have drawn attention from researchers and service providers in recent years, and increasing numbers of research findings have brought us a better understanding of them

(Kinzie, 1985; Lee, 1990). However, there is still much remaining to be studied and better understood. In order to serve these groups appropriately and adequately, it is a necessary prerequisite to have a good appreciation of their background and an accurate assessment of the comprehensive issues with which they are struggling. When a clinician is confronting an individual with major psychiatric illness, s/he may be unable to recognize the presence or absence of the major psychiatric condition without sharing the culture of the client or having a deep appreciation of the culture. There are considerable similarities in the manifestation of psychiatric conditions across cultural boundaries. The belief that human psycho-behaviors are universal and similar across all, or at least most cultures, is termed *etic* (Feleppa, 1986). The opposing view, the thought that human behaviors are non-generalizable or iso-cultural, is termed emic. The case manager should be aware that some behaviors and the psychology of refugee clients may be culturally specific, or *emic* in nature. Individuals' values, coping skills, and perceptions are formed by their life experiences and the cultural environment to which they are exposed. Problem definition and needs prioritization become influenced by these unique norms and value systems. Boehnlein (1987), for example, has commented on how religious rituals function to help Cambodian refugees cope with suffering by re-establishing the concept that there is order in the universe. Since case management is an individualized plan of care to ensure that a person's unique needs are met in a sensitive and culturally appropriate manner, cultural competency in evaluation and interventions is the duty of a case manager. Awareness and sensitivity is critical to ensure appropriate and effective approaches to refugee clients. Judgments about the "appropriateness" of behavior must occur within the cultural context. At the same time, however, while there is a danger of misinterpreting culture-bound behaviors and beliefs as symptomatic of psychiatric illness, care must be taken not to overly attribute symptoms of an illness to cultural influence. Such an error would represent emic bias.

There seems, nevertheless, a meaningful difference in symptom manifestation by the Southeast Asian clients. Kinzie and Boe (1989) observed that there is a higher incidence of psychotic features among refugees suffering from Post-Traumatic Stress Disorder than other comparable groups, such as combat veterans. DSM III-R does not list further psychotic features other than flashbacks. The researchers proposed that diagnostic criteria of PTSD should include more psychotic features such as auditory and visual hallucination and paranoid delusion to better fit the clinical presentation of the Southeast Asian refugee population.

Cultural beliefs can often provide an explanation for the cause of an illness. An idiosyncratic way of presenting a psychiatric condition and its cause can be easily misinterpreted when an evaluator is not familiar with the cultural beliefs of the client, as illustrated by the following:

> A Mien client attributed his severe depression and psychotic symptoms to a supernatural experience of an encounter with an indignant soul and the subsequent spell cast on him. He firmly believed that he would not be able to recover from his condition until the spell was lifted. Initially, to a clinician not familiar with Mien culture, the client sounded very delusional. However, consultation with a Mien mental health worker confirmed that his symptoms were within the norms of Mien belief that illnesses could result from an offended spirit, or from a curse placed by an angry community member.

Socialized behaviors unique to a culture can create confusion in the evaluation process, and must be evaluated within their cultural context before clinical significance is attributed to them, as exemplified below:

> A Cambodian female client interviewed by a non-Cambodian clinician was misunderstood to experience some internal stimulation. She complained of her problem with poor memory. When asked to report concrete examples of her impairment, she smiled and giggled as she reported leaving her purse at a store, burning food, and forgetting to bring her Medi-Cal card to the session. Her smiles and giggling behavior were very mood incongruent and inappropriate to the contents of her report. A less culturally sensitive worker would conclude that the client was resistant to treatment, or in denial of her obvious problems. The clinician in this case consulted a Cambodian

mental health worker regarding how to interpret the client's behavior. The Cambodian mental health worker explained that it was common, especially for women, to laugh or giggle in order to cope with difficult emotions such as frustration, sadness, or anger, especially in the presence of a stranger/outsider.

Language can be an obvious barrier to an accurate assessment. Still, the language issue sometimes becomes ignored or minimized when evaluating a monolingual person or those with limited English skills, at times with serious consequences.

An assessment in her first language brought out surprising findings for a Japanese patient who had been in an inpatient setting for many years. She was initially referred to psychiatric emergency for a suicide attempt and later transferred to a long-term care facility due to her repeated suicide attempts. Her treatment team was convinced that she was suffering from persistent depression in reaction to her husband's death. They believed her behaviors were culturally syntonic for her due to her Japanese heritage. The patient was treated with various anti-depressant medications and electro-convulsive treatment, to no avail. A referral was eventually made to a Japanese bilingual psychiatrist due to her lack of response to years of psychiatric treatment. During the interviews, it was revealed that she was suffering from active hallucinations and delusional thinking, both of which heavily influenced her behaviors.

As this case illustrates, the importance of an assessment in the client's primary language cannot be overemphasized. When a case manager's language and cultural background are different from the client's, it is strongly recommended that a trained translator/cultural broker be present to ensure an accurate assessment of the client. Even when the client has seemingly adequate English skills, it is advisable to get cultural and language consultation until the worker is convinced that the language and cultural differences do not hinder an accurate assessment and the establishment of a positive and trusting relationship between the case manager and the client.

A respectful and sensitive case manager from a different ethnic and cultural background can be very successful in interventions with refugee clients. However, a case manager with the same language and cultural background as the client's has an incomparable advantage in quickly building rapport, earning trust, and subsequently being effective in service. This is especially relevant in an economic environment where resources are scarce and time with which to serve clients is limited.

> A competent and sensitive psychologist worked with a Mien woman with a Mien-speaking mental health worker as her translator/co-therapist over several months. It seemed that a good rapport had developed between the psychologist and the client and the therapy proceeded rather successfully. When the psychologist left the clinic, the Mien client was transferred to the sole care of the Mien mental health worker. The client confided to the Mien worker that she had withheld her substance abuse problem from the psychologist. Since she now had a Mien worker, she stated that she felt safe to disclose the most shameful part of her secrets and wanted to seek help for her substance abuse.

Problem definition and interventions differ depending upon the values and beliefs an individual subscribes to. The importance of considering these values is seen below.

> A Laotian woman was seen in crisis after threatening to kill herself. Her suicidal threat was triggered by her son's suggestion for his family to move out of her house due to a growing space need. She would not acknowledge the issue of her need to search for new housing or the added financial burden until her emotional issues of abandonment and lost face were addressed. This woman believed that an only son should live with and care for his parents, and she was deeply ashamed to face her community with the fact that her son was "abandoning" her. Understanding of this cultural tradition helped the worker process the client's feelings before moving on to other issues.

COMPONENTS OF CULTURALLY
COMPETENT ASSESSMENT

The importance of cultural competence cannot be overemphasized for an accurate assessment of a client's needs. However, genuine interest and empathy from a case manager is equally critical in rapport-building and for a good understanding of a client's situation. Many refugee clients come in with a limited understanding of mental health services. They do not understand how talking about their life history helps their "sickness." Neither are they familiar with the concept of active participation by patients in problem definition and determination of the treatment plan. A continuous educational process on the part of the case manager is required to close the gap in understanding of the helping process and the expectations of roles and service outcomes. This process needs to be bi-directional as both the case manager and the client continue to adjust to one another.

The method whereby refugee clients present their needs and desires may be different from mainstream clients. Refugee clients are only ready to tell stories of their life once they feel safe. They may not articulate their emotions and thoughts or their reaction to their life events. Rather, they offer their emotional reactions and needs by narrating stories about their life in their country, their separations and losses, horrors of war and subsequent escape, etc. Story-telling is indirect and time-consuming. Listening to these stories empathetically can lead to a better understanding of clients and their worldview. It is also therapeutic to most refugee clients. When the worker listens to the client's life stories, s/he may want to structure data-gathering in the following manner: Lee (1990) provided an assessment model for Southeast Asian refugee families, which includes (1) assessment of major family stressors, (2) assessment of family strength, and (3) assessment of culturally specific responses to mental health problems.

A chronological history is also helpful in understanding the refugee client. Three major aspects of the family's migration history are:

1. Premigration experiences: life in the homeland; socioeconomic and educational background; traumatic events; and any significant losses.

2. Migration experiences: the escape process and life in a refugee camp.
3. Postmigration experiences: problems caused by language difficulties; financial worries; culture shock; reception experience; changes in family relationships.

It is very easy for evaluators to become overwhelmed by the multiple stressors in their clients' lives and focus solely on the clients' problems and deficits. However, it is equally important to identify the strengths possessed by clients and their families. The search for inherent strengths in clients will help workers develop interventions for them. The strengths may be endurance and perseverance through hardships beyond the usual human experiences, strong family ties, or strong senses of obligation and achievement orientation. As workers assess the stressors in their clients' lives and their demonstrated strengths, it is also necessary to assess the clients' own understanding of their mental health issues, and their expectations of the role of the service providers. Observation of a client's method of explaining the source of his or her condition and his or her own prescription for it will provide suggestions for interventions palatable to refugee clients. This also opens a door to a working relationship. The following example shows how crucial it is to engage clients in a helping relationship by responding to them on their own terms.

A Laotian male client became very disillusioned about life in the U.S. and stated that all he wanted from his case manager was help in finding information on how to return to Laos. He felt that once he was back in Laos, he would be fine. His case manager agreed to work on the client's priority issue as she coordinated other services for him. Her evaluation indicated a need for mental health services, social services for financial assistance, and a vocational program. As the pressing problems that troubled him eased with the services provided through case management, the client began reevaluating his plan to go back to Laos in a more rational manner.

DEPENDENCE VS. EMPOWERMENT

Transplantation from one society to another is a very stressful experience. The refugee experience is more stressful than voluntary migration, as it involves traumatic departure, unexpected and unwilling separation, and horror of wars and the migration process. One striking difficulty among many others is that these refugees suffer from personal losses in various aspect of their lives. Lee and Lu (1989) identified five types of losses associated with refugee status: (1) material losses, such as properties, business, career, and investment; (2) physical losses, such as disfigurement, physical injuries, hunger, and malnutrition; (3) spiritual losses, such as freedom to practice religion and support from the religious community; (4) loss of community support and cultural milieu; and (5) loss of family members, other relatives, and friends. These losses are traumatic and difficult or impossible to restitute. What probably devastates these people most, however, is their sense of a loss of control over their lives. They feel they have lost all with which they were familiar and had mastery over. Many think they will never again regain a sense of control over their environment, as illustrated below:

> A Vietnamese man in his early fifties said in a group session, "I wouldn't have any doubt in my ability to survive if I were in Vietnam. But I have no confidence at all that I will be able to survive in this country. I have no idea as to what I can do here."

The pressures to learn a new language and to secure financial means for survival in a new country are overwhelming. The culture shock the refugees have to deal with on top of the trauma they bring with them as emotional baggage from the past is often so debilitating that even the most motivated refugee can easily lose a will to fight the multi-layered barriers to survival in a newly adopted country. The strong senses of despair and disenfranchisement felt by refugee clients are sometimes manifested by dependence and adopting a passive sick person role. The level of despair is a good indicator of the prognosis for response to the interventions. Furthermore, an assessment regarding the specific causes of the despair will enhance the intervention strategies.

A successful intervention for refugee clients should involve efforts to help them regain a sense of mastery of their environment. It should include skills building that will enhance a sense of self-reliance or self-sufficiency. An investigation into the skills and experiences of refugee clients helps to prioritize the areas of assistance. The intervention will be most successful when it is directed at restoration of their strengths and value of their self-reliance. The strengths restored through case management will rekindle a hope in their lives and a will to strive. Case management also needs to involve efforts to reconstruct or link a support network. The network, which used to be comprised of extended families and provided emotional support as well as practical information, must be replaced by a new group of informal and formal networks.

TRUST-BUILDING

The establishment of trust is the key ingredient for all successful interventions. While trust is important in all therapeutic interventions, it is especially meaningful for the refugee population. Trust eroded for many refugees during the long years of wars and disintegration of their countries. The civil wars in those Indo-Chinese countries divided people against each other based on ideological differences. As a way of controlling people, political propagandists pitted people against their own people; the poor against the rich, the uneducated against the educated, sons against their fathers. The corruption among government officials during the chaos of wars ingrained the distrust of authority figures into the minds of the refugees. Oppressive governments under dictators and/or Communist regimes taught the refugees not only to distrust but also to fear their leaders.

In life within reeducation camps or under Communist regimes, trusting others and confiding true thoughts freely to others could be a lethal error placing their own lives and the lives of their families at risk. Illustrations of this ongoing mistrust are common:

A Vietnamese client in group therapy whispered to his therapist that another member in the same group had a Northern accent, implying his suspicion of the other person's possible affiliation with the North Vietnamese government.

The mistrust or fear of others is pervasive and affects refugees' daily lives. Life in the camps did not foster trust or communal cooperation. Rather, it reinforced the fear and mistrust of authorities or people in power. The guards of the refugee camps turned to bandits at nights. They terrorized and brutalized the refugees with the power their positions allowed. In order for the refugees to depart the camps for the third countries, some had to lie about themselves, familial relationships, their background, or their affiliation with people already in the third country. All of these past experiences have taught refugees to be cautious with anyone associated with government or similar organizations. They also learn to be slow to trust and not to disclose too much information about themselves. It is difficult for an outsider to earn the trust of refugee clients. First, Asian cultures discourage family problems being shared with outsiders. Problems are supposed to be taken care of within the extended family circle. It brings shame to the family if the problem is revealed to the community or if outside interventions are needed. Also, there is apprehension that outsiders who did not have similar experiences would not be able to understand them. Refugee clients think outsiders may not even believe what they report. Many patients have expressed this concern explicitly in evaluation sessions. They think their traumatic pasts are so extraordinary that few people would believe what they say. This sense of estrangement may also result from the clinical condition of Post-Traumatic Stress Disorder that many refugee clients suffer from. Constricted affect and feelings of detachment are some of the clinical features of PTSD. Those affected with this condition may have difficulty in connecting with someone at an affective level and developing genuine and trusting relationships.

Historical experience influences one's worldview. The last hundred years of Indo-Chinese history is a history of colonialization of the region by Western superpowers. How this history plays itself out in the helping relationship remains to be understood. However, it isn't too difficult to imagine the power disparity a client might feel with a non-Asian service provider and its implication to the trust issue. In order to enhance trust, case managers should pay attention to several areas. First, knowledge of the client's culture and respect for his or her background aids the case manager's understanding of the client and in establishing rapport. Respect for differences and genuine interest in learning about the client needs to be conveyed. At times, this may mean engaging in activities not practiced with other clients. For example, joining meals when invited or participating in cultural practices as simple as taking shoes off in their homes will communicate respect. These actions definitely enhance the relationship between the client and the case manager. Secondly, an understanding of the client's expectations of the service provider should be well incorporated in the intervention strategy. Refugee clients do not make a clear distinction of the different roles of physicians and other mental health professionals. They respect these authority figures and tend to accept their recommendations. In return, they expect the professionals to "take care of" or "cure" their problems. Chao (1992), in reviewing several Southeast Asian cultures, posits the role of a good psychotherapist as an "Expert of the Heart," and looks at role expectations exhibited by different groups. She cites "A good doctor is a good mother" among Vietnamese clients and "expert of the inner heart" among certain ethnic Chinese. The service provider can increase his/her credibility by "taking care of" the client's immediate needs through task-oriented, concrete services. The credibility of the case manager can also be established by credentials, or affiliation with a reputable organization.

The refugee client expects the service provider to assist with the concerns of his or her whole family, not just those of the "identified patient." The refugee client often expects the case manager to take care of all the problems that affect him or her. Flexibility and responsiveness on the part of the case manager is critical in working with refugee clients. The case manager's willingness to stretch his or her professional role and boundaries is again very important. Workers at ACMHS on some occasions have needed to respond to invitations and attend their client's weddings, birthdays, and funerals. The case manager, once he or she is trusted and respected, becomes a part of the extended family circle. The client may become offended if the case manager does not respond to the invitations.

Those occasions also provide the worker a unique opportunity to observe cultural practices, and support systems available, in a setting comfortable to the client.

A final suggestion is to assess the client in his or her own environment:

> A female client was observed to be very passive and helpless in a clinic setting. But later when interviewed at her home, she became a livelier and active participant. The clinic setting was probably intimidating or threatening. Also the setting might have been reinforcing her role as a helpless and sick person.

CULTURE-SYNTONIC TREATMENT INTERVENTION

Treatment intervention is most successful when the client cooperates. This is best elicited when the service is provided in a way that fits the client's expectations. Most of the time, refugee clients come with problems that are acute and require immediate attention. The case manager must respond in a crisis mode and bring resolution to the problems with concrete help. In the initial stage of treatment, task-oriented, timely intervention will help to develop a trusting relationship and increase credibility of the case manager. Cultural understanding of the client's beliefs can be incorporated into the intervention. Many refugee clients believe in fate and karma. Fatalism can be an adaptive coping mechanism when the client has to find ways to explain catastrophic events in his life. Fatalism helps people face and deal with adversities in life gracefully and try to find meaning in them.

Asians draw strength to endure difficult situations from a sense of obligation or sense of mission. By understanding these strengths, the case manager is able to encourage refugee clients to find a new meaning in life through economic success, or through encouraging good education for their children. New missions and dreams give them roles to take on and a sense of direction for the future. Refugee clients suffering from prolonged depression tend to dwell in the past and feel they do not have a future to look forward to.

For most Southeast Asian cultures, work is especially meaningful. A strong work ethic is regarded as a virtue. Work and economic success are a source of pride and self-worth. Particularly, it is the primary responsibility of a male to work and provide for his family. Work also addresses the issues of financial security and self-reliance. Vocational rehabilitation seems an approach that fits expectations of the refugee clients. It addresses the cultural values as well as unemployment issues prevalent among refugees. When leisure activities such as painting were offered to the refugee clients at ACMHS as a method of managing stresses and social isolation, some felt offended, thinking leisure activities were only for children. However, art projects that involved making practical items were better received since they were deemed useful and educational.

Programs that promote learning are especially well received by the refugee clients. For them, education was a means of social advancement in their country. The educated were well respected. Programs addressing various issues can be presented as "classes." Any efforts to help clients re-create their support networks will be well received. Refugee clients come from cultures that provided support from the extended family. The disruptive migration processes dissolved their indigenous support networks. The refugee families often attempt to reconstruct similar support networks by living with or near others from the same country of origin. They create a flexible extended family, maintaining a "comfort zone" for themselves.

Group treatment in a supportive format is well received by refugee clients since it addresses their need for a support system. The group is an effective vehicle to generate emotional support for participants. Unlike many Western groups, participants are encouraged to socialize outside the group. It also serves as a forum to exchange information vital for the recent arrival's adjustment, such as where to get medical care, how to secure affordable housing, and how to understand their acculturated teenagers. The group is also a natural place to practice social skills with other members and to overcome isolation and detachment resulting from PTSD.

Respect for folk healings and cultural practice aid in the relationship between clients and the case manager. Appropriate use of cultural practice along with case management services increases the treatment compliance and positive responses to the interventions.

A Mien male client had persistent depression. He believed his illness was a result of punishment for his failure to fulfill his obligation as the eldest son to his deceased father. He wanted to offer a ceremony conducted by a Mien shaman to appease the indignant soul of his deceased father. The case manager supported the client's plan and assisted him in the planning process, while also encouraging the client to comply with his psychiatric treatment. After the three-day-long ceremony, the client felt lifted from the guilt and became more appreciative of the understanding and support of the case manager.

ADVOCACY

Case management is a mechanism for ensuring a comprehensive program that will meet an individual's need for care by coordinating and linking the components of a service delivery system. The refugee client comes in with layers of problems that require ongoing, multi-disciplinary, and multiple community services. Services required by the refugee client include health and mental health, housing, income support, education, legal aids, transportation, and education. While the needs of the refugee client require access to various service programs, in many instances the programs crucial to meeting the needs of the client are not accessible for him or her due to language and cultural barriers. The case manager must adopt an advocacy role to ensure that the needs of the client are recognized and the services improve accessibility and adequacy. The case manager may need to assume the role of change agent and participate in community organization and resource-development activities to see that the requirements of the client are identified and understood by the service delivery system and that community action is initiated to meet particular needs.

The case manager working with refugee clients must also take an educator role, informing clients about their rights and entitlements, as well as educating them about the use of our political process to get their needs understood and met by the system. Refugee clients are not only unfamiliar with the system and political process but often times feel too insecure about their rights and status in the adopted country to advocate for themselves.

A Cambodian client who participated in a rally to protest the cutbacks in mental health resources experienced anxiety later for fear of government retaliation. Her case manager explained about the rights of every citizen to voice concerns and influence the decision-making process that affects them. The client subsequently became more appreciative of participating in a political process.

The case manager also needs to take on a community developer role. The refugee communities are in an early stage of development due to their newness to this country. There is tremendous need for leadership development and training for bilingual mental health professionals. This capacity-building in the community will contribute to empowerment of the community and adequacy of services. More effort needs to be invested in recruiting bilingual students from the refugee communities into graduate programs in social work and support for them to complete their training. This effort to retain them in the field is as critical. The few bilingual professionals present are very vulnerable to burn out due to the enormous pressure to perform and meet the overwhelming needs of their clients with the few resources available. Training of bilingual/bicultural professionals is critical in dealing with the problems of inadequate and inaccessible services. Cultivating indigenous leadership through advanced training is also the best way of empowering the underserved and underrepresented communities.

CONCLUSION

Working with Southeast Asian refugee groups poses a special challenge to service providers. This chapter has attempted to help professionals to better understand these groups and has suggested some intervention strategies. As one of the newest immigrant groups in the U.S., these refugees have much to teach us about their unique experiences and needs as well as what would constitute effective interventions.The Southeast Asian refugee groups present not only migration stresses common among an immigrant population, but also unprecedented trauma that compounds adjustment and the recovery process. Case managers can be easily overwhelmed when confronted by the multi-layered and all-pressing problems of their refugee clients. Lack of trained bilingual/bicultural professionals and service resources in general highlight the enormity of needs among the refugee groups.

The pre- and post-migration experiences of refugee clients have often exposed them to oppressive practices by government representatives. This history strongly suggests a need on the part of the service provider to empower the client. Many refugee clients resigned themselves to a dependent role after having gone through situations where their destinies were decided by someone else or their well-being was totally determined by others. A case manager needs to foster self-determination in clients through educational processes as well as through respect for their rights.

Comprehensive case management by someone who is clinically competent and knowledgeable about community resources is an essential modality for the successful outcome of services for refugee groups. Effective case managers need to be culturally competent with a good understanding of their clients' culture and life experiences. Bilingual skill is also an invaluable asset in working with refugee clients. The main roles/tasks of case managers can be summarized in three areas: service coordination, empowerment, and advocacy. Service coordination is an effort to facilitate clients' access to much-needed services. This coordination involves not only linking services but also cultural consultation to service providers to help them recognize the needs of a client and also to ensure the cultural appropriateness of the services provided. The bilingual skills of a case manager can open up a wide range of services previously inaccessible to the monolingual refugee client.

A case manager's role as an advocate is as important as the other two above-mentioned roles. Refugee groups are the newest and least established in the U.S. A case manager needs to undertake constant efforts to make the needs and inadequacies of existing resources known to the public and to policymakers and must be an unyieldingly advocate for improvements in service resources.

The final task is for case managers to take care of themselves both physically and emotionally. Working with groups who have such tremendous needs but such a paucity of resources is very exhausting and can become discouraging. It is important to network with other professionals in the same field for support and nurturance as well as to share information.

REFERENCES

Beiser, M. (1988). Influences of time, ethnicity and attachment on depression in Southeast Asian refugees. *American Journal of Psychiatry, 145,* 46-51.

Boehnlein, James K. (1987). Clinical relevance of grief and mourning among Cambodian refugees. *Social Science and Medicine, 25*(7), 766-772.

Chao, C. (1992). The inner heart: Therapy with Southeast Asian families. In: L. Vargas and J. Koss-Chioino (Eds.), *Working with Culture: Psychotherapeutic Interventions with Ethnic Minority Children and Adolescents.* San Francisco: Jossey- Bass.

Feleppa, R. (1986). Emics, etics, and social objectivity. *Current Anthropology, 27*(3), 243-255.

Fox, R. (1985). The Indochinese: Strategies for health survival. *International Journal of Social Psychiatry, 30,* 285-291.

Gong-Guy, E. (1987). California Southeast Asian Mental Health Needs Assessment. California State Department of Mental Health.

Kinzie, J.D. (1985). Cultural aspects of psychiatric treatment with Indochinese refugees. *The American Journal of Social Psychiatry, 1,* 47-53.

Kinzie, J.D. and Boe, J.J. (1989). Post Traumatic Psychosis among Cambodian Refugees. *Journal of Traumatic Stress, 2,* 185-197.

Kinzie. J.D., Sack, W.H., Manson, S., and Rath, B. (1986). The psychiatric effects of massive trauma on Cambodian children. *Journal of American Academic Child Psychiatry, 25,* 370-376.

Knoll, T. (1982). *Becoming Americans.* Portland: Coast to Coast Books.

Lee, E. (1990). Family therapy with Southeast Asian families. In M.P. Mirkin (Ed.), *The Social and Political Contexts of Family Therapy.* New York: Allyn and Bacon.

Lee, E. and Lu, F. (1989). Assessment and therapy of Asian-American survivors of mass violence. *Journal of Traumatic Stress, 12,* 93-120.

Loo, C., Tong, B., and True, R. (1989). A bitter bean: Mental health status and attitudes in Chinatown. *Journal of Community Psychology, 17,* 283-298.

Lorenzo, M.K. and Adler, D.A. (1984). Mental health services for Chinese in a community health center. *Social Casework: The Journal of Contemporary Social Work, 65,* 609.

McGoldrick, M. (1982). Ethnicity and family therapy: An overview. In M. McGoldrick, J. Pearce, and J. Giordano (Eds.), *Ethnicity and Family Therapy.* 3-30. New York: The Guilford Press.

Miller, G. (1983). Case management: The essential service. In C.J. Sanborn (Ed.), *Case management in Mental Health Services.* 3-15. Binghamton, NY: The Haworth Press.

O'Hare, W. (1990). A new look at Asian Americans. *American Demographics, 12*(10), October.

Rozée, P.D. and Boemel, G.V. (1989). The psychological effects of war trauma and abuse on older Cambodian refugee women. *Women and Therapy, 8*(4), 23-49.

Snowden, L.R. and Cheung, F. (1990). Use of inpatient mental health services by members of ethnic minority groups. *American Psychologist, 45,* 347-355.

Strand, P.J. and Jones, W. (1985). *Indochinese Refugees in America.* Durham, NC: Duke University Press.

Sue, S. (1977). Community mental health services to minority groups: Some optimism, some pessimism. *American Psychologist, 32,* 616-624.

Sue, S., Fujino, D.C., Hu, L., Takeuchi, D.T., and Zane, N.W. (1991). Community mental health services for ethnic minority groups: A test of the cultural responsiveness hypothesis. *Journal of Consulting and Clinical Psychology, 59,* 533-540.

Szule, T. (1980). The refugee explosion. *New York Times Magazine,* Section 6, 136-141.

Williams, C.L. (1985). The Southeast Asian refugees and community mental health. *Journal of Community Psychology, 13,* 258-268.

Chapter 7

Clinical Case Management with Severely Mentally Ill African Americans

Valerie Roxanne Edwards

INTRODUCTION

Though the etiology of mental illness may be a mysterious consequence of genetic disorder and/or early life trauma, it has been
firmly established that episodes of the illness are precipitated by
stressful life events. Thus, it is all the more regrettable that persons
with mental illness have more than their share of problems in living.
Many of the psychiatrically disabled do not have the personal
resources to maintain independent living. The inability to provide
for basic needs such as food, shelter, and urgent health care can be
stressful for anyone. For those less able to cope, it is often a disaster.
It is typical to utilize support systems in times of crisis. However,
several studies have shown that characteristics of personal networks
are problematic among chronically mentally ill individuals. For
example, the size of their personal networks are only half of that
which is normal for the general population (13 for the psychiatric as
compared to 25 for the general population). This study by Tolsdorf
(1976) showed that for psychiatric patients, twice as many of their
ties are with kin than is the case with chronic medical patients.
Consequently, hospitalization is often used as compensation for
these deficits in the patient's support network rather than for its
unique therapeutic functions (Cutler and Tatum, 1983). Methods of
disengaging hospitals from this role are a challenge for community
mental health (CMH) systems. For African Americans, this challenge is particularly great. African Americans are overrepresented

among those involuntarily hospitalized, yet underserved in community care. This, as well as the chronic shortage of acute and sub-acute beds in the CMH system, has been the impetus for increased focus on the use of the client's social networks. For African Americans, the community should be particularly well utilized. A ramification of racism and its attendant issues–poverty, dearth of resources, and the strong African value of the community pulling together to support its members–the use of informal networks is a relatively rich recourse for African Americans who suffer from a psychiatric disability (Lawson, 1985). This chapter explores the unique cultural features of African environments in the U.S., and how they can best be employed to help persons with psychiatric illnesses live in the community. How racism has influenced mental health care to African Americans will also be considered, as well as how non-Africans can best provide culturally competent care.

AFRICENTRIC PERSPECTIVE

There is a breadth of family configurations, economic classes, and vocations that make up African-American communities. There is no single profile of any given African American's thoughts or feelings. There is, however, an aggregate of values and a worldview distinctive to Africans that is expressed in their many communities in the U.S. (White and Parham, 1990). Culturally sensitive case management requires adopting methods that are responsive to the values and worldview typically held by people of African descent. This is what is meant by an Africentric approach. A prominent feature of African culture is the priority given to the collective over the individual. Solutions for an individual are not limited to what can be found within an individual, an immediate family, or even an extended family. The strength of any given person is a *function* of his or her community alliance. Power is understood to increase for all if it increases for one. This is in great contrast to the Eurocentric perspective, which implies that power has an economic dynamic; that for one to have more power it must have been taken or lost from someone else. The African-American community takes pride in the successes of it's individuals as well as sharing in the shame of failure. Community resources are pooled to pull a family through economic crises with rent parties, for example, or child care or household duties are taken over by neighbors due to the poor health of a family caretaker. The whole unit, such as a family or a church, will pitch in to support the advanced education of one member.

AN AFRICENTRIC MATRIX OF SUPPORT

The way in which culture is most clearly expressed and transmitted is through family. It is also how the collective value is best demonstrated. Of course, there is not one kind of family configuration for people of African descent. There are families that function primarily on the nuclear level. But in part because of discrimination, extended family networks remain prevalent (Pinderhughes, 1982). Extended family means inclusion of persons other than the parents and direct offspring. It is multigenerational, with central involvement of other relatives whether they live in the home or not (Edwards, 1994). The aspect that best characterizes extended families is the allocation of chores of daily life. This includes help in monitoring and disciplining children, participation in family decisions, and tacit acceptance of wayward relatives into the home. It often means parental tasks for some or all of the children may be filled by grandparents, uncles, aunts, or older siblings or cousins. Collective responsibility involves, when necessary, individuals or the immediate family sacrificing for the sake of the extended family as a whole (Boyd-Franklin, 1989). It would not be unusual for immediate families to double up in a time of crisis such as a loss of job or sudden migration.

African-American families are often a matrix of relationships. Cousins raised together will relate as siblings, grandparents may be closer to their grandchildren than are the parent(s). Family configurations may also include "play relatives." These members are not biologically related yet identify as a family without benefit of a formal adoption process; they are brought together out of mutual need. Such alliances are a result in part of African Americans being denied access to formal social institutions. Because orphaned black children were neglected by society and few black adults could afford or could trust the formal adoption process, new families have been created that in every way are as binding as genetic ties. Many other "play" relationships are an expression of the collective value of African Americans (White and Parham, 1990). Many such alliances were built in the 1940s when there was a mass migration of Southern blacks to the North. Recent transplants, often the first members of their families to arrive in a new state, would seek camaraderie by developing relationships of mutual support similar to those they would have with their own kin if they were present. These relationships are especially likely with folks from their native region or state.

While recognizing its many values, it is important not to idealize the support of extended families and the community. Flexibility can be double-edged. Flexibility in the caretaker role in African-American culture can result in life-long splits between mothers and offspring, or jealousy between siblings due to the mother's decision that one or more of her children is to live with and be raised by someone other than her. The issues of abandonment, favoritism, and self-esteem can arise not only during childhood but can re-emerge throughout the adult years. It is not unusual for stress in the family to exacerbate these issues. A case manager sensitive to these dynamics can recognize the signs early on and help family members deal with them as they arise. In the following case, the case manager took care to consider the client's view of family and to include them in the treatment plan.

Arlene is a 19-year-old African-American female diagnosed with schizophrenia, paranoid type. She had been brought into the emergency room by the Highway Patrol. They found her delusional and disorganized, walking on the freeway. Fairly recompensated after a four-week hospital stay, she returned to her grandmother's home. At baseline she continued to exhibit poor insight, poor judgement, and poverty of speech. She was, however, agreeable to the plan of follow-up once the goal was described as staying out of the hospital. The case manager proposed to Arlene that the people she most relied on be included in the plan and delivery of treatment. She readily agreed. Arlene identified her mother, paternal grandmother, and her grandmother's sister as the people to involve. At 17, several months after the onset of her illness, her mother sent her from their East Coast home to live with her paternal grandmother in San Francisco, whom she had met only once before, ten years earlier. Also in the home was an invalid stepgrandfather who was confined to the bed in the living room, her 11-year-old half sister and her 13-year-old half brother. Her father occasionally lives in the home, but is periodically ordered out by his mother when he once again starts stealing from her to support his drug habit. Her paternal grandmother has a sister with whom she had a close but highly competitive relationship and who lived nearby. Arlene would bounce between her grandmother's and her aunt's home, depending on which one she was getting along with best. Her aunt cared for a three-month-old foster child who suffered from brain damage and was blind in one eye. The aunt also had a son living with her who, by description, had many schizoid and explosive personality traits. These family members were unaware of Arlene's psychiatric illness until after she arrived. They were confused and angered by her behavior. Arlene kept insisting that "they are not my family." Making interventions at the family level was key to successful outpatient care for Arlene.

First, a treatment plan was developed that identified the many problems of the family. Assessment of the medical, substance abuse, and psychiatric concerns of other family members was made and problem solving and linkage to the appropriate referrals was done. The case manager monitored the other family situations, always taking into account how these concerns affected Arlene's mental status. But the case management interventions focused on the issues most directly influencing Arlene. The four most salient issues of the treatment plan were:

1. Educating Arlene and her grandmother and great aunt about the nature of her illness.
2. Building the emotional bond between Arlene and her West Coast family, particularly between Arlene and her grandmother, by scheduling with them weekly meetings to address recent conflicts.
3. The great aunt and grandmother participated in an Africentric multi-family group. They addressed issues between them re-

garding care and the value conflicts around them. They were able to agree on parameters that eliminated the splitting that occurred between them around Arlene's care.
4. Working with the grandmother, Arlene, and, by telephone, Arlene's mother, on the issues of abandonment, dumping, and betrayal that was felt between them.

Arlene's rate of hospitalization dropped from three times in six months to less than one time a year before she moved back with her mother on the East coast. She returns regularly for family visits.

For many non-African families, the lack of contact between Arlene and her paternal family would have precluded an unfamiliar relative who was having some life difficulty from being welcomed to live in their home. The case manager was able to look past the protests of Arlene and her new family and recognize the hidden signs of alliances that were born from shared family and cultural values. It was these values that were the foundation of the relationship and upon which trust was built.

The feature that commands the most attention in the larger society and indeed is the greatest cause for concern in the African community is the growing number of single parent homes and the rise of teenage pregnancies. In 1965, 25 percent of black households were headed by a single parent. It is more than twice that today and continues to rise at a rate that parallels the rise in white communities. Factors contributing to this include the feminization of poverty created by no-fault divorce, the rising divorce rate, and the increase in couples living together without legal marriage. Some teenage girls, many of whom were born to teenaged mothers, view childbirth as the only creative and financial opportunity possible in their life. Typically it perpetuates a cycle of despair.

Twenty-nine-year-old Adrienne was diagnosed with schizoaffective disorder. Three times over the last six months she was in the ICU for failure to follow her diet and insulin regime for her diabetes. This was usually followed by a psychiatric inpatient stay that usually ended by her winning her court hearing. After spending or losing her SSI, she spent most of every month living on the street unless her 31-year-old sister Victoria provided her shelter. Adrienne's case manager made a visit to Victoria's house with the hopes of securing it as a permanent home for Adrienne. The home visit revealed that Victoria was the only adult in a home for her 15-year-old daughter and her infant granddaughter, as well as Adrienne's ten-year-old son, 14-year-old daughter, and infant granddaughter. Victoria had cared for their mother, who was also diabetic and "depressed," after the mother was released from the state hospital until her death ten years later. Victoria felt overwhelmed and resentful of Adrienne, who was often verbally abusive and a significant drain on the family's income. She also felt guilty for not doing more for Adrienne. At first the case manager also felt overwhelmed, but then he decided to take the long view. He validated Victoria's belief that Adrienne would be best served in the hospital. Together they recommended to community mental health practitioners and the courts that Adrienne be stabilized using long-term hospitalization, after which she would be placed in residential care with regular visits to the family.

When working with such families, clinicians may encounter premature grandmothers who are the primary caretakers for several generations of their family. These families may already be stressed to the limit. In addition to helping the individual and family understand and cope with the illness, clinicians must be prepared to address the chronic depression of caretakers overwhelmed by the stress of the family's multitude of problems (Lawson, 1985). African-American nuclear families also have unique features. An example of this is the role of women. Perhaps it is a consequence of black women historically working outside of the home that husband and wife have a more egalitarian relationship, sharing in child care and decisions about how money is used.

Another distinct feature of African-American families is the role of children. The children often take on parental tasks in that they are helpful with chores and take a significant role in the care of their siblings. The assignments are less likely to be gender identified. Though a child may have parental tasks, this does not mean they have a parentified role. Their role is appropriate as long as they do not have responsibilities inconsistent with their age, and power and authority in the family are clearly and properly aligned. A broader distribution of power and authority than is found in many non-African-American families also contributes to the flexibility.

THE INTERSECTION OF FAMILY
AND COMMUNITY SUPPORT

The family and communal roles are so continuous in African communities that it is not possible to address one aspect fully without including features of the other. The point at which the two most overlap is in the role of caretaker of children. It is considered the responsibility of the whole community to oversee the welfare of children. The names of the children and their behavior on the street is considered a public concern. As a result, the parents may hear from several sources on their way home about their child's misbehavior. Depending on the family as well as the community involved, the child may be disciplined several times before the parents have an opportunity to hear about the situation. This sense of investment in the welfare of the family members of others is also evident when illness renders an adult unable to care for themselves.

In the following case every facet of the informal networks was utilized before the community sought help from the formal social service institutions.

> Bernice, a woman who was developmentally disabled and suffered from intermittent explosive disorder, had her first introduction to the community mental health system at age 58. She had lived with her family in Arkansas and reported working in a cafe owned by her family. Her 84-year-old uncle with whom she currently lived, and who was clearly fond of her and valued her company, indicated that she did little more than hold a dishrag all day in the cafe. He reported that the extended family moved her to San Francisco to care and be cared for by this invalid uncle after local familial caretakers died. Bernice's first contact with community mental health was an involuntary hospitalization as a danger to others. She would tease neighborhood children as they passed her home. Once they were no

longer intimidated, the children retaliated by taunting Bernice, provoking in her fear and anger. Upon investigation, it was learned that the hospitalization was initiated by the neighbors, who feared that her behavior was placing her in danger. CMH and social services became involved, providing public health nursing support and transportation to clinic appointments for the uncle, who could no longer walk and was legally blind. Even after arranging this, the neighbors remained vigilant, making sure social workers would not institutionalize Bernice, addressing the problem of individual children with their families, and insisting that the agencies find a solution without involving the police. The community's efforts resulted in Bernice and her uncle moving to senior citizens' housing that created a safe distance between Bernice and school children, was equipped to assist with the uncle's physical disabilities, and was staffed with counselors to intervene regarding psychological and social concerns.

Bernice's situation illustrated the many personal and community resources that may be overlooked by a professional case worker: Bernice's contributions to her family and community by tending to the cafe and caring for her uncle, and the problem-solving capacity of the extended family and the community. These actions made the difference between Bernice being a viable part of the community and being an institutionalized burden to the state.

A negative consequence of this flexibility is that the presence of more options can increase the risk that a problem will be managed–by moving the person (and the problem) from one place to another–but never confronted or resolved.

Denise, a 30-year-old African-American woman with a severe borderline personality disorder that included many cognitive deficits, for several months avoided needed inpatient care by trading on the good will and familiarity her family had built over the last 20 years of living in the community. She was readily taken in, first by family, later by friends. As her behavior became more bizarre and known among her network, she sought the aid of people she knew but had not had contact with for a number of years who thus were unaware of the severity of her difficulties. She eventually was hospitalized, but only after her behavior escalated to enticing neighborhood children from their home for several hours at a time.

It would have benefited Denise and her community if the intervention was done sooner through the community clinic rather than later on an inpatient ward. The laws governing grave disability as well as the community's willingness to accommodate her bizarre behavior contributed to, rather than prevented, her decompensation. An Africentric approach means intervening on a family and community level as well as with the individual. Regular community outreach and education by community mental health was indicated. Such primary prevention would have increased the community awareness of mental illness and its manifestations and perhaps led one of Denise's caretakers to seek help from community mental health.

The matrix of community and extended family creates stability and emotional support. Overall it allows for greater flexibility, role diffusion, stability, and emotional support than a nuclear configuration. Though the stressors too often remain severe, these qualities provide amelioration for the pressures of drug use, premature childbearing, legal difficulties, and other consequences of racism and poverty.

THE DYNAMICS OF BICULTURALISM

Though there are numerous biological and genetic traits that constitute racial identity, their significance bears little weight compared to those created by convention, social policy, and racist laws. Historically the majority of the offspring of mixed African-European ancestry were a result of rape by white men of African women. The North American sanctions against intimate relationships between races has been so great that the union of marriage (so called miscegenation) and therefore of the offspring was illegal in most states until a little more than 30 years ago. Many states created laws that dictated racial assignment. Louisiana, for example, defined Negroes as any persons with 1/32 or more of African ancestry. This climate rendered moot the issue of multiracial identity.

At the present time, however, there is a growing number of people in our society who refuse to identify themselves with just one racial category. Unlike in the past, when a child conceived by one white parent and one African-American parent was as estranged from the dominant culture as other African Americans, multiracial children who are being raised by both parents today are often included, with varying degrees of acceptance, in the extended families of each parent. They are therefore a product of both cultures.

The greatest struggle for multi-racial people is living in a society that refuses to recognize their duality. Even their parents, each of whom can guide them through the issues of his or her own race, are unable to lend insight to the biracial identity. Even in African-American communities, the prevailing thought is that if you look black, the dominant culture will relate to you as they do to all blacks regardless of parentage, and therefore, in their minds, it is only the African ancestry that should have meaning to someone of mixed heritage (Thomas and Sillen, 1971). This assumes that the only importance culture has is political. The elements of culture, however, not only influence one's relation to others, but the relationship with one's self as well.

Preconceived notions of "black ways" are as notorious within African-American communities as in the larger society. Most African Americans, at one time or another, are questioned by their peers about their racial authenticity because of their appearance, their ideas, or their speech. For biracial children, being the target of this form of self-oppression tends to be more extreme and intimidating than for those who do not have a non-African parent. They may also encounter blacks who are attracted to them because of their non-African features. They typically experience parallel dynamics with Euro-Americans who seek them out because they see people of mixed heritage as "exotic." There are others, in many cases family members such as their white grandparents, who accept them when they are toddlers but become critical and ultimately estranged from them when they become teenagers who listen to the kind of music or have the kind of friends the grandparents view as belonging more to their African-American heritage (Ordway, 1973). Such conflicts can provoke a reaction in biracial children of rigid and exaggerated behaviors of one culture or the other in an attempt to force their family and the general public to accept them as monoracial persons. Clinicians working with biracial clients will do their best work if they create an environment in which their client can explore and define their culture for themselves.

THE ROLE OF RELIGION

Spiritual institutions are another major source of social support in the African-American community. Many of our clinical goals for clients–insight, self-esteem, and peace of mind–are among the rewards people find in religion. Traditionally this has been the church. In addition to its role in presenting and describing the Christian ethic, it fuels a cohesion and a strong social identity. The church has been historically unique to African Americans in that it is the only place in which they have been allowed to congregate without fear of reprisal. Though there are many devout Christians in the African-American community, this precious feature significantly contributes to the church being as much of a social as a spiritual forum. It has been able to capitalize on the psychological distance between blacks and whites (we are bound not only by our culture but by our experience of racism). Because African-American church congregations exist with relatively little vigilance from the dominant society, it is a logical ground swell of social networking such as aiding in business development or in finding a potential spouse, and as the source of political action. It is of little surprise that so much of the civil rights movement was founded and operated from countless churches across the nation.

Another more recent development in spiritual congregation of African Americans has been adherence to Muslim traditions as practiced by the Nation of Islam and orthodox Islam. The movement began in the black community in the mid-1930s and has rapidly grown to include millions of African Americans. Both sects preach ethnic pride, self-reliance, and economic independence. It has been the route to freedom from substance abuse, crime, and poverty for many, especially black male youth (Sylvester Monroe Emerge, 1994). Clinicians should help clients access their faith by reinforcing use of the resources that have been helpful in the past as well as exploring new ways to utilize spiritual support.

THE IMPACT OF RACISM ON MENTAL HEALTH CARE DELIVERY

Historically, mental health professionals have been no less immune to racism than the larger society. The professional literature has reflected a commonly held assumption that blacks lacked the intellectual capacity for talk therapy, or "insight." Consequently there has been a high reliance on long-term hospitalization, an over-use of medication, and inordinate use of restraints. To date, racism continues to be a barrier to proper treatment. African-Americans continue to have a higher rate of misdiagnosis and poorer treatment outcomes (Snowden and Todman, 1982). Fueled in part by clinician inability to engage with the client, blacks are over-diagnosed with schizophrenia and underdiagnosed as suffering from affective disorders (Pinderhughes, 1973). Unable to differentiate the higher, but socially appropriate, vigilance of African Americans from clinical paranoia, clinicians further overpathologize this population (Grier and Cobbs, 1968). Blacks are more likely to be overmedicated simply out of their provider's *fear* of violence or agitation rather than for their behavior or for the clinical picture of them that has been established (Adebimpe, 1981). There is unequal access to mental health for all non-white groups in relation to Euro-Americans, but is most extreme for African Americans. Even when access is equal, the treatment is not responsive; that is, not a proper fit between treatment technique and the client's lifestyle, tending to emphasize social control over client-centered treatment.

Racism in mental health is particularly debilitating for African Americans who suffer from severe mental illness. Their healthy counterparts who, through school and work are often immersed in Euro-American culture and its people, become very skilled at navigating the racial divide and are able to facilitate the interaction for their less skilled Euro-American peers. Those African Americans with severe and persistent mental illness, however, have a much more isolative lifestyle. For this segment of the African-American population, negotiating a white-dominated environment is much more perilous. An involuntary hospitalization is a good example. It may be the only time in many years that a member of this population speaks to someone who is not of African descent. For them the food isn't right, the air smells funny. In addition to having a psychiatric disability, they are as poorly skilled as or more poorly skilled than their non-African clinician at cross-cultural communication. Consequently, they are a more severe and more frequent victim of the assumptions and fear and inferior treatment that result from racism. They see societal racial dynamics recreated in the hospital, where people of their own race are most often employed at the lowest levels of the clinical hierarchy and are charged with controlling behavior and forcibly administering medications. Reasonable, culturally sensitive practice dictates that attention be paid to the racial makeup and culture of the residential care facility when making a post-discharge referral, and that this aspect be addressed with the client. Once this gap in treatment is recognized, it is not difficult to see why blacks are more likely to be discharged from the hospital sooner, less likely to be linked to aftercare, and then identified as not being motivated for treatment.

It is not surprising, therefore, that the first contact for many African Americans seeking mental health care is likely to be in the emergency room; that 50 percent of non-white clients drop out of treatment after the first session, or that blacks will drop out 66 percent of the time when they have a white counselor (Sue, 1977). The more similar the race and class is, the more willing the therapist is to explore the inner feelings and behavior of the client. That is not to say, however, that non-African-American clinicians cannot perform culturally competent assessments. Studies show that the clinician's knowledge of the client's social class also influences evaluations (Carkuff and Pierce, 1965), and such factors should be carefully considered.

CONCLUSION

There are many ways to avoid racist practice in mental health care delivery. As a consequence of the *lack of* access to formal institutions and the high reliance on informal networks, an inordinate percentage of African-American clients make their first presentation to the mental health system in the emergency room. Though this is the first time they seek formal help, it does not mean there have not been organized, realistic attempts made to resolve the problem. This information will reveal the support network available to the client, which may be utilized to create a successful treatment plan.

In treatment issues with black clients, it helps to reframe behavior, to view the client as having appropriate reluctance rather than resistance, so that the situation can appear workable for the clinician. Without this, there is little hope of it appearing workable to the client; s/he may have spent years trying to solve the problems without success. There are many barriers to treatment: childcare, transportation, and others. We should treat them as real, solvable, problems. Clinicians should consider home visits, child respite programs, other formal supports, and above all, should respect clients and their families. They are not experts at psychiatry, but in our relationships with them, they are the experts on their culture and their families. We should consider them a resource, and try to be aware of the unique aspects of their community without making unwarranted assumptions. It is also imperative that we consult, on an ongoing basis, with professionals of the same culture.

It is crucial for the case manager to have, for her or himself, a balanced perspective on race and culture. This is necessary for recognizing how racism affects its victims. Essential to quality care is the case manager's ability to engage in discussion and exploration of the subject, particularly how it affects the problems the client has come to solve. Real explorations of the issues may be inhibited by the white clinician's feelings of guilt and shame (another ramification of racism). A therapeutic relationship is possible only if the case manager is able to tolerate the emotions that the client expresses about the bigotry s/he has experienced.

In order for case managers to access the unique environmental features of the African-American (or any other) community, they must "raise the frame" of the usual questions in a way that allows clients to be most responsive. They must ask who lives/lived in the home vs. questions of marriage. The interview must detail who was their primary caretaker and who, if anyone, helped their primary caretaker raise them. The clinician must then juxtapose the parental figures, and explore how their roles affect current family dynamics. If the clinician takes the opportunity to ask questions about who the client consults before making important decisions, otherwise unknown sources of support, spirituality, and power within the family and larger network may be revealed. All of these ingredients combine to contribute to culturally competent clinical case management with African-American clients.

REFERENCES

Adebimpe, V. R. (1981). Overview: White norm and psychiatric diagnosis of black patients. *American Journal of Psychiatry, 138,* 279-285.

Boyd-Franklin, N. (1989). *Black Families in Therapy: A Multisystems Approach.* New York: The Guilford Press.

Carkuff, R. R. and Pierce, R. (1965). Differential effects of therapist race and social class upon patient depth of self exploration in the initial clinical interview. *Journal of Consulting Psychology, 31,* 632-634.

Cutler, D. and Tatum, E. (1983). Networks and the chronic patient. In D. Cutler (Ed.), *Effective Aftercare for the 1980's.* San Francisco: Jossey-Bass.

Edwards, V. E. (1994). Understanding culture as a process. In R. Surber (Ed.), *Clinical Case Management: A Guide to Comprehensive Treatment of Serious Mental Illness.* Thousand Oaks, CA: Sage Publications, Inc.

Grier, W., and Cobbs, P. (1968). *Black Rage.* New York: Bantam Books.

Lawson, W. (1985). Chronic mental illness and the black family. In M. Fullilove (Ed.), *The Black Family: Mental Health Perspectives.* San Francisco: Proceedings of the second annual Black Task Force Mental Health Conference.

Ordway, J. (1973). Some emotional consequences of racism for whites. In C. Willie, B. Brown, and B. Kramer (Eds.), *Racism and Mental Health.* Pittsburgh, PA: University of Pittsburgh Press.

Pinderhughes, C. (1973). Racism and psychotherapy. In C. Willie, B. Brown, and B. Kramer (Eds.), *Racism and Mental Health.* Pittsburgh, PA: University of Pittsburgh Press.

Pinderhughes, E. (1982). Afro-American families and the victim system. In M. McGoldrick, J. Pierce, and J. Giordano (Eds.), *Ethnicity and Family Therapy.* New York: The Guilford Press.

Snowden, L. and Todman, P. (1982). The psychological assessment of blacks: New and needed developments. In E. Jones and S. Korchon (Eds.), *Minority Mental Health* (193-226). New York: Praeger.

Sue, S. (1977). Community mental health for minority groups: Some optimism, some pessimism. *American Psychologist, 32,* 616-624.

Sylvester Monroe Emerge (1994). *The Fruits of Islam: Muslim Faith Grows in Followers and Respect.*

Thomas, A. and Sillen, S. (1971). *Racism and Psychiatry.* New York: Carol Publishing Group.

Tolsdorf, C. (1976). Social networks, support, and coping: An exploratory study. *Family Process, 15*(4), 407-417.

White, J. and Parham, T. (1990). *The Psychology of Blacks: An African-American Perspective* (Chapter 2) Englewood Cliffs, NJ: Prentice-Hall, Inc.

Chapter 8

Gender as Culture: Competent Case Management for Women with Major Psychiatric Disorders

Joanne R. Wile
Anna M. Spielvogel

INTRODUCTION

It is with good reason that we introduce clients by their age, ethnicity, and gender, as in "this is a 45-year-old African-American female." All three variables work together to provide a context for the psychosocial understanding of the person. Age has a profound influence on psychiatric issues. The female's life cycle is more extended and medically complex than that of the male. Ethnicity influences the formation of psychiatric symptoms, social circumstances, and reproductive issues. Finally, in some cases gender will provide a protection and in others a vulnerability to the development of certain medical and psychiatric disorders.

Because male research subjects and men's psychological experiences have been considered the normative standard, the content of medical and psychiatric assessment and treatment has failed to address the complex variables affecting women's lives.

This chapter will include examples of how a woman's psychological development contributes to certain strengths and vulnerabilities in her social relationships; the reproductive issues that emerge through her life cycle; the impact of violence against women; and gender differences in psychiatric disorders, substance abuse, and HIV infection.

MAJOR AREAS OF EVALUATION

The gender-sensitive case manager needs to take into account how the following factors develop and interact in women's lives.

Biological Factors

A woman's hormonal changes affect both physical and psychological symptoms. This is most commonly seen in presentations of late luteal phase dysphoric disorder, also known as premenstrual tension syndrome. Hormones influence medication levels and medication responses. Recent research (Yonkers et al., 1992) suggests that young women may require lower doses of antipsychotic agents and benzodiazepines than young men.

Women's reproductive functions, family planning choices, course of pregnancy, childbirth, and the postpartum, and passage through menopause all require special consideration. Since psychotropic medication is prescribed for women twice as frequently as for men (Ashton, 1991), psychiatrists, therapists, and case managers need to discuss each female client's pregnancy plans. Physicians and others need to be aware of the effects of various medications on the fetus during the course of the woman's pregnancy.

General health monitoring for women should include regular screening for breast and cervical cancer and a complete pelvic examination. The need for HIV screening should be carefully evaluated with each woman.

Psychological Factors

Women's early development, with the close early bond to the mother, usually leads to a greater attentiveness to interpersonal relationships, and furthermore, to a lesser expression of physical aggression (Jordan, Surrey, and Kaplan, 1991). These empathic abilities present both a strength and a vulnerability. Women's self-esteem is often strongly influenced by vicissitudes in their relationships. Repeated disappointments, losses, and traumas contribute to higher rates of depressive, borderline, somatoform, phobic, and anxiety disorders (Waites, 1993).

Social Factors

Gender biases which continue to keep women's roles restricted contribute to the high level of poverty among women. When women live alone or with their children, they will either receive limited public assistance payments or, if they are employed, will earn less than men. In 1990 women earned 66 cents for every dollar earned by men (Sprague, 1991). This means that single female heads of households have lower earnings than both male heads of households and two-parent households. The National Coalition for the Homeless estimates that single mothers and children comprise 40 percent of the homeless population (Sprague, 1991). The feminization of poverty is a result of both social and economic forces. Sidel (1986) identifies "the weakening of the traditional nuclear family; the rapid growth of female-headed families; the continuing existence of a dual-labor market that actively discriminates against female workers; a welfare system that seeks to maintain its recipients below the poverty line; the time-consuming yet unpaid domestic responsibilities of women, particularly child care" (p. 15) as contributory. The high societal tolerance for the sexual abuse, harassment, and battering of women also fosters the disadvantaged position of women.

HEALTH CARE NEEDS

A number of health care settings throughout the country have developed treatment programs that incorporate the biological, psychological, and social factors in women's lives. Since women utilize both hospital and community services, clinicians must be familiar with the range of interventions in both settings.

One hospital-based group, the Women's Issues Consultation Team, established in 1984 in the Department of Psychiatry at San Francisco General Hospital, initially focused on providing optimal care to pregnant women with severe and persistent mental disorders. Since its inception, the group has expanded to study the effects of trauma; the impact of pregnancy, birth, and other reproductive events; the needs of special subpopulations of women; and gender-related patterns of substance abuse. The patient population has included women from each of the major psychiatric diagnostic classifications. The treatment team has developed gender-sensitive protocols for medical, reproductive, and diagnostic evaluations. Much of the case material for this chapter is drawn from the experience of this team and its community providers.

Clinicians in both hospital and community settings have expressed concern that individuals with severe mental disorders receive inadequate medical care. Koranyi (1979) found that service providers were unaware of approximately half of the medical illnesses of the patients treated at a community mental health outpatient clinic. In a study of 42 outpatients in a Baltimore community mental health program, Roca, Breakey, and Fischer (1987) found that nearly half of the women clients had cervicitis or vaginitis, usually due to trichomonads. The 22 female subjects had a total of 76 problems. Only 26 percent of these problems were given appropriate attention and treatment. Handel (1985), in a survey of both state and general hospital psychiatric units, found that pelvic examinations were routinely deferred for female patients. The Women's Issues Consultation Team therefore asks all female patients whether they have had complete gynecological examinations and mammograms within the past year and, if they have not, offers this service.

> A European American woman with a diagnosis of schizoaffective disorder developed cervical cancer at age 50. At the time of detection it was inoperable. In spite of over 20 psychiatric hospitalizations and continuous outpatient treatment, she had not had a pelvic examination or pap smear in the last ten years. An intrauterine device had been in place for the last 15 years.

This client illustrates the difficulties some women will have obtaining gynecological care in the community. It is essential that case managers include these medical appointments in their outpatient care plans, so that they will make repeated efforts to remind or even accompany female clients to their appointments.

Some women are more receptive to examinations during a psychiatric hospitalization. After the initial inquiry about the last check-up, members of the Women's Issues Consultation Team will make daily requests for the patient to attend the women's clinic in the hospital to obtain these examinations. In addition to the frequent invitations to the patient, the psychiatric staff works closely with the gynecological service so that waiting periods will be short and the optimal treatment approach for a particular patient can be utilized.

Research on gender differences in medication responsiveness remains limited. Review of a number of studies suggests that the presence of estrogen and progesterone during women's reproductive years may contribute to their improvement on lower doses of neuroleptics and benzodiazepines compared to men in the same age group (Yonkers et al., 1992).

Since psychotropic medications affect the menstrual cycle, many female clients become confused and upset about menstrual abnormalities, such as amenorrhea. Studies indicate that from 50 to 90 percent of women on antipsychotic medication are amenorrheic (Sullivan and Lukoff, 1990). Apfel and Handel (1993) describe how a woman client and her psychiatrist agreed to monitor her psychotic symptoms closely and taper her neuroleptic medication until menstruation resumed. This may not be possible with all clients. The case manager must be familiar enough with these concerns to advocate for the female client with her psychiatrist.

FAMILY PLANNING

Studies indicate that since the era of deinstitutionalization, fertility rates of severely mentally ill women are beginning to approximate those of the general population. Coverdale and Aruffo (1989) found that 73 percent of 80 female psychiatric outpatients had been pregnant at least once. Thirty-three percent of these women had not used birth control at the time of their last intercourse, even though they stated that they did not wish to become pregnant. In a recent review of 93 women admitted to the Women's Issues Consultation Team in a one-year period, 67 percent had been pregnant at least one time, with an average of 2.6 pregnancies per woman. Twenty-one percent of the births of these subjects were terminated by therapeutic abortion. Seventy-four percent of the women did not have custody of their children.

Women's difficulties in effective family planning have a number of sources. The following example illustrates one such source: how the precipitous wish to have another child can be an attempt to fix other problems by becoming pregnant.

> Ms. D, a 41-year-old Asian-American married female, was living with her husband, eight-month-old daughter, and 19-year-old developmentally disabled son when she was admitted to the Women's Issues Consultation Team in an acute manic state. She was irritable, agitated, and combative.

Ms. D had stopped taking her lithium carbonate and neuroleptic medication two months prior to this admission when she made the decision to have another child. A number of factors influenced this plan. She felt jealous of her husband for spending more time away from home and assumed he was having an affair. She was feeling increasingly inadequate in taking care of their daughter. When her son began to pressure her for more spending money, she struck him. This led to the hospital admission.

After it was determined that she was not pregnant, Ms. D was re-started on lithium carbonate and the medication was titrated to a therapeutic level. Ten days after her admission, she informed the staff that she had sexual intercourse with another patient on the unit because she still wanted to get pregnant and was angry at her husband. Her medications were suspended until laboratory tests could confirm whether or not she was pregnant.

Mr. D, her 45-year-old Asian-American husband of 20 years, was invited to a conjoint meeting at the hospital with the case manager. The motivation to have a child was explored by both members of the couple in greater depth. Mr. D hoped that the pregnancy would stabilize his wife's mood and increase her satisfaction with him and the children. In response to her questions, he stated that he was not having an affair, but acknowledged that he had been more withdrawn. Ms. D spoke of her fear of losing her daughter to an involuntary placement because this had happened with her previous child. She wanted to get pregnant in anticipation of losing their daughter. Neither partner had shared their concerns this completely with the other or with the case manager.

Ms. D's history of decompensating when discontinuing her medication was reviewed with the couple. They also talked about the possible effects of lithium carbonate on the fetus in the first trimester and the risks of cardiovascular malformations (Spielvogel and Wile, 1986). The husband acknowledged his concerns about financial support of another child and wondered about whether they could do more to strengthen the family unit.

After several days of discussion, the couple decided not to have another child, and instead to improve their current family life. Ms. D re-entered her day treatment program and began attending parenting classes. The couple also requested that the case manager join them in a meeting with the extended family. Relatives had been actively supportive of the couple's wish to have another child. Mr. and Ms. D felt that further explanation of the possible exacerbation of Ms. D's psychiatric illness and the risks of medication effects on the fetus would help the family understand their change in plans. The case manager agreed, knowing the value of engaging the extended family in treatment issues (Gaw, 1993).

In a follow-up interview two years later, Ms. D reported that she and her husband were using birth control. She was continuing her medication and day treatment program, requiring no further hospitalizations. The two children remained in their care with even greater involvement from the extended family.

This individual and family crisis illustrates several issues relevant to the treatment of female clients:

1. Having a child and being a competent mother is as much a concern for women with major psychiatric disorders as it is for women in the general population. The case manager must be aware of the central importance of this issue.
2. Women with bipolar affective disorders are prone to impulsive sexual activity while in manic states. Repeated pregnancy screenings may be necessary during these episodes.
3. Lithium carbonate, the most effective medication for the treatment of bipolar affective disorders, is teratogenic, causing cardiovascular malformations in about seven percent of fetuses (Miller, 1991). Clients' decisions to discontinue medication need to be made in conjunction with the case manager and psychiatrist.
4. The sexual partner of the client needs to be involved in family planning discussions. The couple's wishes and fears and knowl-

edge of safe sex practices should be explored with the case manager in order to make fully informed decisions.

5. As much as possible, the case manager and psychiatrist should jointly meet with the couple to discuss information about genetic components of mental illness and risks and benefits of pregnancy and childbirth for the woman and her family.

MOTHERHOOD

The profound wish of the client to be "normal" by giving birth may lead to conflicts with family members and health care providers.

Ms. R, a 33-year-old single African-European-American woman with a diagnosis of schizoaffective disorder, conceived after being raped by a man she had met in a neighborhood bar. After receiving counseling and the opportunity to press legal charges against the man, she insisted that she wanted to give birth and be "like other women." She acknowledged to her case manager that since it was hard to care for herself that she could not really imagine taking care of a baby and that she knew she would have to give it up for adoption.

The family members were very troubled by the client's decision and met with members of the Women's Issues Consultation Team and the client to encourage her to consider an abortion. The client remained firm in her wishes to have the child. She met legal criteria for competence to make such a decision. The family explored the possibility of adoption, but no one was in a position to be able to raise a child.

After the birth, Ms. R requested foster adoption, enabling her son to be placed with a family who would be able to later adopt him if her psychiatric disability remained unchanged. Ms. R eagerly awaited the pictures of him that she received each year. In this way he remained an important part of her life and she treasured the success of her pregnancy.

Ms. R exemplifies a remarkable recovery following two severe traumas: rape and the loss of a child through relinquishment. Hamilton (1989) describes the particular vulnerability for self-hatred in women from minority racial subgroups when they are the object of discrimination and abuse. Ms. R's family, although initially disagreeing with her decision to have the baby, were clearly loving and supportive and central to her recovery. Although she was extremely sad in saying good-bye to her baby, the pictures reinforced her feeling of having achieved a successful pregnancy and delivery.

Women who have severe mental disorders and who attempt to raise their children have few formal resources to help them. They often have to depend on the support of friends and family. Test and Berlin (1981) have observed that there is an over-representation of research on the effects of maternal mental illness on children in comparison to the negligible research on the resource needs of mentally ill mothers. Nicholson et al. (1993) found that only a few states had programs that provide parenting education, mother-infant programs, day care, or specific residential treatment settings for mentally ill mothers and their children. Case managers must be particularly skillful in locating and coordinating the variety of services that are needed. Because many referrals involve families with multiple problems, a team consisting of a health professional, case manager, psychiatrist, infant-parent therapist, and Child Protective Services worker must collaborate to deliver an effective treatment plan, as illustrated by the following case:

> Ms. P is a 32-year-old single Latina who was involuntarily hospitalized after she had passed out on the floor of her hotel room. She had serious burns on her arm, having fallen on a hot plate. Ms. P was incoherent, disheveled, and acutely intoxicated with alcohol. Upon admission to the Women's Issues Consultation Team, she learned that she was 30 weeks pregnant. After withdrawing from alcohol, Ms. P was suicidal, severely depressed about being pregnant, and displayed paranoid ideation.

Ms. P had been raised in a strict Catholic family in which she was given harsh physical punishment from an early age by her alcoholic parents. She had difficulties in school, dropped out, and ran away at age 17. Ms. P supported herself as a striptease dancer in cheap clubs and through sex trade work. Her family refused to have contact with her even though they lived in the same city.

In the hospital, Ms. P was given small doses of neuroleptics. Her depressive symptoms and suicidal and paranoid ideation abated. She was discharged back to her hotel to be followed by the case manager. Ms. P was 34 weeks pregnant.

Ms. P came back to the obstetrics unit at the time of delivery, which actually was relatively uncomplicated. After the delivery, the case manager requested an evaluation by Child Protective Services. The infant girl was made a ward of the court and placed in Ms. P's care. The case manager also initiated contact with the Infant-Parent Program at San Francisco General Hospital.

Ms. P felt intruded upon and controlled by the treatment and supervision, yet she acknowledged her need for both. In the work with the Infant-Parent therapist, she learned to manage her angry outbursts and depressive episodes so that she could attend to her daughter's needs without the interference of major mood shifts. She constantly complained about the requirements to obtain full custody of her daughter, but consistently refrained from using alcohol or doing sex trade work. In spite of her protests, she clearly experienced the expectations, structure, and care from the health care team as necessary and helpful. The teaching about her daughter's needs and responses helped her develop an identity as a competent mother while her own needs for approval, interest, and containment were partly met by the treatment team through the coordination of the case manager.

The health care team focused on the mother-infant dyad, helping the mother recognize her own needs and way of relating while at the same time learning about the needs and communications of her child. This facilitated the development of the unique features of the mother-daughter relationship, which involves "more frequent mirroring, mutual identification, and more accurate empathy" (Jordan, Surrey, and Kaplan, 1991).

SEQUELAE OF EARLY SEXUAL TRAUMA

A number of studies (Beck and van der Kolk, 1987; Bryer et al., 1987; Craine et al., 1988; Goodwin, Cheeves, and Connell, 1990) indicate that childhood physical and sexual abuse may be under-recognized and lead to misdiagnoses in female psychiatric clients. Symptoms may be ignored and the psychological sequelae of certain traumas in women may not be addressed.

In this example, the Women's Issues Consultation Team was able to incorporate knowledge of the client's history of sexual abuse as they treated her through her pregnancy, voluntary relinquishment, and decision to have a tubal ligation.

> Ms. L is a 24-year-old European-American single woman, admitted to the treatment team for the third time in three months after a drug overdose of 35 tablets of phenobarbital, 20 milligrams of methadone, cocaine, and intravenous amphetamine. She was 35 weeks pregnant, had been beaten by her boyfriend and kicked out of their living situation, and now had no place to stay.

Following admission and review of her recent situation, a thorough history was taken. She reported that she knew nothing about her father. Her mother had used drugs, supported herself by sex trade work, and was killed by a customer when Ms. L was three years old. She then lived with her mother's sister and husband until age nine, when she was gang-raped and ran away from home. After that she lived in a series of foster homes. In her early teens, she started supporting herself by sex trade work and began using a variety of drugs: heroin, amphetamine, and cocaine, depending on their availability.

Ms. L quickly developed a high profile on the psychiatric unit. She would become enraged at seemingly slight frustrations, threatening staff and other patients. She required seclusion and restraint on numerous occasions until she could voluntarily contract to take time in her room when she began to lose control. She complained about visual and auditory hallucinations. At night she would see dark figures around her bed who would try to grab her and call her derogatory names.

Knowing the association of behavioral problems and sexual delusions in clients with childhood sexual trauma (Beck and van der Kolk, 1987), the staff helped the patient understand how her behavior was a desperate attempt to ward off the helplessness, intrusive memories, and intense feelings associated with her past traumas. She spoke of feeling compelled to follow the path of her mother in a life of risk, suicide attempts, despair, and substance abuse.

The staff attempted to help her decrease her risk-taking behaviors by discussing safe sex practices, use of bleach with needles, and decrease of needle sharing. Ms. L then countered that the risk of unprotected sex was worth the higher income she obtained for offering sex without condoms. She felt that her daily exposure to life-threatening risks was high but unchangeable.

In contrast, she wanted something better for her baby. She arranged a voluntary private adoption by her infertile cousin and her husband with the help of the social worker. In order to reduce the risk of fetal exposure to drugs and the perils of the streets, she agreed to stay in the hospital until the baby was born. Ms. L also decided that she wanted a tubal ligation to avoid future pregnancies and painful separations.

The birth of her daughter and the voluntary adoption were remarkably uncomplicated. Ms. L accepted placement in a substance abuse treatment program, but soon left and returned to her previous lifestyle on the streets. She refused all outpatient services, but periodically would return to the hospital to visit the staff. Two years after the birth, she informed the team that she was HIV-seropositive, using heroin, living in various hotels, and visiting her daughter on a monthly basis. She said that she experienced the birth and voluntary adoption as "one of the few positive things I've done in my life."

Faced with her chaotic and dangerous life situation, the members of the treatment team might have become discouraged and judgmental. They were able to avoid withdrawing from her by discussing the intense reactions they experienced in working with her during weekly treatment planning meetings with other staff members.

RELATIONSHIPS

Women's greater emphasis on affiliation and interdependence (Surrey, 1991) yields particular strengths and vulnerabilities. In their study of young adults with schizophrenic disorders living in community settings, Test, Burke, and Wallish (1990) found that compared to men, women were more likely to be heterosexually active, involved in parenting, and living with a partner of the opposite sex. Similar male-female differences are found in the homeless population. Many studies (Calsyn and Morse, 1990; Bahr and Garrett, 1976) show that compared to homeless men, a higher percentage of homeless women have been previously married. Women are more likely to have responsibility for children (Calsyn and Morse, 1990; Crystal, 1984; Maurin, Russell, and Memmott, 1989). In their study of men and women entering an intensive case management program for homeless shelter residents, Goering et al. (1992) found that women had more supportive relationships, larger social networks, and listed service providers as network members more often than men. Goering et al. concluded, "Women clients may be more reluctant and distrustful initially, but once they are engaged, they may not drop out as frequently as men" (1992, p. 164).

It is known that married, in contrast to unmarried, men have a considerably smaller risk of developing psychiatric symptoms or requiring psychiatric hospitalization. The effect of marriage for women, however, is more variable. Women who are unhappy in their marriages experience more depressive symptoms than either unhappily married men or unmarried women (Aneshensel, Frerichs, and Clark, 1981). Epidemiological studies indicate high rates of depression in married women aged 25 to 45 who have children (Paykel, 1991).

Nolen-Hoeksema (1987) has suggested that the discontinuity in women's caretaker roles, from the intense investment in the raising of children to the shift when they leave home, creates stresses unique to women.

The case of Ms. V illustrates some of the benefits and problems of the caregiver role.

Ms. V is a 54-year-old European-American divorced woman who had worked as a cook. She had just been hospitalized for suicidal ideation following a number of losses: the death of her common-law husband of 14 years after a prolonged illness, and deaths of her father and granddaughter. She felt that she had always "lived for others," and after these deaths could not imagine living for herself. Ms. V also had numerous medical problems that she had ignored.

As she responded to the anti-depressant medication and therapeutic milieu, Ms. V became more aware of her denial of her own needs and medical problems. It was clear that attending to others had occurred at her own expense. In the community halfway house which specialized in the treatment of clients in middle- and late-life transitions, she continued to explore her feeling of being used-up and useless. She was able to experience the caring and interest of other residents in the house and share similar reactions, especially to losses.

Ms. V decided to enter a volunteer program to do what she considered to be meaningful work in a health care setting. She was able to re-direct her skills in making interpersonal connections in a way that was not self-denying or self-neglectful.

For Ms. V, as for many other women, her role as caretaker and her awareness and responsiveness to others were the only ways she had of experiencing her own worth. It is within that relational context that she needs to make the necessary adjustments. The volunteer program provided that opportunity for her.

Women's reactions to aging and the feeling of being less sexually attractive may exacerbate conflicts with their adolescent daughters. As their biological life cycles intertwine, rivalries and, in more psychotic clients, delusional ideas may emerge. The case manager can evaluate whether individual, conjoint, or family sessions will be most helpful in sorting out the individual and family issues.

SUBSTANCE ABUSE

We know that chemical dependency in women often has an onset, course, and response to treatment which is different from that of men. "Addicted women are far more likely than addicted men to be married to, or romantically attached to, other addicts" (Unger, 1988, p. 747). Physiological, hormonal, and dietary factors affect women's course of alcoholism. Even though they begin misusing alcohol at a later age and in smaller amounts, they will become alcohol dependent at the same life stage as men.

We also know that most treatment programs do not make women welcome. The majority of clients are male and sexual hustles are part of the environment. Furthermore, child care needs are generally not considered. Finally, heavy reliance on techniques of confrontation flood women with guilt, producing less successful outcomes than with men (Fullilove, Lown, and Fullilove, 1992).

Service providers struggle with countertransference reactions of disapproval or withdrawal when dealing with pregnant substance abusers. They often share the conventional view that women should rise above their addictions either by preventing pregnancy, or if that fails, by stopping drug use during the pregnancy. Staff often find themselves adopting a greater interest in the fetus than in the client (Eastwood, Spielvogel, and Wile, 1990).

Women who jeopardize the health or life of the fetus are particularly difficult for caretakers to treat.

> Ms. M is a 30-year-old single Eurasian woman, 36 weeks pregnant, who was brought by her case manager to the high-risk obstetrics clinic. Ms. M described increasing depressive symptoms, extreme anxiety, and disorganized thinking over the last six weeks when the father of the baby had left her. Her thoughts of suicide were not acted upon because she wanted to live for her baby. Ms. M had been using crack cocaine for the last five years on a weekly basis. Even though she had decreased the amount, she was unable to quit completely on her own or get into a treatment program.

Ms. M had been raised in foster homes because her schizophrenic mother had been unable to care for her. As a child, she had been the object of both physical and sexual abuse. Her first hospitalization occurred at age 16 when she cut her wrists. Since then hospitalizations were required every two years.

Ms. M had a series of relationships with abusive men in which she would feel suicidal after they left her. Diagnostically the client was assessed by the consulting psychiatrist as having a borderline personality disorder and suffering from an adjustment disorder with depressed mood and cocaine abuse. She was started on a low dose of a neuroleptic and strongly encouraged to avoid using cocaine. Two weeks after this contact, the client called her case manager and was admitted to the labor and delivery unit with vaginal bleeding. No fetal movements were found. It was determined that she had *abruptio placentae.* She delivered a stillborn fetus.

Ms. M was extremely tearful and requested to be seen by the consulting psychiatrist. She admitted to heavy cocaine use 12 hours earlier. The urine toxicology screen confirmed the presence of cocaine. Ms. M stated, "I know what I did to my baby, but I do not want the doctor talking to me about what went wrong with the baby. I want you to tell me."

The consulting psychiatrist urged her to talk directly to the obstetricians, since they were the experts in such situations, and the client consented. Both the case manager and psychiatrist then met with her and talked about the power of cocaine addiction. They acknowledged that Ms. M had tried to break her addiction and now felt very bad that the baby had died and that it was possible she had some responsibility for the baby's death. With encouragement she was able to hold the dead baby and say goodbye. She was able to talk about her hopes for the baby. The next day the case manager again discussed how attached she was to the baby. She was encouraged to care about herself as much as for the baby and to pursue her wish to stop drugs and get into a treatment program. On follow-up one month later Ms. M was drug-free and living with her family.

As this case illustrates, the clinician must speak clearly about the risks of the addiction for the fetus and be able to deal straightforwardly with whatever tragedies result from the addiction. Ms. M felt that she had killed her baby by continuing to use drugs. She needed to be allowed to openly express her deep feelings of self-blame and horror without being given superficial reassurances. Then the grief work about the meaning of the loss of the baby, the power of the cocaine addiction, and possible new beginnings can be explored.

HIV DISEASE

Women who are intravenous drug users or sexual partners of intravenous drug users are the largest subgroup of women with AIDS (Stuntzner-Gibson, 1991). As studies have shown, HIV-infected men in contrast to HIV-infected women are more likely to be homosexual, white, and middle class, whereas women are more likely to be heterosexual, of color, poor, and uneducated (Centers for Disease Control, 1990; Shaw, 1988).

HIV disease affects members of social classes and minority ethnic groups disproportionately. Members of lower socioeconomic classes with less access to health care services have a high prevalence of the disease. African Americans constitute 27 percent of adult and 53 percent of pediatric AIDS cases, while comprising only 11 percent of the total American population. Latinos constitute 16 percent of adult and 25 percent of pediatric AIDS cases, while comprising only seven percent of the general American population (CDC, 1990; Painter, 1989). Such disproportionately high percentages also occur for African-American and Latina women, in comparison to lower rates for Asian and European-American women.

AIDS infection is not limited to women who have had multiple sexual partners. Women with AIDS acquired heterosexually report a median number of three sexual partners (Walker, 1993). Because women's symptoms are usually not recognized early, every woman should be considered an appropriate candidate for HIV screening. A sexual history should include questions about partner characteristics, sexual practices, and number of partners. Gynecological information about menstrual disorders, recurrent genital herpes, history of sexually transmitted diseases, recurrent vaginal yeast infections increasing in severity, and increasingly abnormal pap smears should be obtained. Questions about intravenous drug use as well as use of non-injection drugs need to be asked, since under the influence of drugs, partners are less likely to adopt safe sexual practices.

A number of authors recommend developing groups for women who are HIV seropositive so that they can discuss questions about medical treatment and care of children, share feelings about social isolation, and deal with the effects of discrimination (Chung and Magraw, 1992).

VIOLENCE

Hamilton has observed that "sexual and physical abuse is so prevalent that it has been characterized as a normative aspect of female development" (1989, p. 36). Battering may occur in 25 to 50 percent of women and attempted to completed rape in 46 percent of women (1989, p. 36).

The danger of internalizing a sense of unworthiness from such experiences is high. In addition, the woman may suffer from affective instability and depressive symptoms.

The case manager is frequently in the position of needing to deal with the effects of violence in female clients' lives while simultaneously trying to contain volatile and dangerous partners.

> Ms. R is a 20-year-old single Latina with a long history of polydrug abuse. Her case manager had assisted her with keeping visits to a drug treatment clinic to decrease her use of speed, cocaine, and PCP.

Ms. R's mother left her husband and children when the client was five years old. She was raised in a series of foster homes and reported instances of sexual abuse. She made frequent attempts to run away from the homes. At age 15 she met her current boyfriend, Mr. O, and began living with him. Her sex trade work helps support both of them financially.

The goal of the case manager has been to help Ms. R remain HIV negative and to decrease her use of drugs. Ms. R has made it clear that she wishes to remain with Mr. O even though he hits her periodically when he is intoxicated.

During one visit to her case manager, Ms. R arrived in tears, severely bruised about her face. She had been raped and beaten by a sex trade client who was high on drugs and who also refused to pay her. Her fear was that Mr. O would not believe her and would be enraged that she had failed to get money from the client.

The case manager took Ms. R to the emergency room, where she was given a physical examination and counseled about how to press legal charges against the rapist. She insisted on taking no action. Her fear was that Mr. O would not take her back.

The case manager, operating on the principle that a therapeutic alliance needs to be maintained with both members of the couple to prevent the escalation of abuse, arranged to accompany her back to the apartment where Mr. O was waiting. To her relief, he expressed concern for her and anger at the rapist.

Knowing that it was important to Ms. R that she stay in the

relationship, the case manager underscored the protective reaction Mr. O had and emphasized how important his role would be in her recovery from the rape. They openly discussed the need for her to have time off the streets to recover emotionally and physically from the assault. The case manager helped the couple develop a strategy to borrow money temporarily from relatives to give her time away from the sex trade work.

Experience has shown that we cannot attack the woman's partner when she feels dependent on him and chooses to remain with him. We can work with her to recognize signs of impending violence and to evaluate her choices with her if she should decide to leave. Case managers who attack the abusive partner may actually increase the vulnerability of the client to retaliatory measures (Walker, 1993).

Group work is another vehicle for women in the community setting to hear about experiences of violence and self-defense.

> Ms. C is a 29-year-old single African-American woman who had been attending the women's group at her neighborhood mental health clinic for the past year. One year before starting the group she began to live with Mr. M, who was physically abusive to her. They subsisted on income from General Assistance.

In the group, Ms. C told the members that when she was nine years old her mother died and the nine children were placed with relatives. Starting at age 12 in her aunt and uncle's home, she was sexually abused by the uncle, even after complaining to her aunt of his assaults.

Ms. C became involved with her current boyfriend, Mr. M, from age 12 to 15. He was 23 years old at the time, seemingly successful and wealthy. Ms. C ended the relationship because of his increased drug use. She completed high school and attended two years of community college.

After ending a relationship with another man, Ms. C resumed her involvement with Mr. M. During the interim years, he had been in prison for sexual assault and tax evasion.

Following one abusive episode by Mr. M, she came to the group and reported that she had superficially cut her wrist, but didn't need medical attention. Group members expressed concern about her welfare. She continued to state that she preferred being with him to being alone.

Ms. C's ability to attend the group regularly was seen as a strength and a reflection of an ability to value her own activities. Two months after being in the group, Mr. M inflicted a serious bite to her cheek, which required medical attention. Ms. C left him and entered a shelter, but when Mr. M came and begged her to return, she did.

Six months later, while intoxicated, Mr. M attempted to choke her and said he would kill her. Ms. C grabbed a kitchen knife and stabbed him. She immediately called the police and was arrested for murder. After the court determined that she had acted in self-defense, she was released from jail.

Upon her return to the group, members were initially speechless as they listened to the story of the murder. Gradually members spoke of their admiration for her determination and ability to save her own life. Ms. C said that she felt there had been no other way to save herself, but she missed Mr. M terribly. The other women sympathized with her, many reporting their own attachments to violent men. They encouraged her to enter a residential treatment program to deal with the loss and work on her wish to "start over again."

In assessing indicators for physical violence in a couple relationship, the clinician should evaluate the frequency of references to the partner's anger, the presence of suicide attempts, the frequency of references to the partner's jealousy and accusations of infidelity, indications of sexual and/or physical abuse of the children, severe social isolation, a fear of harming the partner, and the expectation that the woman will "follow orders" in the relationship. As the two case examples illustrate, the case manager is usually involved in a long-term assessment of the woman's ongoing concerns and risks to her safety.

"TREATMENT-RESISTANT" WOMEN

Service providers may have particular difficulties with female clients who deal with issues of sexuality, reproduction, aggression, and dependence in nontraditional ways. Waites (1993) observed that women who "exhibit the kinds of difficulties in impulse control more readily accepted in males" (p. 17) are often considered "undesirable" as clients and denied access to treatment.

> Ms. A is a 24-year-old European-American lesbian who was admitted to the hospital after destroying property and threatening to kill her hotel manager and Child Protective Services social worker.

Ms. A has a history of multiple brief hospitalizations following either suicide attempts or property destruction. Her affective lability, low frustration tolerance, internal feeling of emptiness, brief psychotic states, and personal identity struggles indicate a diagnosis of borderline personality disorder.

Her early childhood was marked by both physical and sexual abuse. She ran away from home at an early age and began using street drugs to dampen her psychological and physical reality. Following an unsatisfactory relationship with an older man, she became pregnant, left him, and moved in with her female lover, who supported her emotionally and financially.

After the birth of the baby, Ms. A continued to use street drugs. Her lover told her that her destructive behavior and drug use had reached an unacceptable level and they needed to separate. At the same time, the Child Protective Services Unit had placed the baby in a temporary adoptive home. Ms. A, feeling angry and bereft, moved into a hotel. When the social worker arrived to discuss the adoptive review plan, Ms. A exploded, throwing objects against the wall, and threatened to harm the social worker and manager. The police were called and she was hospitalized.

A case manager began to meet with her in the hospital. Ms. A denied any need for help and denigrated all staff who attempted to work with her. Her only concern was in finding and maintaining housing for herself. The case manager respected this circumscribed arrangement and helped Ms. A negotiate a contract with her new hotel manager. Together they established a mutually satisfactory arrangement for how either the manager or the client could discuss any problems with the hotel arrangement. The case manager made no attempt to obtain outpatient treatment for Ms. A, respecting her ability to receive help only in specific concrete arenas.

The case manager first analyzed her own responses to the client.

She began with a review of any homophobic prejudices she might be harboring against Ms. A (Falco, 1991), and then shifted to a broader focus to analyze the countertransference responses Ms. A's threats and aggression engendered. Once she had understood her own responses of anger, fear, and rejection, she could help other service providers work more effectively with Ms. A.

Case managers are frequently called upon to develop ways of interacting with "treatment-resistant" clients that respect their fears of intrusion and control and yet allow them to maintain their living situations in the community.

CONCLUSION

Some of the complexities of the lives of women in the public mental health system are illustrated in the presentations and discussions in this chapter. Clearly much is demanded of the gender-sensitive case manager: knowledge of developmental theory; health care needs; reproductive issues; awareness of the meaning of motherhood; knowledge of the psychological sequelae of sexual and physical trauma; and an appreciation of the implications of women's capacity for affiliation.

Many of the women we treat evoke feelings of fear, fascination, and avoidance. Maxine Harris (1991) relates these responses to a warding off and denial of certain qualities in women. "The disowned parts of modern woman are her vulnerability, her alienation, her aggressiveness, and her rebelliousness. And so, in this latter half of the twentieth century, I would argue that the feminine shadow consists of a combination of the victim, the exile, the predator, and the rebel" (p. 45).

As resources for severely and persistently mentally ill individuals continue to shrink, the role of the case manager becomes even more central. It will not be sufficient to command an extensive knowledge of women's treatment issues. The truly competent case manager must call upon this specialized knowledge and, much like an alchemist, combine it with a street-wise craftiness to provide counseling, education, advocacy, and coordinated services for the female client.

REFERENCES

Aneshensel, C., Frerichs, R., and Clark, V. (1981). Family Roles and Sex Differences in Depression. *Journal of Health and Social Behavior, 22,* 379-393.

Apfel, R. and Handel, M. (1993). *Madness and the Loss of Motherhood.* Washington, DC: American Psychiatric Press, Inc.

Ashton, H. (1991). Psychotropic Drug Prescribing for Women. *British Journal of Psychiatry, 158*(10), 30-35.

Bahr, H. and Garrett, G. (1976). *Women Alone: The Disaffiliation of Urban Females.* Lexington, MA: Lexington Books.

Beck, J.C. and van der Kolk, B. (1987). Reports of Childhood Incest and Current Behavior of Chronically Hospitalized Psychotic Women. *American Journal of Psychiatry, 144,* 1474-1476.

Bryer, J.B., Nelson, B.A., Miller, J.B., and Krol, P.A. (1987). Childhood Sexual and Physical Abuse as Factors in Adult Psychiatric Illness. *American Journal of Psychiatry, 144,* 1426-1430.

Calsyn, R.J. and Morse, G. (1990). Homeless Men and Women: Commonalities and a Service Gender Gap. *American Journal of Community Psychology, 18*(4), 597-608.

Centers for Disease Control. (1990). U.S. AIDS Cases Reported Through February 1990. HIV/AIDS Surveillance Report, 11-18.

Chung J. and Magraw, M. (1992). A Group Approach to Psychosocial Issues Faced by HIV-Positive Women. *Hospital and Community Psychiatry, 43*(9), 891-894.

Coverdale, J. and Aruffo, J. (1989). Family Planning Needs of Female Chronic Psychiatric Outpatients. *American Journal of Psychiatry, 146,* 1489-1491.

Craine, L.S., Henson, C.E., Colliver, J.A., and MacLean D.G. (1988). Prevalence of a History of Sexual Abuse Among Female Psychiatric Patients in a State Hospital System. *Hospital and Community Psychiatry, 39,* 300-304.

Crystal, S. (1984) Homeless Men and Homeless Women: The Gender Gap. *Urban and Social Change Review, 17*(2), 2-6.

Eastwood, J., Spielvogel, A., and Wile, J. (1990). Countertransference Risks When Women Treat Women. *Clinical Social Work Journal, 18*(3), 273-280.

Falco, K. (1991). *Psychotherapy with Lesbian Clients.* New York: Brunner/Mazel, Publishers.

Fullilove M., Lown, A., and Fullilove, R. (1992). Crack 'Hos and Skeezers: Traumatic Experiences of Women Crack Users. *The Journal of Sex Research, 29*(2), 275-287.

Gaw, A. (1993). Psychiatric Care of Chinese Americans. In A. Gaw (Ed.), *Culture, Ethnicity, and Mental Illness* (245-280). Washington, DC: American Psychiatric Press.

Goering, P., Wasylenki, D., St. Onge, M., Paduchak, D., and Lancee, W. (1992). Gender Differences Among Clients of of Case Management Program for the Homeless. *Hospital and Community Psychiatry, 43*(2), 160-165.

Goodwin, J.M., Cheeves, K., and Connell, V. (1990). Borderline and Other

Severe Symptoms in Adult Survivors of Incestuous Abuse. *Psychiatric Annals, 20,* 22-32.

Hamilton, J. (1989). Emotional Consequences of Victimization and Discrimination in 'Special Populations' of Women. *Psychiatric Clinics of North America, 12,* 35-51.

Handel, M. (1985) Deferred Pelvic Examinations: A Purposeful Omission in the Care of Mentally Ill Women. *Hospital and Community Psychiatry, 33,* 25-34.

Harris, M. (1991). *Sisters of the Shadow.* London: University of Oklahoma Press.

Jordan, J., Surrey, J., and Kaplan, A. (1991). Women and Empathy: Implications for Psychological Development and Psychotherapy. In J. Jordan, A. Kaplan, J. Miller, I. Stiver, and J. Surrey (Eds.), *Women's Growth In Connection* (27-50). New York: The Guilford Press.

Koranyi, E. (1979). Morbidity and Rate of Undiagnosed Physical Illnesses in a Psychiatric Clinic Population. *Archives of General Psychiatry, 36,* 414-419.

Maurin, J.T., Russell, L., and Memmott, R.J. (1989). An Exploration of Gender Differences Among the Homeless, *Research in Nursing and Health, 12,* 315-321.

Miller, L. (1991). Clinical Strategies for the Use of Psychotropic Drugs During Pregnancy. *Psychiatric Medicine, 9*(2), 275-298.

Nicholson, J., Geller, J., Fisher, W. and Dion, G. (1993). State Policies and Programs That Address the Needs of Mentally Ill Mothers in the Public Sector. *Hospital and Community Psychiatry, 44*(5), 484-489.

Nolen-Hoeksema, S. (1987). Sex Differences in Unipolar Depression: Evidence and Theory. *Psychological Bulletin, 101*(2), 259-282.

Paykel, E. (1991). Depression in Women. *British Journal of Psychiatry, 158*(10), 22-29.

Roca, R., Breakey, W., and Fischer, P. (1987). Medical Care of Chronic Psychiatric Outpatients. *Hospital and Community Psychiatry, 38*(7), 741-745.

Shaw, N. (1988). Preventing AIDS Among Women: The Role of Community Organizing. *Socialist Review, 100,* 76-92.

Sidel, R. (1986). *Women and Children Last.* New York: Viking.

Spielvogel, A. and Wile, J. (1986). Treatment of the Psychotic Pregnant Patient. *Psychosomatics, 27*(7), 487-492.

Sprague J. (1991). *More Than Housing: Lifeboats for Women and Children.* Boston: Butterworth Architecture.

Stuntzner-Gibson, D. (1991). Women and HIV Disease: An Emerging Social Crisis. *Social Work, 36*(1), 21-28.

Sullivan, G. and Lukoff, D. (1990). Sexual Side Effects of Antipsychotic Medication: Evaluation and Interventions. *Hospital and Community Psychiatry, 41*(11), 1238-1241.

Surrey, J. (1991). The Self-in-Relation: A Theory of Women's Development. In J. Jordan, A. Kaplan, J. Miller, I. Stiver, and J. Surrey (Eds.), *Women's Growth In Connection* (51-66). New York: The Guilford Press.

Test, J. and Berlin, S. (1981). Issues of Special Concern to Chronically Mentally Ill Women. *Professional Psychology, 12*(1), 136-144.

Test, M., Burke, S., and Wallish, L. (1990). Gender Differences of Young Adults with Schizophrenic Disorders in Community Care. *Schizophrenia Bulletin, 16*(2), Schizophrenia Research Branch, NIMH, Washington DC, 331-344.

Unger, K. (1988). Chemical Dependency in Women. *The Western Journal of Medicine, 149*(6), 746-750.

Waites, E. (1993). *Trauma and Survival.* New York: W.W. Norton and Company, Inc.

Walker, L. (1993). Domestic Violence. *News for Women in Psychiatry, 11*(2), 4-5.

Yonkers, K., Kando, J., Cole, J., and Blumenthal, S. (1992). Gender Differences in Pharmacokinetics and Pharmacodynamics of Psychotropic Medication. *American Journal of Psychiatry, 149*(5), 587-595.

Chapter 9

Culturally Competent Health and Human Services for Emotionally Troubled Children and Youth: Only Through Intensive Case Management

Abner J. Boles III
Harriet A. Curtis-Boles

INTRODUCTION

The needs of children and youth with serious emotional difficulty are varied and multitudinous. Institutions designed to serve children and youth along with their families have often struggled with legal mandates, the limited and categorical nature of funding, ethnic and cultural diversity, diverse manifestations of emotional difficulties and in many cases mislabeling, ineffective approaches to treatment that provide too little in the way of the "50-minute hour" and too much in the way of hospitalization (Knitzer, 1982), isolated services and assessments, and a huge gap between level of need and actual service to children and youth.

Efforts to better serve children and youth have increasingly centered around systems of care and coordinated treatment (Smith, Attkisson, and Boles, 1993). A common component of recent efforts to serve children and youth through systems of care has been case management. Due to the complex manner in which services are provided and the often complex needs of emotionally troubled youth, the use of case management to attempt to coordinate and orchestrate services for this particular population is well founded, even though necessary in large part because of fragmented service systems and the uncoordinated nature of the care that is currently in place to serve children and families. Recent efforts by the Children Adolescent Systems Service Program (CASSP), funded in 1989 by the National Institute of Mental Health (NIMH), have encouraged the development of coordinated systems of care in 40 states across the country and are setting new standards in care for children and families. Many of the efforts utilize case management approaches as the means toward enhanced coordination and effective service delivery.

Case management services and approaches are not new to Health and Human Services care. The field of Social Work has employed case management in the form of case-specific care since the early to mid-1960s along with the 1960s human services growth movement. With a recent resurgence of case management as a main component of service delivery to children and families, interest in the functions and styles of case management has increased. Models of systems of care have incorporated case management, while researchers and evaluators are beginning to report the efficacy of various models, the value of certain approaches, the training needs of staff, and target population effectiveness.

Much discourse has occurred over the past 34 years regarding the functions of case management and the diverse roles that case managers have undertaken. The roles have been representative of models that utilize individuals who are personally uninvolved and casually referred to as service brokers, to individuals who have multiple functions, including brokering, but often accomplish hands-on, direct service integration and advocacy on the behalf of the client and family. In this chapter we will focus on the current thinking regarding case management for children and families from a system of care perspective and report on a model program in San Francisco, California that exemplifies aspects of case management care in an ethnically diverse urban setting. Individual case management will be discussed in conjunction with team case management; individualized care approaches will be discussed; obstacles to systems change and coordinated care delivery will be examined; and recommendations for the future in case management for children and families will be proposed.

SYSTEMS OF CARE

In 1986, Beth Stroul and Robert Friedman delineated the core values and principles for systems of care for emotionally disturbed children and youth. They identified two main values, which were:

1. that systems of care should be child centered and family focused, with the individual needs of the child and the family determining the nature of the services; and,
2. that systems of care should be community based, implying that the services be located in the community, that responsibility of decision making be that of the community, and that the management of the array of services rest in the community as well.

The term community-based takes on a slightly different meaning then previously delineated in the literature in that it refers to location and function (Patterson, 1993). A service or agency can be located in the community and not be community based if it is not a part of the community in the eyes of the neighborhood or community residents, or in the eyes of the recipients of care. To be a part of the community means to also represent and participate in the happenings of the community as a staff, an agency, and a resident. Often this means activity beyond the scope of just mental health or service delivery, but includes recreational activities, political activities, social activities, and local church and civil involvement. To value and target children for service delivery has not been difficult for most service delivery systems, but to provide services targeting children in family-focused ways is a step beyond where most institutions of care tread. Family-focused may suggest targeting key members of a family, thereby indirectly affecting the identified child in need. By securing the needed services for a primary caregiver, the needs of an identified child may be better addressed, hence family-focused services result in individual care to the child (Collins and Collins, 1990).

To realize systems of care for emotionally troubled children Stroul and Freidman (1986) outlined ten guiding principles. These guiding principles are seen as benchmarks against which system of care networks are judged (see Table 9.1).

TABLE 9.1. System of Care Guiding Principles*

1. Children with emotional disturbances should have access to a comprehensive array of services that address the child's physical, emotional, social, and educational needs.
2. Children with emotional disturbances should receive individualized services in accordance with the unique needs and potentials of each child and guided by an individualized service plan.
3. Children with emotional disturbances should receive services within the least restrictive, most normative environment that is clinically appropriate.
4. The families and surrogate families of children with emotional disturbances should be full participants in all aspects of the planning and delivery of services.
5. Children with emotional disturbances should receive services that are integrated, with linkages between child-caring agencies and programs and mechanisms for planning, developing, and coordinating services.
6. Children with emotional disturbances should be provided with case management or similar mechanisms to ensure that multiple services are delivered in a coordinated and therapeutic manner and that they can move through the system of services in accordance with their changing needs.
7. Early identification and intervention for children with emotional problems should be promoted by the system of care in order to enhance the likelihood of positive outcomes.
8. Children with emotional disturbances should be ensured smooth transitions to the adult service system as they reach maturity.
9. The rights of children with emotional disturbances should be protected, and effective advocacy efforts for children and youth with emotional disturbances should be promoted.
10. Children with emotional disturbances should receive culturally competent services that are sensitive and responsive to cultural differences and special needs and are provided without regard to race, religion, national origin, sex, physical disability, or other characteristics.

*Stroul, B.A. and Friedman, R.M. (1986). *A System of Care for Severely Emotionally Disturbed Children and Youth.* Washington, DC: Georgetown University Child Development Center, CASSP Technical Assistance Center.

As is evident by the System of Care principles, the nature of service delivered to children and their families, the manner of service delivery, and the extent to which the services are specific to the individual needs of children and youth are crucial elements. The service deliverers and key stakeholders are necessary in the determination of services and in the design and delivery of services. The stakeholders include policymakers, professionals, service deliverers, and most especially parents and primary caregivers.

For effective service delivery to emotionally troubled children and their families, services must be integrated and coordinated within and across health and human service systems. Integrated services can only exist if linkages are made between child-focused agencies and programs. These linkages need to be both formal and informal with written memorandums of understanding detailing the purpose and nature of linkages. The philosophy, goals, and principles of child-focused organizations must reflect the importance of integrated care and agency linkages so that service deliverers in their day-to-day activities support and develop informal methods of participating collectively with others in care delivery. Mechanisms must be established that allow for active planning regarding services to ensure the best possible outcomes in each situation. Along with planning, collective service development must occur to ensure the proper service and client match, to ensure that the respective resources, skills, and needs of the serving agencies are identified and collectively put into place, and to ensure that specific agency needs are met. Coordination of collaborative efforts is vitally important and requires at least mid-management-level focus of the linkage, planning, and often budgetary issues necessary to ensure that the partnership across agencies is fruitful for the sake of the children and their families, but also for the sake of the agencies themselves.

Many successful systems of care establish methods to ensure coordination and integration. In situations where the service needs are multiple, the service providers are multiple, and the children with their families have complex needs and issues that demand across-agency and across-discipline collaboration, the method of choice is often case management.

The context in which we would like to discuss issues related to effective case management, individualized care, obstacles to systems change, and future recommendations to address the health and human services needs of emotionally troubled youth is that of the Family Mosaic Project.

FAMILY MOSAIC PROJECT

The Family Mosaic Project is one of eight system of care demonstration projects funded in part by the Robert Wood Johnson (RWJ)

Initiative entitled the Mental Health Services Program for Youth. Over 20 million dollars over five years to eight states across the country have been committed to support the development of community-based comprehensive systems of care for children. The site for the state of California is the Family Mosaic Project, which is located in the city and county of San Francisco. The seven remaining sites funded by this initiative are located in Pennsylvania, Wisconsin, Ohio, Oregon, Kentucky, Vermont, and North Carolina. The Family Mosaic Project has taken the initiative and developed a health and human service approach to providing comprehensive care to severely emotionally and/or behaviorally disturbed children and their families. The overarching features of the project include increasing inter-agency collaboration, reducing fragmentation in service delivery, providing "wrap-around" services, and serving in partnership with parents and children. In addition, the project goals include: (1) developing and coordinating service provider relations across help-giving disciplines; (2) implementing automated data management systems; and (3) increasing federal participation in the funding of local services for children and families; while (4) developing flexible services through the pooling of categorical health and human service agency dollars.

In the city and county of San Francisco, the Family Mosaic Project (FMP), housed in the Department of Public Health, has taken the lead in guiding the multi-agency collaboration of Health, Social Services, Juvenile Probation, Education, and Mental Health on behalf of children and their families. This effort draws heavily form the values and principles of the Ventura Model (Jordan and Hernandez, 1990), the National Institute of Mental Health's Child and Adolescent Service System Program (CASSP) (Stroul and Friedman, 1986), "wrap-around" care as exemplified by the Alaska Youth Initiative (VanDenBerg, 1993) and effective managed care models as developed through technical assistance from the Robert Wood Johnson Foundation and the Washington's Business Group on Health (Uribe de Mena, 1992).

The goals of the Family Mosaic Project are to:

- develop focused community services that bring professional health and human services into the home, classroom, and other nontraditional settings;

- develop a school transition support project for middle school-aged children;
- involve parents as active partners in helping their children and families;
- provide continuous training to support cross-disciplinary interventions within a framework that is appropriately responsive to cultural differences;
- develop a culturally competent system of care and enhance diversity in the provider population;
- develop a coordinated and comprehensive emergency response effort;
- ensure stable foster care placements by providing clinical support;
- provide comprehensive and intensive case management services

The Family Mosaic interagency collaboration features comprehensive service planning across agencies with parents and children, and the pooling of agency resources and in kind staff. Coordinated case management, the development of flexible services, and maximization of federal participation in the financing of mental health services for children across all partner agencies also define Family Mosaic. The benefits of this interagency collaboration include appropriate treatment planning for children involved with multiple agencies, particularly children in school and in the juvenile justice systems. Moreover, interagency collaboration permits the development of individualized service interventions that are necessary to be effective with inner-city children. Finally, the expansion of existing resources and the revitalization of community ownership for the service and care of special-need children and their families is heightened through this collaboration among agencies.

COORDINATED CASE MANAGEMENT

The nature of service delivery to children and families in the Family Mosaic Project is guided through coordinated case management. Initially, the project developed individual case management that featured: small caseloads; extensive psychological and psychiatric consultation; multi-agency, cross-disciplinary input; access to culturally competent service systems and professionals; an automated data record keeping system; traditional and non-traditional services, and flexible funds. Most case management models employ individual case management, which allows for one individual to manage and develop care plans for a caseload of families. The Family Mosaic Project has attempted to develop coordinated case management following particular principles. The principles that best describe case management as depicted by the project include:

- Providing the continuity of one person to support and empower a family across all systems;
- Providing access to services by locating personnel in neighborhoods, with schedules that meet people's needs and a response capacity that is available 24 hrs. a day;
- Recognizing that each family and child is unique, exhibiting a service approach that is flexible to accommodate the new and individual circumstances presented;
- Working with parents as partners in the development of plans and strategies to help their children and strengthen the family;
- Making services community identified by locating them where they are physically and psychologically accessible to families;
- Providing and recommending services that are meaningful and practical for the family;
- Maintaining an attitude that constantly approaches creative solutions from an interagency perspective with clear resolve to work as an ally for the family and to never give up;
- Demonstrating a culturally competent style of case management that will appropriately guide aspects of communication and relationship with families.

For such a model to be effective, the case manager must gather the relevant information available, coordinate with the existing service providers across disciplines and agencies, interview and thoroughly assess the needs of the child and family, access additional data when necessary, develop a relationship with the child's primary caregivers so as to involve them in the planning and development of the primary care plan, and oversee the implementation and maintenance of the care plan. The job of the case manager is difficult at best and some of the issues that can arise to complicate matters include: the diversity of family and child needs and issues, the complexity of agency bureaucracy and institutional inefficiency, the lack of flexible funds to creatively serve individual needs, poor ethnic and cultural match, a lack of knowledge and experience in the multiple health and human service arenas that impact the lives of children, a lack of trust among parents and caregivers including case managers, the prevalence of philosophies and practices that intimate that parents are the causes of childhood dysfunction and shouldn't be allowed to guide the care of their children, and in many cases simply the lack of services and resources for the treatment of emotionally troubled children.

These issues and other factors have led the Family Mosaic Project to redirect its case management structure from individual case management to TEAM case management. Team case management as it is being developed in San Francisco has been modeled after the team case management approach exemplified by a Chicago-based program called KALEIDOSCOPE. Kaleidoscope was founded and is directed by Karl Dennis, who has emerged as one of the premier authorities on "wrap-around care." Like Kaleidoscope, the Family Mosaic Project has pulled together five staffs to form teams that manage up to 50 families. Particular Family Advocates (term used instead of care manager) are assigned primary responsibility for ten to twelve families, but share information, cross-consult, cross-support, and become generally involved in all 50 families. This particular case coordination structure allows for families to have individuals aware of their unique situation and individuals who have come to know them provide the back-up, coverage, and support for them when their primary family advocate is unable to. This structure allows for better matching of client needs and staff strengths, better ethnic and cultural matching, staff support both emotional and informational, reduction of staff burn-out and isolation, enhanced creativity in problem solving and enhanced continuity and smoother follow through. Although a team case management approach addresses many of the issues that have been identified in individual-focused case management, there are some unique issues that need attention because of this approach. Some issues that need attention include: a greater need for intense and ongoing routinized communication; a greater need for detailed documentation and easy but protected access to case information; consistent case alerts to predict as much as possible those cases that are potential problems, and ready access to untapped resources for emergencies.

SERVICES

Luckily for the city and county of San Francisco and for the Family Mosaic Project, an extensive array of services are available. The array of services available and being developed include in-home and out-of-home respite care, parenting education, psychiatric evaluation and medication, conflict resolution training and interventions, emergency assessment and evaluation, crisis response and care, tutoring, transportation, parent advocacy, community support, recreational enhancement, shadowing (specialized mentoring), health screens, follow-up health care, family and individual psychotherapy, day treatment, select residential care, and short-term acute hospitalization. Many of the services identified are fairly new and some are in the process of being developed and expanded to be available to all emotionally troubled youth receiving care in the city and county, whether in the Family Mosaic are not. The array of services clearly crosses over the lines of health, mental health, social services, and education to provide for the comprehensive needs of the child. More attention is being directed toward the development and the coordination of substance abuse services for children and parents, the enhancement of services for homeless youth and families in the way of temporary and permanent housing, along with better coordination of recreational and correctional resources on behalf of Mosaic kids.

INDIVIDUALIZED CARE

The norm in providing care to children and families focuses around the development of an array of services, when the resources exist, and the provision of that array in a continuum to allow for graduated treatment as needed. Unfortunately, a continuum of services with an elaborate array does not guarantee effective service delivery. An array of services often implies pre-established programs that have specific modes of operating with particular treatment practices. If a child's needs and issues fit the program design, then effective services may be provided, however, if the child has needs and issues that are beyond or just different from what the program is able to handle, then services will be ineffective and often the child or the child's family are targeted for blame or are expected to change to accommodate to the needs of the program. Individualized care has as its main goal the delivery of services to individual children according to their unique needs and the particular needs of their families. To better understand the concept of individualized care, perhaps it would be useful to examine the purported principles and elements of such a care delivery approach.

MacFarquhar, Dowrick, and Risley (1993) conducted a nationwide survey of identified individualized service delivery models that resulted in consistent features and particular aspects of success. Table 9.2 shows the key features they identified in the survey after reviewing some 15 programs across 12 states. As the features indicate, individualized care is complex and comprehensive with a clear

TABLE 9.2. Key Features of an Individualized Assistance Approach

1. Program services must be tailored to fit the youth, not the youth fit into the existing services.
2. Services must be youth- and family-centered.
3. Funding needs to be flexible to permit flexibility in programming.
4. Programs must work under an unconditional care policy.
5. Use of a treatment team for collaborative planning and management is a must.
6. Normalization should be stressed throughout all phases of treatment planning and implementation.
7. Programs should use a community-based care approach.
8. Intensive case management is essential.
9. Funding must be extensive enough to provide whatever services are needed for significant effect with an individual.
10. Treatment planning and implementation must strive toward less restrictive alternatives.
11. An accountability component is essential.
12. Services should be based on appropriate outcome data.

emphasis on meeting the needs of the recipient of care and on providing and ensuring effective care. The financing of individualized care is important in that funding has to be flexible and sufficient. To maintain quality care, youth- and family-centered care, and coordinated care, intensive case management with the use of treatment teams that provide collaborative planning and management are essential. Collaborative planning and management has to include children and their parents to a large degree to ensure buy-in and to ensure client-family treatment plan compatibility.

Those factors that tended to contribute to the success of the surveyed models of individualized care included: the use of an interagency team; talent and commitment of staff; commitment to values of the agency; adherence to an unconditional care policy; and to a lesser degree, willingness to take risks and implementation of a youth-focused approach. What emerged as the greatest challenge to individualized care approaches was the reeducation and the changing of attitudes of providers because of their training, prior experience, and philosophies. It would appear that traditional care providers may have attitudinal barriers to individualized care because of longstanding commitment to pre-designed programming, categorical funding that results in categorical services, and mere resistance to change (Burchard and Clarke, 1990).

Driving the service model of the Family Mosaic Project are the concepts of family preservation, wrap-around services, cultural competence, flexible funding, and use of natural environments for service delivery. It is useful to view the primary goal of health and human service provision to children in a system of care as delivering individualized care that meets the specific needs of any one child and family. In a system of care, individualized services address the unique needs of a particular child as opposed to requiring the child to fit a pre-determined service. The concept of wrap-around individualized care has been pioneered by such programs as Kaleidoscope in Chicago and the Alaska Youth Initiative. The main principles of wrap-around services that influence FMP services are its mandate to provide unconditional child-family centered care in the least restrictive environment.

"WRAP-AROUND CARE"

The Family Mosaic Project provides individualized services via a wrap-around care approach. The term wrap-around evolved from the concept of identifying the needs of a particular child and with access to flexible funds literally setting up services and resources that can be molded and flexed to respond to that child's needs, and to be able to follow that child wherever he/she may be to continue that individualized service. Specific principles of wrap-around care have been developed and are consistent with the general individualized care philosophy. Generally stated, the principles include: building and maintaining normal lifestyles for children and families; ensuring that services are client-centered; providing services to children unconditionally; planning for the long term when designing and providing care; implementing services that help children and families move and work toward less restrictive environments; having competent and well-trained providers of care; establishing consensus among key decision makers in the client's treatment; funding of services with flexible budgets; installing a "gatekeeper" function, and developing measurable accountability.

The Family Mosaic Project has been most successful with implementation of the majority of the wrap-around principles. More success can be seen in the building and maintaining of normal lifestyles, the training and hiring of competent staff and providers, gaining access to flexible funding, providing gatekeeper functions, and developing measurable accountability.

MEASURING SUCCESS

The primary goal of the Family Mosaic Project is to provide San Francisco's children and youth who have serious emotional problems with a local system of culturally competent services that will enhance family unity, capability, and responsibility. The system will provide for stability in placement, in the least restrictive setting, to enable these children and youth to engage in behavior that is appropriate for their age and their community and to attend and progress in local schools. To gauge progress toward these goals and to guide program staff in service design, a set of outcome objectives was established. The basis for four key outcome objectives included: assisting children to remain in school, keeping children at home and in their community, which meant reducing hospital stays, and reducing incarceration. Initial data evaluations along the lines of these outcome objectives have indicated that the project is meeting with some success. By focusing on school attendance and school performance, detention days, and acute hospitalization, a number of indicators of service impact were identified (Glazer and Morgenstern, 1993). After about one year of involvement in the Family Mosaic Project, significant trends were identifiable, such as increased school attendance by approximately 50 percent (Boles, Martinez, and Marx, 1993). Those individuals who went to school more often showed significant increases in school performance as reported by their parents, teachers, and case managers (Lourie and Katz-Levy, 1991). Children in the project who were attending school regularly showed some increases in attendance and also improved in school performance. The school attendance and school performance trends were gathered based on a population of 120 children and families with current and prior enrollment in the project. Focusing on the detention history of a population of 25 children involved in the juvenile justice system revealed a clear trend in reduced incarceration rates following one year of project involvement. The trend indicated an approximate decrease in detentions of 50 percent (Boles, Martinez, and Marx, 1993). Acute hospitalization rates of the 120 children reviewed hovered around 25 percent prior to the project and after one year of service the hospitalization rates hovered around 2 to 4 percent. Although the findings reported here are preliminary, they are certainly promising and indicate clear trends of service success.

CULTURAL COMPETENCE

To provide culturally competent care, the Family Mosaic Project focused on the skills and ability of the staff, the nature of the services provided, and the context for delivery of the services. The definition of cultural competence that guided the project was derived from the work of Terry Cross and others in the 1989 monograph entitled *Towards a Culturally Competent System of Care*. The definition reads as follows:

> Cultural competence is a set of congruent behaviors, attitudes, and policies that come together in a system, agency, or among professionals to work effectively in cross-cultural situations. A culturally competent system of care acknowledges and incorporates–at all levels– the importance of culture, the assessment of cross-cultural relations, vigilance towards the dynamics that result from cultural differences, the expansion of cultural knowledge, and the adaptation of services to meet culturally-unique needs" (*Focal Point*, 1988)

Staff were carefully selected due to experience, knowledge, commitment to children and families, and ability to grow and change. It was imperative that staff reflect the ethnic make-up of the client population with consideration being given to degree of community need (Cross et al., 1989). Staff training was and is a major priority with parents, outside agencies, consultants, and staff contributing their particular knowledge to enhance staff abilities. Since the case management staff of the project consists of child welfare workers, juvenile probation officers, psychiatric social workers, public health nurses, teachers, and counselors, staff also participate in the sharing of across-disciplinary knowledge and skills. Designing services that are geared to keeping children at home and to helping families stay together is paramount to culturally competent care. Helping primary caregivers utilize existing resources and utilize natural resources available in the community and among family can aid in family preservation while enhancing individual child functioning. Services have to be community-based by being located in the neighborhood and responsive to the needs of the community setting and environment.

Cross et al. would argue that cultural competence is not ultimately attainable and can be only approached. Key aspects of any case management approach that will help to move any system toward cultural competence must include: the provision of services by recognized and credible case managers that are from and of the community, services that are effective and meet the particular needs of any child and the child's family, and the provision of services in the least restrictive environment.

By providing case management services in a Team Model, FMP has been able to combine agency-trained and agency-identified staff with indigenous staff who have cut their teeth in the community and among children and families representing the target populations served by the project. The indigenous staff provide almost immediate credibility to the case management team that has the charge of working with, and on behalf of, children and families that have become disenchanted with the agencies designed to serve them.

Some major tasks of the case management team are to gather data and information, conduct extensive interviews and meetings with the targeted child and family to understand their needs and issues, and identify the potential resources necessary to serve the child and family.

Following this information-gathering period focusing on the comprehensive health and human service needs of the child, a plan of care meeting is held with the parent, child, teachers, service providers, physicians, probation officer, therapists, and others to agree on a specific individualized care plan for the identified child and the family. A culturally competent service plan can be approached if all participants agree to the plan and recognize their respective roles in carrying it out, if adequate flexible funds are available to drive the plan, if the plan is designed to meet the individualized needs of the child, and if the multiple needs of the child are addressed by the plan.

The major goal of any culturally competent approach to care for children is to provide services in the least restrictive and most natural environment possible. The desire of the FMP is to provide that care whenever possible in the child's home and family of origin. The desire to enhance the family environment and give the necessary resources to ensure the enhanced functioning of the family is paramount to quality care. When it is not appropriate to serve children in their homes, the next best environment may be a home-like situation such as foster care or relative care. Keeping children in homes and in the community has to be a primary objective of any culturally competent approach.

FLEXIBLE FUNDING

Funding for the Family Mosaic Project for the first four years of operation included combined Robert Wood Johnson grant dollars, California State Department of Mental Health block grant funding, and local city and county dollars. A primary objective of the project was to secure by the end of four years stable and long-term funding that hopefully would bring additional revenue to San Francisco and maximize existing city and county revenue. In seeking to maximize existing dollars, the basic premise that local dollars could be pooled across health and human service agencies, creating a richer reservoir of funds that could be used to match Federal Medicaid dollars for emotional disturbed youth, was a guiding principle that encouraged the local departments of mental health, social services, juvenile probation, the school district, and public health to contribute in kind dollars to support the project. By acknowledging that the children and families that exist in the multiple health and human service agencies are for the most part the same, and that regardless of where they show up in the system their needs often are multiple and span across health, mental health, education, social services, and probation, the contributors toward the Family Mosaic Project were able to increase their identified funds by using them to match Medicaid dollars, initially through targeted case management and currently through capitation.

In May of 1993, the California State Department of Health Services entered into a contract with the Family Mosaic Project, the Department of Public Health in the City and County of San Francisco, to provide Medicaid billing services to an emotionally disturbed population of children in a capitated model of financing. This agreement meant that for every child enrolled in the project who was on Medicaid or Medicaid eligible, the project would receive a finite amount of money to address their mental health needs. The payment for services for each child would be monthly and would be up front. By receiving capitated funds, the project was able to receive Medicaid dollars that were restricted to certain modes of service delivery and use those dollars to fund flexible services. The primary restrictions were that the funds had to be used for predetermined service arenas and additional funds could not be received beyond the capitated amount. By captivating funds, the project has to track every dollar that comes for each child, ensure that the services provided are effective and accomplishing their intended goals, track and monitor the service cost for each child and family, and intertwine clinical decision making with fiscal planning, never losing sight of the reality that quality care, and not necessarily cost control, was the main objective.

OBSTACLES TO CHANGE

In implementing wrap-around care principles, the Family Mosaic Project has struggled most in the area of consensus-building among key decision makers in the client's life (Uribe de Mena, 1992). More specifically this struggle has focused on the interagency level of treatment planning and service design, with providers and traditional agencies competing with parents and primary caregivers for the final say as to what is needed and necessary for appropriate treatment and adequate expenditure of funds. The primal dilemma for FMP has been its desire to operate in true partnership with parents and the need to co-exist and represent in certain situations both providers and health and human service agencies. Take for example a scenario where an FMP family advocate has to assume the role of providing support and advocacy for a parent or child who needs to take legal action against a service provider to get the discharge process to stop so that the parent can access additional resources, and/or gain time to be better able to support or actively fight placement recommendations for their child. Generally it is in the area of parent and community involvement in a meaningful and empowering way that most service delivery systems meet obstacles and impasses. Often it is in this area that professionals and parents find it difficult to work as members of the same team; they may find it difficult to ensure that the needs of emotionally troubled youth are met without pointing the finger of blame or engendering anger. Yet one true benefit of a system of care is the potential to bring together the identified resources in the service delivery sector and make them available to the primary caregiver, often the parent, to allow them to control and influence along with the child the appropriate degree and direction of movement toward more positive functioning. As is the case in the State of California and in particular in San Francisco, parents and service providers often find themselves on the opposite side of the table fighting for control of resources, shouting to be heard and to be acknowledged as the authority of the identified child. This adversarial situation gets in the way of real partnership and true empowerment, and in most cases does a severe disservice to the emotionally troubled child. Coordination of service delivery and to some degree service orchestration can be severely compromised in such an atmosphere and continues to be a challenge for Family Mosaic. The struggle to meet this challenge will continue with three process goals clearly at the forefront to continue to guide the Family Mosaic Project: (1) providing equal access for parent and child in decision making regarding treatment and service delivery; (2) ensuring that children and parents have a voice and are listened to at all junctures of planning and implementation; and (3) acknowledging that true ownership can only come from child and parent agreement and commitment to any plan that concerns them by seeing to it that no plan is funded or accepted unless there is clear parent/child buy-in.

Since the inception of the Family Mosaic Project, there were hopes that a model pilot program would have considerable influence on the existing systems it represents in terms of service delivery, financing of care, principles and philosophy, agency and provider relationships, service system structure, parent empowerment, computerized record keeping, and interagency collaboration. At this point in the history of the project, a number of system changes can be identified as well as a number of successful and unsuccessful struggles.

The city and county of San Francisco will benefit from the establishment of a system of care that will be the foundation for the development of Health and Human Services for children and their families across agencies, community-based organizations, neighborhoods, parents, and children. A real commitment to collaboration and reducing fragmentation has become the mainstay of daily interactions and basic functions among the major child services players and advocates. The entire Children's Mental Health System has embraced the concepts of wrap-around care, pooled financing, automated record keeping, ongoing evaluation and assessment to ensure accountability, and collaboration with health and human services agencies on behalf of children and families. A city-wide effort is underway that receives sanction from the Mayor's office and is guided through the Mayor's Office of Children, Youth, and Families. This city-wide effort focuses on neighborhood-based planning, interagency collaboration, development of comprehensive cross-agency data and information sharing, revenue enhancement, violence prevention, determinination of the needs of communities and neighborhoods to develop a healthier city, and efforts to de-categorize health and human services funding with the help of state legislation.

Institutions are difficult to change and often change is possible only when major fiscal or structural catastrophes occur. This resistance has resulted in pockets of hesitancy that exemplify the struggles yet to be overcome. One such struggle has to do with the degree to which health and human services agencies that serve children and families communicate on a regular basis and attempt to break down the barriers of child ownership, turf, and philosophical issues (Uribe, Boles, and Morimoto, 1993). Without regular sharing of philosophical stances and motivational foundations, it is difficult to understand why certain actions are taken and why certain attitudes may prevail. Different professional disciplines are often aligned with certain agencies and therefore find it necessary to protect their professions and to some degree their professional egos. Unfortunately, this turf bantering only results in conflictual approaches and poor if any coordination. Responsibility for children has become an issue that legal statutes and federal/state mandates dictate all too well. Agencies who are directed by these regulations get caught up in the child ownership war when clearly the parents/ legal guardians/primary providers are the necessary and natural child "owners," if such a term is appropriate. What the agencies need to come to terms with is the fact that they and their staff are the servants, the children and their parents are the recipients of the services, and therefore the parents are the ones to have the ultimate and final say.

RECOMMENDATIONS

In the current national climate where health care reform is a major topic of debate, case management and forms of case management such as primary care coordination are of major concern. As with the many factors that have catapulted this nation into the health care reform debate, many similar factors force us to utilize case management to address the needs of emotionally disturbed children and youth. Perhaps a health care crisis would not exist in this nation if the health care delivery system were more coordinated, if it were designed in such a way that all Americans had equal access, if services were less fragmented, and if the cost of care were manageable.

REFERENCES

Boles, A.J., Martinez, M., and Marx, L. (March 1993). *A New Wave of Caring: A Collaborative Approach to Keeping Kids in the Community, at Home and Out of Trouble,* the 6th Annual Research Conference, A System of Care for Children's Mental Health: Expanding the Research Base, March 1-3, 1993, Tampa, Florida.

Burchard, J.D. and Clarke, R.T. (1990). "The Role of Individualized Care in a Service Delivery System for Children and Adolescents with Severely Maladjusted Behavior." *The Journal of Mental Health Administration, 17,* 48-60.

Collins, B. and Collins, T. (1990) "Professional Responses to Parent Involvement in Treatment Planning," in A. Algarin and R. Friedman (Eds.), *3rd Annual Research Conference Proceedings–A System of Care for Children's Mental Health: Building a Research Base,* 247-256. Tampa, FL: Florida Mental Health Institute.

Cross, T., Bazron, B., Dennis, K., and Isaacs, M. (1989). *Towards a Culturally Competent System of Care,* CASSP Technical Assistance Center. Washington.

Focal Point. (1988). What does it mean to be a culturally competent professional? Portland, Oregon: Portland State University Research and Training Center. 3-17.

Glazer, W.M. and Morgenstern, H. (1993). "The Impact of Utilization Management on Hospital Length of Stay and Illness." *Administration and Policy in Mental Health., 21,* 41-50.

Jordan, D.D. and Hernandez, M. (1990). "The Ventura Planning Model: A Proposal for Mental Health Reform." *The Journal of Mental Health Administration, 17,* 26-47.

Knitzer, J. (1982). *Unclaimed Children.* Washington, DC: Children's Defense Fund.

Lourie, S.I. and Katz-Levy, J. (1991). "New Directions for Mental Health Services for Families and Children." *Families in Society, 72,* 277-285.

MacFarquhar, K.W., Dowrick, P.W., and Risley, T.R. (1993). "Individualizing Services for Seriously Emotionally Disturbed Youth: A Nationwide Survey." *Administration and Policy in Mental Health, 20,* 165-172.

Patterson, D.Y. (1993). "Twenty-First Century Managed Mental Health: Point-of-

Service Treatment Networks." *Administration and Policy in Mental Health,* *21*(1), 27-34.

Smith, L., Attkisson, C.C., and Boles, A.J. (March 1993). *Systems of Care Research in California: Current Results and Future Directions: A Symposium,* the 6th Annual Research Conference, a System of Care for Children's Mental Health: Expanding the Research Base, Tampa, Florida.

Stroul, B.A. and Friedman R.M. (1986). *A System of Care for Severely Emotionally Disturbed Children and Youth.* Washington, DC: Georgetown University Child Development Center, CASSP Technical Assistance Center.

Uribe de Mena, J. (1992). "Multiagency Staffing: The Challenge." *In Focus: Family Matters.* Winter.

Uribe, J., Boles, A.J., and Morimoto, C. (1993) *Making It Work When the Ground Keeps Moving Under Your Feet: Administration and Management of the Family Mosaic Project.* Virginia Beach Conference, Children and Adolescents with Emotional or Behavioral Disorders, October 3-6, 1993, Richmond, Virginia.

VanDenBerg, J.E. (1993). Integration of individualized mental health services into the system of care for children and adolescents. *Administration and Policy in Mental Health,* 20(4), 247-257.

Index

Abandonment, 155-156,172,174
A-B-C-D cognitive restructuring
    method, 132
Abramson, J., 5
Abuse
    and post-traumatic stress disorder,
      194-196
    sexual and physical in women,
      178,194-196,201-204. *See*
      also Sexual abuse
    substance. *See* Substance abuse
Accessibility, 4
    racism and, 181-182
    to Southeast Asians, 149
Acculturation continuum, 19-20
Ackerson, L. M., 80,91,93
Acosta, F. X., 1,111,121,128,135
Adebimpe, V. R., 1,181
Adler, D. A., 150
Adler, P., 45
Advocacy, 62,64,66,150
    as function of case manager,
      22-23
    for homeless
      major principles, 68-69
      in shelters, 60
    for Southeast Asian refugees,
      164-165
    system-level, 23
AFDC (Aid to Families with
    Dependent Children), 130
Affective disorders. *See* Bipolar
    disorder; Depression
African Americans
    and AIDS/HIV, 201
    biculturalist dynamic and,
      178-180
    biracial children of, 179

African Americans *(continued)*
    "falling out" syndrome, 10
    family/community support,
      176-178
    gender roles, 175-176
    language, 27
    medication effect differences, 23
    "play relative" concept, 171-172
    premature grandmothers, 175
    racism and service delivery,
      180-181
    religion and, 180
    social supports, 171-175
    special problems of, 169-170
    stereotyping of, 179-180
    teenage pregnancy and single
      parent homes, 174-175
    worldview, 170-171
Age
    and assertiveness, 135
    and depression in Native
      Americans, 85,91
Aguilera, D., 107
AICPP (Native American Cancer
    Control Project), 83-96
Aid to Families with Dependent
    Children (AFDC), 130
AIDS/HIV, 200-201
Alaska Natives, 81. *See also* Native
    Americans
Alaska Youth Initiative, 216,222
Alcohol. *See* Substance abuse
Alcohol, Drug Abuse, and Mental
    Health Administration, 52
Alienation, 52,59. *See also*
    Disaffiliation
Allen, G., 61,65
Alpert, M., 27,104

American Psychiatric Association, 119
American Psychological Association, 123
Andranovich, G. D., 61,62
Aneshensel, C. S., 90,91,197
Anthony, W., 4
Anthropology, 26
    cultural, 8
Antipsychotic medications, 23
Apfel, F., 189
"Appropriate" behavior, 21,152-153
Arce, A., 53
Arewa, B. D., 42
Armas, R., 122
Armstrong, E., 106
Aruffo, J., 189
Ashton, H., 186
Asian Americans, 190-192. *See* Southeast Asians and individual nationalities
    medication effect differences, 23
Asian Community Mental Health Services (Oakland, CA), 146-147
Assertiveness, Southeast Asian attitudes toward, 150
Assertiveness training, 135-137
Assessment
    acculturation continuum, 19-20
    cultural appreciation and, 151-156
    cultural bias in approach, 11
    culturally syntonic of Southeast Asians, 157-159
    environmental, 20
    functional behavioral, 12-13
    goal setting, 21-22
    personal interaction and, 18-19
    planning/prioritizing, 20-21
    in women, 186
Ataques de nervios syndrome, 10-11
Atkinson, D. R., 102,103,104,105
At-risk
    individuals, 62
    populations, 2

Attkisson, C. C., 93,211
Availability of services, 3-4
    racism and, 181-182
    and Southeast Asian refugees, 148-150
Axis I vs. Axis II disorders, 3

Bachrach, L. L., 1,6,24,42,43, 46,47,54,55,129
Bag ladies, 58-59
Bahr, H., 197
Bahr, J. M., 57
Ballentine, R., 1,4
Balwin, B. A., 107
Baron, A. E., 80,91,93
Barrera, M., 121
Barrow, S. M., 58,66,67
Bassuk, E. L., 42,47,52
Batchelder, W. H., 8
Baumohl, J., 14,52
Baxter, E., 47,50,56,57,58,68
Bazron, B., 225
Beals, J., 80
Bean, G. J., 53
Beck, A. T., 124,125,126
Beck, J. C., 194,195
Beech, R. P., 106
Behavior
    "appropriate," 21,152-153
    culturally specific expressions, 16
Behavioral assessment, 12-13
Beiser, M., 147
Belcher, J. R., 51,65
Belle, D., 48,49
Ben, R., 11
Bender, M. G., 3
Bereavement, 154
    and depression, 122-123
    Latino practices, 107-110
Berenson, B. G., 107
Bergman, L. I., 4,17,18
Berlin, S., 193
Berry, J., 11
Berry, J. W., 127

Berry, S., 119,120
Bestman, E. W., 42,43
Bias
    gender, 187. *See also* Gender
        roles; Women
    Western cultural,
        9-10,15-16,79,92,170-171
Biculturalism of case manager, 25
Bifurcated approach, 2
Biggs, J., 24
Bilingualism
    compound, 27-28
    and refugee services, 150-151
    and schizophrenia, 104
    subordinate, 28
Billig, N., 17,61
Bipolar disorder, 190
Biracial children, 178-179
Birth control, 189-192
"Black English," 27
Blaming the victim, 79
Blau, J., 50
Bloom, B. L., 105
Blumenthal, R., 102
Blumenthal, S., 186,189
Boat people, 145-167. *See also*
        Refugees; Southeast Asians
Boe, J. J., 152
Boehnlein, J. K., 152
Boemel, G. V., 148
Boque, D. A., 57
Boles, Abner J. III, 211-231
Bond, G. R., 4,61
Borland, A., 62
Boulette, T. R., 135
Bowery (New York City), 47,57
Bowman, J. T., 110,111
Boyd-Franklin, N., 171
Brammer, L. M., 107
Breadwinner role, 12,13
Breakey, W. R., 41,46,51,188
Breslin, R., 10
Breton, M., 60
Brown, G., 124
Brown, K. S., 52

Bruce, M. L., 120
Bryer, J. B., 194
Buckner, J. C., 47
Buddhism, 21
Budman, S. H., 106
Bui, A., 11
Bulimia, 11
Burchard, J. D., 222
Bureaucracy
    and entitlement, 122,123
    and mentally ill, 101
Burgess, A. W., 107
Burghardt, E., 26
Burke, S., 196
Burnham A., 3,41,47,53,119,120
Burns, D., 126,132
Bush, C. T., 64

Cairns, V., 124
California Department of Mental
        Health, 227
California Psychological Inventory
        (CPI), 81
California State Department
        of Health Services, 227
California studies
    Asian Community Mental Health
        Services (Oakland), 145-167
    Family Mosaic Project (San
        Francisco), 215-231
    of Native American depression,
        79-96
    Women's Issues Consultation
        Team (San Francisco General
        Hospital), 187-206
Calsyn, R. J., 61,65,197
Cambodians, 147,165. *See also*
        Asian Americans; Southeast
        Asians
Campbell, R., 45
Cancro, R., 24
Caper, R. A., 121
Caplan, G., 107,109
Caplow, T., 57

Caribbean Africans "falling out"
syndrome, 10
Carillo, C., 99,102
Carkuff, R. R., 107,182
Carlos, M. L., 121
Carter, G. W., 100
Casas, J. M., 102,103,104,111
Case management. *See also* Case
managers
characteristics, 4-7
clinical defined, 6-7
communication aspects
cultural reframing, 31-33
language, 27-29
metaphorical usage, 29-31
conclusions about, 33-34
contemporary conceptualizations,
4-5
and crisis intervention, 100-101
cultural aspects
activities and, 16-25
case manager as culture broker,
2-3,5-6,25-27,151
and mental illness, 15-16
psychiatric (medical) model,
8-15
role of culture, 7-8
culturally competent, 25
and deinstitutionalization, 100
developmental acquisition model,
5-6
emergence, 3-4
historical background, 1-3
in homelessness, 41
models
Community Support Program,
61-62
engagement, 63
intensive case management,
62-63,68-69
multidisciplinary continuous
care, 63
person-in-environment approach,
2
public sector, 5

Case management *(continued)*
rehabilitation-oriented, 64
service brokerage model, 5-6
and Southeast Asian refugees,
148-150
Case managers
advocacy role, 22-23,164-165
biculturalism of, 25
community developer role, 165
as culture brokers, 2-3,5-6,25-27,
151
educational role, 164-165
gatekeeper role, 23
linking function of, 22-23,66,151
Caseness concept, 84
Caseness rates of Native American
depression, 84,92-95
Casework vs. psychotherapy debate,
19
CASSP (Children and Adolescent
Systems Service Program),
212,216
Caucasians
depression compared with Native
Americans, 81
health insurance, 103
mean number of therapy sessions,
107
medication effect differences, 23
Causality, supernatural, 15-16,153
Census Bureau. *See* U. S. Bureau
of the Census
Center for Epidemiologic Studies
Depression Scale (CES-D),
81,83-96. *See also* CES-D
Centers for Disease Control (CDC),
201
Cervical cancer, 188
CES-D
discussion
caseness rate, 92-95
risk factors, 90-91
smoking, 91
subgroup differences, 91
in Native Americans

CES-D, in Native Americans
  (continued)
    cutoff scores, 93
    instrument to measure
      depression, 82
    results, 85-90
    study design, 83-85
    reliability coefficients, 87
Chafetz, L., 52
Chamas, J., 45
Chamberlain, R., 1,5,64
Chan, F., 122
Chao, C., 161
Cheeves, K., 194
Cheung, F., 1,2,3,149
Chicago
  homeless study, 53
  KALEIDOSCOPE project,
    219,222
Chicanos. *See* Latinos
Children and Adolescent Systems
    Service Program (CASSP),
    212,216
Children and youth
  biracial, 178-179
  case management background,
    211-212
  Family Mosaic Project, 215-216
    coordinated case management,
      217-220
    cultural competence in, 224-226
    funding of, 227-228
    goals of, 216-217
    individualized assistance
      approach, 220-222
    measuring success in, 222-224
    obstacles to change, 228-230
    recommendations, 230-231
    services available, 220
    "wrap-around care" concept,
      221
  systems of care, 213-215

Chinese Americans, 146
  family involvement, 32
  medication effect differences, 23
Chronicity, 15-16
Chung, J., 201
Church, G. J., 101
Clark, V., 90,91,197
Clarke, R. T., 222
Clemons, J. R., 64
Clients
  experiences with mental health
    system, 18,19,56
  positive relationships with, 17-18
  reciprocal relationship triangle,
    6-7
Clinical case management defined,
    6-7
Clothing. *See* Material needs
Cobbs, P., 181
Cocaine. *See* Substance abuse
Cognition deficit, 177
Cognitive-behavioral therapy
  advantages of, 123-124
  in depressed Latinos
    assertiveness training, 135-137
    assessment, 126-128
    beginning services, 130-131
    cognitive restructuring, 132-133
    comorbidity and, 120
    conclusions, 139-140
    cultural barriers, 121
    integration with case
      management, 126-138
    interventions, 128-130
    pleasant activities
      ("distracciones"), 133-135
    prerequisites, 126-127
    in primary care, 122-126
    problem themes and gender
      issues, 128
    psychoeducation, 131-132
    psychosocial stressors, 121-122
    socioeconomic status and,
      120-121
    termination, 137-138

Cognitive-behavioral therapy
  (continued)
  in depression, 17
Cognitive restructuring, 132-133
Cohen, B., 4
Cohen, C. I., 57
Cohen, M., 4,55,56,63
Cohen, N. L., 58
Cole, J., 186,189
Collins, B., 213
Collins, T., 213
Colliver, J. A., 194
Colson, P., 49,51,52,53,54,58
Comas-Diaz, L., 1,126,128,135,136
Communication
  culturally specific expressions, 16
  in forming positive relationships,
    18
  interpretors vs. translators, 28
  language, 27-29
  metaphorical usage, 29-31
Community studies, 47
Community Support Systems
    (NIMH), 61-62,64-65
Community worldview of African
    American, 170-171
Comorbidity
  Latinos at high risk for, 120-121
  National Comorbidity Survey,
    120-121
Compliance/noncompliance. *See
    also* Underutilization
  and language, 30-31
  Latino, 103
Compound bilingualism, 27-28
Connell, V., 194
Conover, S., 46
Constantino, G., 102
Continuity of care, 6,22,63
Contraception, 189-192
Corrigan, F. V., 80
Countertransference, 6,25
Cournos, F. C., 58
Coverdale, J., 189
Cowan, C. D., 46

Cox, G. B., 103
CPI (California Psychological
    Inventory), 81
Craine, L. S., 194
Crisis/crisis
  cultural variations in defining,
    107-110
  as danger and opportunity, 109
  defined, 107
  reduced defensiveness concept,
    109-110
  sequence of crisis events, 109-110
Crisis intervention
  cultural variations in defining,
    107-110
  defined, 106-107
  and deinstitutionalization,
    100-101
  duration, 107
  effectiveness, 106
  ethnic help-seeking patterns and,
    111-113
  Latino studies, 99-114. *See also*
    Latinos
  summary and conclusions about,
    113-114
  theories and models
    eclectic theory, 110-111
    psychosocial transition theory,
      110,112
  therapeutic alliance in, 111
Cross, L., 123
Cross, T., 225
Crystal, S., 197
Cultural anthropology, 8,26
Cultural reframing, 23,31-33
  intra-cultural, 32-33
Culture
  defined, 7,42,48
  disease and, 7
  of homeless, 42,43
  intracultural vs. intercultural
    differences, 7-8
  of poverty, 44

Culture *(continued)*
 systems approach, 8
 of underclass, 44
 vs. language, 27
 work, 12,13,162,163
Culture-bound syndromes, 10-11
Culture brokering, 2-3,5-6,25-27,151
Curanderos, 112-113
Curtis, H. C., 106
Cutler, D., 169

D'Andrade, R. G., 7,8,44
Davis, G. L., 81
Day treatment programs, 14-15
Deinstitutionalization, 3-5
 and fertility rates of mentally ill,
  189
 and need for case management,
  100-101
Deitchman, W. S., 1,4,18,21
De La Cancela, V., 12
Delgado, M., 128
Delpa, C., 124
DelVecchio-Good, M. J., 10-11
Demoralization vs. depression
  in Native Americans, 79-96
Dennis, D. I., 47
Dennis, D. L, 46,47,61
Dennis, K., 225
Dependency
 in refugee populations, 158-159
 vs. gratitude in Latinos, 138
Depression, 17,154,164,175,194,
  199-200. *See also* Depression
  scales
 and bereavement in Latino client,
  107-110
 clinical vs. demoralization
  and epidemiology, 82
  and primary prevention, 82
 cognitive therapy in, 17
 comorbidity in, 120
 DSM-III-R Western cultural bias,
  79-80

Depression *(continued)*
 epidemiology, 119-120
 Latino study of cognitive-
  behavioral therapy, 119-140
 in Native Americans, 79-96
  caseness rate, 92-95
  and health status, 94
  risk factors, 90-91
  and smoking, 91
  subgroup differences, 91
  and symptom expression, 94-95
Depression Guideline Panel, 119
Depression scales
 California Psychological
  Inventory (CPI), 81
 CES-D, 81,83-96
D'Ercole, A., 45,49
De Snyder, 102
Developmental acquisition model,
  5-6
Developmental disability,
  176-177,190
Diabetes, 174-175
Diagnosis/diagnoses
 cultural bias in, 10-11
 multiple, 19
Diagnostic and Statistical Manual.
  See DSM-III
Dick, R. W., 80,91,93
Dietzen, L., 61
Digest of Education Statistics, 101
DiNitto, D., 124
Dion, G., 193
Disability
 developmental, 176-177,180
 as socioeconomic value, 13-14
Disaffiliation, 52,53,56,59,67
Discharge planning, 100-101,
  137-138
Distracciones, 134-135
Dixon, L., 61,62
Dohrenwend, B. P., 80,81,82,90,92
Dorn, F. J., 110
Dowrick, P. W., 221
Draguns, J. G., 2,19

Drake, R. E., 26,42,48
Drug abuse. *See* Substance abuse
DSM-III
 Axis I vs. Axis II, 3
 Western cultural bias, 10
DSM-III-R, 123
 and post-traumatic stress disorder,
  152-153
 Western cultural bias, 79-80
Dual diagnosis, 3
Duncan, G. J., 44
Duncan, J. W., 135,136
Dworkin, R. J., 24
Dwyer, Eleanor Valdes, 119-140

Eagle, P. F., 59
Eastwood, J., 199
Eclectic model of crisis intervention,
  110-111
Education
 and Latinos, 101
 psycho-, 20,24-25,131-132
 role of case managers, 164-165
 for Southeast Asian refugees,
  164-165
Edwards, Valerie Roxanne, 169-184
*Effective Psychotherapy
  for Low-Income and Minority
  Patients*, 121-122
Egri, G., 80,81,82
Elisabeth, M., 42
Ellis, A., 132
Elpers, J. R., 3
Emergency room use, 182
Emery, G., 124,125,126
Emic perspective, 10-11,47,152
Employment, 12-13. *See also*
  Unemployment; Work culture
 and depression, 122-123
 and depression risk in Native
  Americans, 85,91-92
Empowerment in refugee
  populations, 158-159
Engagement, 63,66,67

"Enmeshment"
 vs. interdependency, 16
 vs. involvement, 32-33
Entitlement, 122-123
Environmental assessment, 20
Epidemiologic Catchment Area
  Survey, 120-121
Eshleman, S., 120,139
Espiritistas, 112
Espiritualistas, 112
Estroff, S., 13
Ethnic minorities compared with
  mentally ill, 2
Ethnographic research, 47
Etic perspective, 10,56,152
 imposed, 11-12
Euro-Americans, medication effect
  differences, 23
Eurocentrism, 9-10,15-16,79,92,
  170-171
Evans, L. A., 1,121
External vs. internal causation,
  15-16

Fabrega, H., 1,7,8,9,11,16,17
Fairweather, G. W., 12
Falco, K., 206
Falicov, C. J., 131
"Falling out," 10-11
Family/families
 advocacy with, 22-23
 African-American, 171-176
  caretaker roles in, 176
  role of children in, 175-176
 "enmeshment" of
  vs. interdependency, 16
  vs. involvement, 32-33
 homeless, 52-53
  family lodge shelters, 60
 Latino as natural supports, 60
 migration history of refugee,
  156-157
 and Native American social
  homogenity, 94-95

Family/families *(continued)*
  privacy/reticence issues
     in refugees, 160
  schizophrenogenic, 24-25
  of Southeast Asian refugees, 148
  strengths, 157-158
Family lodges, 60
Family Mosaic Project (Robert
     Wood Johnson Initiative)
  background, 215-216
  coordinated case management,
     217-220
  cultural competence in, 224-226
  funding of, 227-228
  goals of, 216-217
  individualized assistance
     approach, 220-222
  measuring success in, 222-224
  obstacles to change, 228-230
  recommendations, 230-231
  services available, 220
  "wrap-around care" concept, 219,
     221,222-224,228
Family planning, 189-192
Farkas, M., 1,4,64
Farr, R., 3,41,47,53
Fay, J. S., 92
Fay, S. W., 92
Federal Task Force on Homelessness
     and Severe Mental Illness,
     60,63
Feitel, B., 45
Feleppa, R., 152
Fellin, Phillip, 41-69
Feminization of poverty, 174
Field-ground perception (Gestalt
     concept), 31
First, R. J., 42,45,49,65
Fischer, P., 41,45,46,49,51,188
Fisher, W., 193
Fiske, J., 44,45,59
Flaskerud, J. H., 102
Fleming, C. M., 80,91,93
Flexibility, negative consequences
     of African American, 177

Fodor, I., 60
Folks, D., 23
Fox, R., 150
Frank, J. B., 114
Frank, J. D., 80,81,114
Franklin, J. L., 64
Freddolino, P. P., 56,61,64
Fredricks, L., 80,81
Freedman, J., 22
Frerichs, R., 90,91,197
Freudenheim, M., 50
Friedman, N., 61,62
Friedman, R. M., 213,214,216
Fujino, D. C., 103,121,127,149
Fullilove, M., 199
Fullilove, R., 199
Functional behavioral assessment,
     12-13
Functional (rehabilitation) model,
     12-15

Gang rape, 195
Garfield, S. L, 107
Garrett, G., 197
Gatekeeper role of case managers,
     23
Gaw, A. C., 42,191
Gaxiola, S., 126
Geller, J., 193
Gender as culture, 185-206
Gender bias, 187. *See also* Gender
     roles; Women
Gender differences. *See also* women
  in depression in Native
     Americans, 85,87-89,90
  Latino in assertiveness, 135-136
  in marriage rates of homeless, 197
Gender roles
  African Americans, 170-171,
     175-176
  breadwinner, 12-13
  and caregiver responsibilities,
     32-33
  and depression in Latinos, 128

Gender roles *(continued)*
  and distractional activities,
    134-135
  and pain relief, 137
General Accounting Office (GAO),
    46
George, L. K., 54
Gerhart, U. C., 100
Gewirtzman, R., 60
Giamo, B., 47,57
Gibbs, J., 1
Giggling behavior in Cambodian
    women, 153-154
Gilliland, B. E., 110,111
Gilmore, S., 44
Glazer, W. M., 224
Goal setting, 21-22
Goering, P. N., 1,4,64,65,197
Goldfinger, S. M., 41,42,59,60
Goldman, H. H., 24,54,61
Goldstein, A. P., 126
Goldstrom, I., 1,5
Gong-Guy, E., 148
González, G., 123,125,129
Good, B. J., 10,11,17
Goodwin, J. M., 194
Gory, M. L., 50
Gounis, K., 47,59
Grandmothers, premature, 175
Gratitude vs. dependency in Latinos,
    138
Greenfield, S., 119,120
Greenfield, T. K., 93
Greenlee, R., 65
Greenstone, J. D., 50
Grieger, R., 132
Grier, W., 181
Griffith, E., 1,62
Grimson, R. C., 84
Grossman, D. C., 79
Grossman, S., 49,51,52,53,54,58
Group orientation, 14-15
Group therapy, 129-130,131
  for African Americans, 173
  in sexual abuse, 203-204

Group therapy *(continued)*
  for Southeast Asian refugees, 163
Grunberg, J., 59
Guardar (repression), 136-137
Gurman, A. S., 111
Gurza, R., 122
Gutt, W., 64
Guzman, J., 126

Haggard, L. K., 42,45,55,61
Hallucinations, 153
Halpern, H. A., 109
Hamburg, J., 57
Hamilton, J., 192-193,201
Handel, M., 188,189
Harding, C. M., 15
Hardwood, A., 108
Harris, M., 1,4,6,17,18,45,129,206
Harrod, J., 1,17
Harsch, H., 24
Harwin, B., 124
Hays, R. D., 119,120
Health, D. B., 79
Health beliefs, 111-113
Health insurance
  and depression risk, 92
  Latinos and, 103
Health status
  and depression, 85,89-90,122,
    136-137
  and depression risk, 90-91,94
  mental health/physical health
    comorbidity, 120
Helman, C. G., 112
Henson, C. E., 194
Hernandez, M., 216
Herrera, A. E., 135
Herrera, Rafael, 99-114
Hill, M. S., 44
Hirschfeld, R., 123
HIV/AIDS, 200-201
Hodge, Felicia Schanche, 79-96
Hoffman, R. G., 81
Hoffman, S. D., 44

Hollon, S. D., 120
Holloway, S., 51
Holt, R., 24
Holzer, C., III, 120
Homelessness. *See also* Homeless
    persons
  conclusions about, 67-69
  and cross-cultural relationships,
    42
  as culture, 43-46
  cultural characteristics
    disaffiliation, 45
    general lifestyles, 45
    poverty, 45
  cultural traits
    disaffiliation, 44-45,52-53
    general lifestyles, 50-52
    poverty, 48-50
    service/treatment avoidance,
      53-57
  defined, 43
  demographics, 41-43,45
  diagnosis, duration, disability, 42
  evaluation of, 63-67
  heterogeneity of clients, 43
  research and study design, 46-48
  "shelter culture," 59-60
  skid row, 57-59
  stereotypes of, 45-46
  subcultures, 60-63
Homeless persons. *See also*
    Homelessness
  and bureaucracy, 56
  case management, 61-67
  disaffiliation, 58-59
  heterogeneity of, 43
  lifestyles, 50-52,67
  long-term vs. short-term needs
    group, 48
  marriage rates, 197
  material needs, 50-51
  mobility and health service
    delivery, 51-52,65
  personal appearance as problem,
    51

Homeless persons *(continued)*
  priorities vs. mental health
    workers', 55-57
  safety needs, 51,56
  social bonds, 48
  social integration, 48
  social support/social networks,
    52-53
  stigmatization of, 49
  street subculture, 58-59
  unemployed, 48-49
Homeless shelters. *See*
    Shelterization; Shelters
Hopper, K., 47,50,56,57,58,68
Hospitals. *See* Institutionalization
Hu, L., 103,121,126,149
Huang, L., 1
Huebner, R. B., 45
Hughes, M., 120,139
Humm-Delgado, D., 128
Hutchinson, W. J., 60

Ibrahim, F. A., 107
Illiteracy, 146-147
Illness as socioeconomic value,
    13-14
Illness beliefs, 111-113
Illness metaphor, 13-14
Imposed etic, 11-12
Infidelity, 108
Insight therapy, 31
  for African Americans, 181
  vs. crisis intervention, 111
Institute of Medicine, 41
Institutionalization
  of African Americans, 169,
    181-182
  homeless persons' resistance to,
    54-55. *See also* Disaffiliation;
    Service resistance
  internal culture of hospitala, 22
  reduction by intensive case
    management, 64
Intagliata, J., 17,22

Intensive case management, 62-63, 68-69
Interdependence vs. "enmeshment," 16
Intermittent explosive disorder, 176-177
Internal vs. external causation, 15-16
Interpersonal relating, 18
Interpretor vs. *translator*, 28
Interventions
    environment-focused, 128-129
    lithium carbonate therapy, 190-192
    medications and menstrual cycle, 189
    overmedication of African Americans, 181
    patient-focused, 128-129
Intracultural reframing, 32-33
Intracultural vs. intercultural differences, 7-8
Isaacs, M., 225
Isolation, 18,52
Isolative behavior, 14
Isolative lifestyle and racism, 181-182

Jaco, E. G., 102
James, R. K., 110,111
Janosick, E. H., 115
Javier, R. A., 27
Jencks, C., 44,50
Job loss, 122-123
Johnson, A. B., 54,57
Johnson, E., 76
Johnson, M., 29
Johnson, P. J., 5
Johnson, T. M., 112
Jones, E., 1
Jones, W., 146
Jordan, J., 186,194
Jordon, D. D., 216

KALEIDOSCOPE project (Chicago), 219
Kamerow, D. B., 119
Kando, J., 186,189
Kanfer, F. H., 115
Kanter, J., 1,6,17,101,128
Kaplan, A., 186,194
Kaplan, B. H., 84
Karno, M., 105,121
Kass, F. I., 47
Kates, B., 59
Katon, W., 119
Katz, M. H., 91
Katz-Levy, J., 224
Kaufman, M. S., 58
Keane, E. M., 80
Keefe, S. E., 102,104,121
Keigher, S. M., 45
Keltner, N., 23
Kendler, K. S., 120,139
Kesselman, M., 104
Kessler, R. C., 120,139
Kim, Yeunhee Joyce, 145-167
Kinzie, D., 81
Kinzie, J. D., 11,148,150,152
Kipnis, Patricia, 79-96
Kirkeby, J., 103
Kirmayer, L. J., 17
Kirschner, M. C., 54
Kleinman, A. M., 15,17
Knitzer, J., 211
Knoll, T., 147
Koegel, P., 3,41,46,47,53,55
Kogan, L. S., 105,106
Koranyi, E., 188
Korchin, S., 1
Koss, M. P., 105
Kozol, J., 45,47,60
Kraus, S., 65
Krol, P. A., 194
Krumweid, R. D., 4
Kutza, E. A., 45

Lai-Bitker, Alice Y., 145-167
Lakoff, G., 29

Lamb, H. R., 1,6,47,53,56
Lancee, W., 64,65,197
Langford, M. W., 64
Language, 27-29. *See also*
Communication
African American, 27
interpretors vs. translators, 28
vs. culture, 27
Language barriers, 154-155
and health care underutilization,
102
and Southeast Asian refugees,
149-151
Lankton, C., 29
Lankton, S., 29
Laotians, 147-148,157. *See also*
Southeast Asians
La Raza, National Council of, 101
Lasso, B., 104
Latinos
and AIDS/HIV, 201
bereavement practices and
depression, 107-110
bureaucracy and entitlement,
122-123
cognitive-behavioral therapy
in depressed
assertiveness training, 135-137
assessment, 126-128
beginning services, 130-131
cognitive restructuring, 132-133
comorbidity and, 120
conclusions, 139-140
cultural barriers, 121
integration with case
management, 126-138
interventions, 128-130
pleasant activities
("distracciones"), 133-135
prerequisites, 126-127
in primary care, 122-126
problem themes and gender
issues, 128
psychoeducation, 131-132
psychosocial stressors, 121-122

Latinos, cognitive-behavioral
therapy in depressed *(continued)*
socioeconomic status and,
120-121
termination, 137-138
demographic data, 101
dependency vs. gratitude, 138
duration of health care encounters,
105-106
effectiveness of crisis
intervention, 106
health and illness beliefs, 111-113
intracultural differences, 8
medication effect differences, 24
natural support systems, 112-113
respeto concept, 130-131
stigmatization of mental illness
by, 131-132
substance abuse by, 193-194
underutilization of services,
101-102,121
utilization of health services,
101-103
barriers to, 104-105
Lawson, W., 23,170,175
Leaf, P. J., 62,120
Leavitt, S. S., 5,20
Lee, E., 3,152,156,158
Lefley, H. P., 15,16,24,42,43,80
Lehman, A., 61,62
Leisure activities
and gender roles, 134-135
Latino attitude toward, 133-135
Southeast Asian attitudes toward,
163
Leland, J., 79
Leshner, A. I., 41,42,46,49,51,53,
60,63
Leukefeld, C. G., 5
Leung, P., 11,81
Levine, I. S., 41,42,45,47,54,55,61
Levinson, C., 17,61
Lewinsohn, P. M., 126
Lewis, R. G., 79
Lezak, A. D., 54,61

Leberman, M., 124
Lifestyles of homeless persons,
    48,50-52,67
Lin, K. M., 15
Lin, T., 23
Linguistic matching of service
    providers, 126-127
Link, B., 80,81,82,90,92
Linking function of case manager,
    22-23,66,151
Lipman, C., 45
Lipsedge, M., 10,11
Lipton, F. R., 47,52
Lithium carbonate therapy, 190-192
Littlewood, R., 10,11
Littman, S. K., 29
Lloyd, C., 123
Lo, T., 15
Lo, W. H., 15
Locus of control, 21
Loneliness, 18
Lonner, W., 10
Loo, C., 149
Lorenzo, M. K., 150
Loring, M., 1
Lourie, S. I., 224
Lown, A., 199
Lu, F., 3,158
Luborsky, L., 111
Lukianowicz, N., 104
Lukoff, D., 189
Lum, D., 131
Lycan, C., 62

MacFarquhar, K. W., 221
MacLean, D. G., 194
Madsen, W., 102
Magraw, M., 201
Malgady, R. G., 102
Mallinckrodt, B., 135
Mammography, 188
Manderscheid, R. A., 1,5

Manoleas, Peter, 1-34,41,42,43,45,
    99
Manson, S., 80,81,91,93,148
Marcos, L., 24,27,58,104
Margetson, N., 45
Marin, B. V., 91
Marin, G., 91
Marital status, 85
Martin, M. A., 55
Martinez, M., 224
Martinez, R., 8
Marx, L., 224
Mason, E. P., 80
Mason, M., 64
Material needs
    assessment, 21-22
    and crisis intervention, 111
    and depression risk, 87,92-93
    of homeless persons, 50-51
Maurin, J. T., 197
May, Phillip A., 79
McCafferty, D., 61
McChesney, K. Y., 52
McCreath, J., 3
McGlashan, T. H., 25
McGoldrick, M., 148
McGonagle, K. A., 120,139
McGrath, E., 120
McKinney (Stewart B.) Homeless
    Assistance Act, 43
McRae, J., 62
Medicaid funding, 227
Medical (disease) model, 26-27
Medications
    antipsychotic, 24
    case manages as gatekeepers, 23
    intercultural differences in effects,
        23
    lithium carbonate therapy,
        190-192
    and menstrual cycle, 189
    and noncompliance, 31
    overmedication of African
        Americans, 181

Medications *(continued)*
  psychotropic, 31
  sedative, 23
Memmott, R. J., 197
Mendelsohn, F. S., 80,81,82
Mental health, problems in defining, 92
Mental health services. *See* Service providers; Service resistance
Mental health system, client experiences with, 18,19
Mentalistic structures, 17
Mentally ill persons, ethnic minorities compared with, 2
Messick, J. M., 107
Metaphorical usage, 29-31
Metonymy, 29
Mexican Americans. *See also* Latinos
  health insurance, 103
  linguistic matching study, 127
Mien culture, 153,155,164. *See also* Southeast Asians
Migration
  history of refugee families, 156-157
  of Southern blacks, 172
Milburn, N., 45,49
Millen, L., 8
Miller, A. G., 1
Miller, G., 64,146
Miller, J. B., 194
Miller, L., 4,65,191
Minkoff, K., 12
Minuchin, S., 25
Miranda, J., 122
Miranda, M. R., 125
Mirowsky, J., 10
"Miscegenation," 178-179
Mistrustfulness of refugees, 159-160
Mobile mental health case management (NIMH), 65

Mobility of homeless and service delivery, 51-52,65
Modrcin, M., 5,64
Morales, A., 105
Morgenstern, H., 224
Morimoto, C., 230
Morin, R. C., 1,4,
Morrissey, J. P., 24,46,47,54
Morse, G., 61,65,66,197
Motherhood, 192-194
Moxley, D. P., 56,61,64
Mulligan, B. C., 79
Mullis, J., 50
Muñoz, R. F., 120,122,123,125, 126,129
Murphy, H. M., 15
Muslim religion, 180

National Association of Social Work, 120
National Cancer Institute Northern California Native American depression study, 83-96
National Coalition for the Homeless, 187
National Comorbidity Survey, 120-121
National Council of La Raza, 101
National Institute of Medicine, 41
National Institute of Mental Health (NIMH), 46,61,212
  Community Support Program, 61-62,64-65
  homelessness research, 55
  mobile mental health case management, 65
Nation of Islam, 180
Native American Cancer Control Project (AICCP), 83-96
Native Americans
  historical nature of research, 79
  depression vs. demoralization, 81-83

Native Americans *(continued)*
Northern California depression
study, 83-96
discussion, 90-95
results, 85-90
study design, 83-85
social homogeneity of, 94-95
validity of research instruments,
80-83
Natural support systems. *See* social
supports
Nelson, B. A., 194
Nelson, C. B., 120,139
Nestadt, G., 51
New York City
Bowery subculture, 57
Project HELP, 58
shelterization study, 59
Newman, K. S., 44
Nicholson, J., 193
NIMH. *See* National Institute
of Mental Health (NIMH)
Nolen-Hoeksema, S., 197
Noncompliance. *See*
Compliance/noncompliance;
Underutilization
North American EuroAmericans,
bulimia as exclusive to, 11
Northern California study of Native
American depression, 83-96

O'Hare, W., 145
Olfson, M., 64
Ordway, J., 179
Organista, K. C., 123,125,129
Osher, F. C., 48,54
O'Sullivan, M. J., 103,104

PACT (Program for Assertive
Community Treatment),
62-63
Padilla, A. M., 102,121
Padilla, Y. C., 44

Paduchak, D., 65,197
Painter, 201
Parham, T., 170,172
Parron, D. L., 121
Patterson, D. Y., 213
Paykel, E., 123-124,197
Pearlin, L., 124
Pedersen, A., 1
Pedersen, P., 1
Pensee, M., 61
Pepper, B., 54
Perez-Stable, E. J., 91,122
Personalismo, 131
Personality disorders, 177,199-200
Personification, 29
Person-in-environment approach, 2
Peterson, P. D., 103
Peterson, P. E., 44,50
Pierce, R., 182
Pinderhughes, C., 181
Pinderhughes, E., 171
Planning/prioritizing, 20-21
Platica (small talk), 131
Poertner, J., 5,64
Police, case manager interaction
with, 14-15
Ponterotto, J. G., 111
Post-traumatic stress disorder, 148
in abused women, 194-196
in Southeast Asian refugees,
152-153,160
Poverty
feminization of, 174
and homelessness, 48-50
Powell, B., 1
Pregnancy/motherhood
and self-concept, 192
substance abuse in, 199-201
teenage and single parent homes,
174-175
Pregnancy/motherhood, 192-194
Premature grandmothers, 175
*President's Commission on Mental
Health*, 121
Prioritization, 152

Problem definition, 152,155-156
Program for Assertive Community Treatment (PACT), 62-63
Progressive relaxation, 11
Project HELP (New York City), 58-59
Psychiatric illness
  in African Americans, 169-184. *See also* African-Americans
  and child rearing, 193
  in women, 185-206. *See also* Women
Psychiatry
  client experience with, 9
  emic perspective, 10-11
  etic perspective, 10
  functional (rehabilitation) model, 12-15
  medical (disease) model, 8-12
  mentalistic structures, 17
  Western cultural bias, 9-10
Psychodiagnostics, 10-11
Psychodynamic therapy, 25
Psychoeducation, 20,24-25
  in depressed Latinos, 131-132
Psychologizing, 16-17
Psychosocial transition model of crisis intervention, 110,112
Psychotherapy
  as alien to Southeast Asian culture, 148
  cognitive-behavioral, 119-140. *See also* Cognitive-behavioral therapy
  cognitive restructuring, 30
  combined with casework, 18-19
  Effective Psychotherapy for Low-Income and Minority Patients, 121-122
  insight ("talk"), 21,111,181
  psychodynamic, 25
  reframing in, 31
  structural family, 25
Psychotropic medications. *See* Medications

Public sector case management, 5
Puerto Ricans. *See also* Latinos
  and assertiveness, 136
  ataques de nerios syndrome, 10-11
  bereavement practices, 107-110
  gender roles, 32-33
Putnam, J. F., 58
Putsch, R. W., 28

Racism
  and isolative lifestyle, 181-182
  and mental health service delivery, 181-182
Radloff, L. S., 83,87,90
Rae, D. S., 90
Rafferty, Y., 45
Rakos, R. F., 135
Rape. *See also* Sexual abuse
  of African American women, 178
  gang, 195
  pregnancy following, 192
Rapp, C. A., 1,5,64
Rath, B., 148
Recidivism, 4
Reciprocal relationship triangle, 6-7
Reduced defensiveness concept, 109-110
Referral, 66,67,122
Reframing. *See* Cultural reframing
Refugees, 127-128
  Southeast Asian
    advocacy for, 164-165
    Asian Community Mental Health Services (ACMHS) experience, 146-166
    assessment and cultural appreciation, 151-156
    assessment model for, 156-157
    case management issues, 151
    conclusions about, 165-167
    culturally competent assessment, 156-157

Refugees, Southeast Asian
  (continued)
    culture-syntonic treatment
      intervention, 162-164
    dependence vs. empowerment,
      158-159
    losses suffered by, 158
    service delivery strategies,
      150-151
    trust-building, 159-162
    world view of, 160-162
    vs. immigrants, 145-146
*Regional Differences in Indian
  Health*, 79
Rehabilitation (functional) model,
    12-15
Rehm, L. P., 120
Religion
  of African Americans, 180
  Latinos and, 132-133
  Southeast Asian refugees and, 152
Religious preoccupation, 21
Remission, 15
Repression (guardar), 136-137
Research
  cognitive-behavioral therapy
    in Latinos, 127
  NIMH homeless studies, 55
  study design
    community studies, 47
    ethnographic research, 47
    social program evaluation, 48
Respeto concept in Latinos, 102,
    130-131
Rhoades, H. M., 87
Rhodes, L. A., 30
Ridgely, M. S., 54
Ridgway, P., 61
Rife, J. C., 65
Riffer, N., 22
Risk factors for depression in Native
    Americans, 80,85-89
Risley, T. R., 221
Ritchley, F. J., 50
Ritualistic cures, 15

Rivera, C., 24
Robert Wood Johnson Initiative,
    215-231
Roberts, C. R., 90
Roberts, J. M., 8
Roberts, R. E., 87,90,120
Robins, L. N., 139
Robinson, G. K., 129
Roca, R., 188
Roessler, R. T., 100
Rog, D. J., 41,42,55,61,62,63
Rogers, W., 119,120
Rogler, L. H., 102
Roll, S., 8
Rollinson, P. A., 52
Romanoski, A., 51
Romney, A. K., 8
Rose, S. M., 1,61
Rosen, P., 64
Rosenblum, S., 61,62
Rosenthal, B. G., 80
Ross, C., 10
Ross, R. N., 121
Rossi, P. H., 42,43,45,47,48,
    49,51,52,54,56,57
Roth, D., 42,52
Rothman, J., 61
Rousseau, A. M., 59
Rozée, P. D., 148
Rubin, A., 5
Rubin, L., 47,52
Rubin, S. E., 100
Ruiz, R. A., 111
Rumbaut, R. G., 80,81
Rush, J. R., 124,125,126
Russell, L., 197
Ryglewicz, H., 54

Sabatini, A., 52
Sack, W. H., 148
Safety needs
  and depression risk, 89
  of homeless persons, 51,56
  of refugees, 159-160

Sanborn, C. J., 100
Sanchez, A. R., 105
Sanchez, V. C., 135
Sands, R. G., 3
San Francisco Family Mosaic
    Project, 211-231
San Francisco General Hospital
    Women's Issues Consultation
    team, 187-206
Sargent, C. F., 112
Sargent, M., 55
Sartorius, N., 15
Scheffler, R. M., 1
Schizophrenia, 16,172-173,181,188,
    195,199
    communication techniques, 29-30
    disorder, 174-175,192
    family, 24-25
    noncompliance in, 30-31
Schoenbach, V. J., 84
Schwab, B., 26,42
Searight, P., 60
Sedative medications, 24
Segal, S., 14,50,52
Seidman, E., 1,4
Self-concept, 95,109
    and depression, 80
    pregnancy as source, 192
    sick person vs. worker, 12-13
Self-disclosure, 105,131,156,
    159-160
Self-image and breadwinner role, 13
Service brokerage model, 5-6
Service delivery, racism and,
    181-182
Service providers
    attitudes toward women, 206
    cultural bias of, 56
    ethnicity and Latino utilization,
        104
    linguistic matching, 126-127
    priorities vs. homeless people,
        55-57
    refugee views of, 161-162

Service providers *(continued)*
    therapeutic alliance and crisis
        intervention, 111-113
Service resistance. *See also*
    Underutilization of services
    and intensive case
        management, 62-63
    in Latinos, 106
Sexual abuse. *See also* Rape
    group therapy in, 203-204
    and post-traumatic stress disorder,
        194-196
    of women, 178,201-204
Shapiro, S., 53
Shaver, P., 135,136
Shaw, B. F., 124,125,126
Shaw, N., 201
Shelterization, 47,59-60
Shelters, 67
    daytime, 60
    family lodges, 60
    hostels, 65
    nighttime, 60
    safety, 56-57
    safety of, 51
    transitional, 51
    welfare hotels, 60
    women's drop-in centers, 60
Shepard, M., 124
Shinn, M., 45
Shrout, P. E., 80,81,82
Sick role, 26,158-159,162
Sillen, S., 179
Silverman, C., 14
Silverman, W. H., 106
Singer, B., 111
Skid row, 47,51,57-58
Smith, L., 211
Smoking and depression in Native
        Americans, 84,85,91
Snowden, L., 1,2,3,149,181
Snyder, Birgitta Oey, 145-167
Sobadoras, 112
Social bonds of homeless, 48

Social intervention of homeless, 48.
    See also Disaffiliation
Social program evaluation, 48
Social Security, 13
Social Security Disability Income
    (SSDI), 13
Social supports
  of African Americans, 171-175
  of homeless persons, 52
  natural support systems of
      Latinos, 112-113
  of Southeast Asian refugees, 148
  of women, 196-198
Social surveys, 46-47
Socioeconomic status
  and comorbidity, 120-121
  and depression in Native
      Americans, 85
  and depression risk, 91
  *Effective Psychotherapy
      for Low-Income and Minority
      Patients*, 121-122
  and symptom expression, 93-94
Solovitz, B., 64
Somervell, P. D., 81
Sosin, M. R., 49,51,52,53,54,58
Soto, E., 135,136
Southeast Asians, 11,21
  Asian Community Mental Health
      Services (ACHMS)
      experience, 146-167
  attitude toward psychotherapy,
      148
  diversity of population, 145-146
  refugee populations
    advocacy for, 164-165
    assessment and cultural
        appreciation, 151-156
    assessment model for, 156-157
    case management issues, 151
    conclusions about, 165-166
    culturally competent
        assessment, 156-157
    culture-syntonic treatment
        intervention, 162-164

Southeast Asians, refugee
    populations *(continued)*
    dependence vs. empowerment,
        158-159
    losses suffered by, 158
    service delivery strategies,
        150-151
    service unavailability, 148-150
    trust-building, 159-162
    world view of, 160-162
  underutilization of services
      by, 150
  work ethic of, 162-163
Spielvogel, Anna M., 185-206
Spitz, B., 5
Spoerl, O. H., 105
Sprague, J., 187
SSDI (Social Security Disability
    Income), 13
SSI (Supplemental Security Income),
    13-14,137
St. Onge, M., 65,197
Staples, R., 12
Steenbarger, B. N., 106
Stein, L. I., 62,63
Steinberg, R. M., 100
Stereotyping of African Americans,
    170-180. *See also*
    Stigmatization
Stewart, A., 119,120
Stier, H., 49
Stigmatization, 131-132. *See also*
    Stereotyping
  of homeless persons, 49
  of mental illness
    by Latinos, 131-132
    by Southeast Asians, 149
Stoner, M. R., 60
Strand, P. J., 146
Strauss, J. S., 15
Street culture, 58-59
Stress
  and chronicity, 16
  and crisis intervention, 111
  evaluation of client stressors, 20

Stress *(continued)*
  family expectations and, 102-103
  high-risk indicators, 102
Stretch, J., 60
Stroul, B. A., 213,214,216
Structural family psychotherapy, 25
Structural unemployment, 13
Struening, E. L., 46
Study design
  community studies, 47
  ethnographic research, 47
  social program evaluation, 48
  social surveys, 46-47
Stuntzner-Gibson, D., 200
Subcultures of homeless, 57-60
Subordinate bilingualism, 28
Substance abuse, 3,30,31,137,155,
      193-194,195,202
  and HIV/AIDS, 200-201
  in pregnancy, 199-201
  tricyclic overdose, 24
  in women, 198-200
Substance abuse programs, 20
Sue, D., 8,104,107
Sue, S., 102,103,107,111,121,127,
      129,149,182
Suicide/suicidal ideation, 154,155-156,
      193-194,197-198,199-200.
      See also Depression
Sullivan, A. M., 58
Sullivan, G., 189
Supernatural cause, 15-16,153
Supplemental Security Income (SSI),
      13-14
Support systems. *See* Family/
      families; Social supports
Surber, R., 1,6,127
Surrey, J., 186,194,196
Susser, E., 42,46,47,59,60
Swayze, F. V., 41,61
Symptom expression, 93-94
Symptom management, 21
System-level advocacy, 23
System of Care principle, 213-215

Systems approach to culture, 8
Szule, T., 146

Tadlock, M., 53
Takeuchi, D. T., 103,121,127,149
Talbott, J. A., 54
Talmon, 105,106
Taplin, J. R., 107
Task Force on Homelessness and
      Severe Mental Illness, 60,63
Tatum, E., 169
TEAM case management, 219
Teehee, K., 80,81
Teenage pregnancy and single parent
      homes, 174-175
Tempelhoff, B., 61,65,66
TenHoor, W. J., 5,61
Tessler, R. C., 61
Test, J., 193
Test, M., 62,196
Therapeutic alliance, 111
Thomas, A., 179
Thompson, K. S., 62
Thornburg, H. D., 80
Thorndike, R., 10
Tienda, M., 49
Todman, P., 181
Toff, G., 42
Toff-Bergman, G., 129
Tolsdorf, C., 169
Tong, B., 149
Toomey, B. G., 45,49
Toomey, G. G., 65
Toro, P. A., 43,53
Toronto (Canada) homeless hostel
      program, 65
Torres-Matrullo, C., 126,128,135
Transference, 6,25
Translators, 28
Treatment. *See* Intervention
Treatment resistance, 53-57. *See
      also* Disaffiliation; Service
      resistance
  giggling misperceived as, 153-154
  in women, 204-206

Triangle of reciprocal relationships, 6-7
Trickett, E. J., 43,53
Tricyclic antidepressants, 24
Tricyclic overdose, 24
Trimble, J. E., 95
True, R., 149
Turner, J. C., 5,61
Tyhurst, J. S., 109

Underclass compared with homeless, 50
Underutilization of services
  by homeless persons, 54
  by Latinos, 101-105,121
  by Southeast Asian refugees, 150
Unemployment
  and depression, 130
  and depression risk in Native Americans, 91-92
  of homeless, 48-49
  of Latinos, 101-102
  of mentally ill, 49
  of Southeast Asian refugees, 147
  structural, 13
Unger, K., 198
Urcuyo, L., 104
Uribe de Mena, J., 230
U.S. Bureau of the Census, 99,101
U.S. Department of Health and Human Services, 41
U.S. Federal Task Force on Homelessness and Severe Mental Illness, 60,63
U.S. General Accounting Office (GAO), 46

Valentine, C. A., 27
Valle, R., 25,112
VanDenBerg, J. E., 216
VandenBos, G. R., 120
van der Kolk, B., 194,195
VanderVoort, D. J., 50

Vega, W. A., 80,81
Ventura Model, 216
Vergare, M., 53
Vernon, S. W., 87
Victim blaming, 79
Vietnamese, 147,158. *See also* Southeast Asians
Visions, 21
Visual acuity loss, post-traumatic, 148
Vocational rehabilitation model, 12-13
Voice tones, 11

Wagner, E. H., 84
Waites, E., 204
Walker, L., 201,203
Wall, D. D., 43,53
Wallace, S. E., 57
Wallach, M. A., 48
Wallish, L., 196
Ward, S., 4
Ware, J., 119,120
Washington's Business Group on Health, 216
Wasylenki, D., 1,4,64,65,197
Weidman, H. H., 10,26
Weissman, M. M., 120
Welch, W. M., 42
Welfare hotels, 60
Welfare programs
  and depression risk, 92
  homeless persons' nonutilization, 54
Weller, S. C., 8
Wells, K. B., 119,120
Westermeyer, J., 1,11
Western cultural bias, 9-10,15-16, 79,92
White, A., 42,59,60
White, J., 170,172
Whites. *See* Caucasians
Wile, Joanne R., 185-206
Wilkinson, C. B., 1
Williams, C. L., 146

Wilson, W. J., 44,50
Wittchen, H., 120,139
Women
  and assertiveness, 136
  assessment of psychiatrically ill, 186
  drop-in shelters for, 60
  family planning, 189-192
  gender roles and depression in Latinas, 128
  giggling behavior in Cambodian, 153-154
  health care needs, 187-189
  HIV/AIDS in, 200-201
  homeless
    Chicago study, 53
    safety needs, 51
    social support/social networks, 52-53
  Native American and depression risk, 85,87-89,90
  post-traumatic stress disorder in, 194-196
  pregnancy/motherhood, 192-194
  sexual and physical abuse, 178, 194-196,201-204
  social support/relationships, 196-198
  socioeconomic status and depression, 122
  substance abuse by, 198-200
  treatment resistance in, 204-206
  utilization of services by, 55-57

Women's Issues Consultation Team (San Francisco General Hospital), 186-206
Wood, P. S. 135
Work culture, 12-13,162-163
Work metaphor, 13-14
World view, 107,113
  African American, 170-171
  of Southeast Asian refugees, 160-162
"Wrap-around care" concept, 221. *See also* Family Mosaic Project (Robert Wood Johnson Initiative)

Yamamoto, J., 1,111,121
Yerberas, 112
"Yes-but" technique, 132-133
Ying, Y. W., 122
Yokopenic, P., 91
Yonkers, K., 186,189

Zane, N., 103,111,121,127,149
Zawadaski, R. T., 100
Zeigler, V., 24
Zhao, S., 120,139
Zich, J. M., 93
Ziefert, M., 52
Zirkel, P. A., 80
Zubin, J., 15
Zuniga, M., 29